THE
CHRISTIAN
CONFERENCE
PLANNER

Organizing Effective Events
Conferences ◆ Retreats ◆ Seminars ◆ Workshops

ANGELA YEE

SummitStar Press

The Christian Conference Planner: Organizing Effective Events, Conferences, Retreats, Seminars, and Workshops
©2003 Angela Yee
All rights reserved.
Printed in U.S.A.

ISBN 0-9728098-0-5

This book is available at bulk discounts for organizations and companies. Please contact the publisher for more information.

All unattributed quotes, examples, interior photos, design, and artwork (except for symbols on left margins) are by Angela Yee. Attributed examples from other individuals or organizations have been used by permission.

Published by SummitStar Press
2140 Sunsprite Drive
Union City, CA 94587
510-487-8511
www.summitstarpress.com
info@summitstarpress.com

C O N T E N T S

DO YOU WANT A SUCCESSFUL CONFERENCE?

As soon as I opened the door, I knew I was in trouble.

If you'd asked me what I remember most about the retreat, you'd probably hope I'd say something like, "An awesome time of fellowship with God," or "Spending time talking with people," or "Great worship!" But the main thing I remembered was the bugs. Lots of them. BIG ones.

Crawling all over the floor were inch-long, black ants. Cobwebs dangled in the corners of the cabin. Maybe the situation would not intimidate the average camper, but unfortunately I have a great aversion to bugs. (That's why I have a vacuum cleaner at home—because I can easily get rid of an insect from ten feet away. No fuss. No muss.)

As my husband went to get the luggage, I quickly hauled my young children directly from the door to the bed so they wouldn't have to step on the ants. Then I headed to the top bunk bed in order to get as far away from the ants as possible. As I climbed up, I almost got into my bed—until I noticed the dead spider curled up in the middle of my mattress.

The children, who seemed not at all bothered by the fact that their bed was perched precariously over an army of ants, cheerfully laughed and wiggled in their bed, tossing pillows, blankets, and clothes on the floor.

"Children," I said reasonably. "Please get some sleep so we will be well-rested in the morning." But instead my ears heard my voice saying, "YOU KIDS GO TO SLEEP AND STOP SQUIRMING BECAUSE YOU ARE GETTING YOUR STUFF FULL OF ANTS!!!! DON'T YOU UNDERSTAND WE ARE HAVING A NATIONAL EMERGENCY HERE!!!"

As I hyperventilated in my bed, I closed my eyes, but all I could see were visions of dark ants and spiders crawling up and down the walls. To add to the ambience, the toilet in our bathroom flushed every ten minutes. I'm sure I didn't get a wink of sleep all night. But somehow my brain must have deceived me, because in the middle of the night I jerked awake when I heard a loud thud.

My husband turned on the light and discovered our daughter had fallen out of bed and was lying face down on the floor, sleeping. On the ants.

The next morning I dragged myself around. I have no idea what the speaker said, what the worship was like, or even what we ate. Even though there was still another day to the retreat, all I remember was my husband taking one look at me and saying, "We are going home now."

We did.

PLANNING FOR SUCCESS

Every conference planner wants an event that is inspiring, encouraging, and even life-changing. A myriad of details goes into planning a conference but no one thinks about them . . . until something goes wrong. A conference planner's job is to oversee every aspect of a conference, directly or indirectly, so that the attendee can be ready to learn and receive. As I discovered at that retreat, a person who is focused on details totally irrelevant to learning can't really benefit from the teaching and fellowship. That's why this book was written—to help people involved in planning these types of events aim for success and effectiveness.

WHY A BOOK ON CHRISTIAN CONFERENCES AND RETREATS?

Conferences abound in every area of our society: the corporate world, educational institutions and even the government. Just do an Internet search on www.google.com and you'll find over seven million references to conferences!

Christian conferences and retreats have a special twist to them, though: many Christian organizations are nonprofit and have the double challenge of 1) limited financial resources and 2) primarily being volunteer-run. Most of these organizations just can't afford to hire an entire staff to oversee the planning and implementation of a conference. If your organization can, consider yourself one of the fortunate few!

This book was written with these needs in mind. Sprinkled throughout the book are references to how to save on costs and suggestions on how to use volunteers rather than hiring people to do everything. But if you have a little extra money to spend, then please use it in an area that will help your conference be more effective!

The other major difference between Christian conferences and the secular world is the emphasis on the spiritual aspect. This changes the perspective of how Christian conferences are planned since every step ultimately points to trusting God and seeking His direction. This book approaches conference planning from a foundation of prayer and reliance on God.

In my experiences planning conferences, I kept running into people asking, "Do you know where I can find out how to plan a conference?" As I did research, I found plenty of resources about organizing a conference, but most of them were directed at professional planners. Sadly, I couldn't find a single book devoted to the topic of planning a Christian conference, especially to the average volunteer planner. That's why I wrote this book—so that Christian conference planners can learn from one another!

WHO CAN USE THIS BOOK?

Whether you're planning a small intimate retreat or a large conference, this book will help you cover every detail. This book is for anyone involved in conference planning: the head of the organization that sponsors the event, the director who coordinates the entire conference, as well as the conference staff team that oversees individual areas.

Because many of you reading this book are not professional meeting planners, I've purposely tried to stay away from jargon in the meeting industry—most of you won't know what RevPAR, resold language clauses, or fam trips are (and if you do, you're probably a professional!). If I do use a term, it's explained in everyday English so you can easily understand it.

For professional planners who want to find more technical information, I have included a list of conference organizations in the back of the book. Even though parts of this book will be obvious to you, my hope is that you can still learn from the advice of many experienced people around the country!

HOW DO YOU USE THIS BOOK?

This book is written in a loose sequential order of the conference planning process. Given the multitude of different conference formats, audiences and staff planning styles, it's almost impossible to list a specific order for planning conferences. This book covers the process in a general order of events that most conference planners can use, but if you find an alternative order is more useful, by all means go with what works for you!

Although team members who have specific responsibilities may want to read only the sections pertaining to their area, I encourage everyone on the planning team to read the entire book. This enables all the people to know where they fit in and how a conference is put together.

I've had the privilege of speaking to a number of people around the country about their conference planning experiences. Their wisdom is shared in the quotes throughout the book. (Quotes with no names are written by me.)

Throughout the book, you'll see little symbols on the side to draw out points of particular interest:

COMPUTER HELPS

- Computer helps. Computers make life much easier for conference planners. If you have access to a computer, these little notes will give you ideas on how to streamline your planning process.

EXAMPLES

- Examples. Forms, diagrams, sample lists—explanations about these helpful items are referred to with the Examples symbol.

MONEY SAVERS

- Money savers. Everyone wants to save money! Check out these tips that help you stretch your dollar.

RESOURCE TOOLS

- Resource tools. If there is a company or organization that can help provide a resource, it is listed by this symbol. Be aware that Web sites change frequently, so although I've tried to be accurate in my information, the URL addresses are subject to change.

SCHEDULING

- Scheduling. Scheduling tips give information on how to construct a well-planned timetable.

STEP-BY-STEP

- Step-by-step. Here you'll find a summary list of what you need to do.

TIPS FOR SUCCESS

- Tips for success. This symbol points out important notes that can make the difference between whether your conference is successful or not.

At the beginning of each chapter for a coordinator, there is a sample job description page. Time commitments for the position are not listed because the commitment varies depending on the scope of your conference. Add your own requirements for time commitment at the end of the job description.

At the end, I've included an appendix of resources which can provide helps for planning.

This book's goal is to help people coordinate events both simple and complex. If you have an event that is relatively small or simple, please don't be overwhelmed! Just skip the information that doesn't apply to your event. You might even want to look through those chapters for future reference in case next year you want to try something new.

Another note: don't feel like you have to implement every idea in this book. The information in these chapters serves as a guideline and suggestion on ways you can make your conference more effective. Don't feel intimidated by all the information and think that your event is a failure if things don't go by the book. Every event and situation is different, so pull out what will help *you!*

FINALLY...

When I first began coordinating my first retreat, I didn't have a clue as to how to get started. I was fortunate to help an organization called MESA (Ministries for English Speaking Asians) begin conferences for women. These conferences have been held on the East and West Coast and impacted thousands of women.

This book is the result of those experiences as well as over fifteen years of experience in coordinating special events, graphic design, worship leading, speaking and teaching, and past experience working for an audiovisual company and as a marketing coordinator. The saying, "Jack of all trades, master of none" unfortunately applies to me but I count it a blessing that all of these experiences have helped me understand the entire conference planning process more fully.

By the way, I'd love to hear how this book has helped you or if you have suggestions for improvement of future editions. Also, if you have any interesting conference experiences, please write me so I can hear about them!

As you plan your conference, I hope that you will learn and grow as much as I have, and that your faith will be strengthened. It's my prayer that you will find this book to be a great help to your conference planning. May God's blessings and grace be over you and your event!

Angela Yee
angelay@summitstarpress.com
SummitStar Press
2140 Sunsprite Drive
Union City, CA 94587

P.S. Well, it seems like almost everything these days has a disclaimer, so here we go, joining the crowd:

In this book, the author has made references to companies and organizations in order to assist conference planning. Although every effort has been made to be accurate, neither the author nor the publisher is responsible for the reliability of the references or the quality of performance of the references listed in this book. Listing of the references does not imply endorsement of the company or organization.

NOTABLE PEOPLE

Now, there is a reason why I didn't title this section "Acknowledgements," and that is because every person I know skips the acknowledgements page. So I changed the title with the hope that you somehow would not notice that this really is the acknowledgements section and would read it eagerly, but you didn't hear that from me.

Actually, this section also lists the names of some very knowledgeable conference people who shared their wisdom. Their quotes are scattered through this book. If you don't read this section, you won't know who they are!

First I want to thank my husband Albert, the person in this world who I love the most, even though he is nothing like me. And that's a good thing, because I would have never married anyone like myself because I would have gone crazy! What with all this book writing (which is hard work!), *somebody* had to make sure our family had fun and relaxing times. He's the one that kept our family sane and pitched in with laundry and dishes and playing with the kids while my eye was twitching from staring at the computer screen too long. God has blessed me with a wonderfully supportive and loving husband! I would not be able to do this book without him!

I also want to thank my mother, Carmen Lin, and my in-laws, Kane and Maxine Yee, whose love and support meant so much to me. My mother helped introduce me and help me grow in my relationship with Christ, but her major part in this book was when she rescued me on a week that I had to work on this manuscript; she drove like mad to get my laptop computer for me while I anxiously waited to catch a plane. She's also helped immensely with babysitting! My in-laws are wonderful; they encouraged me and helped watch the kids (spoil them, actually). I count myself blessed to have such wonderful family members!

Over the years I've had the opportunity to learn by working on many special events. But the most I learned about conference coordinating was with my experiences with MESA. Many thanks to Louis Lee who helped mentor me in this area.

My experience is limited compared to the many people who have been coordinating conferences for a lifetime, but I've been fortunate to learn from many of these experienced people. You'll find their quotes throughout the book. (All quotes without a name are written by me.) Together they represent hundreds of years of experience in coordinating conferences and retreats. It's been awesome to learn learn something new from every person!

Andrew Accardy started out as a director of conference operations at a conference center, coordinated conferences for Vision New England, and currently is Director of Operations at Purpose Driven at Saddleback Community Church in California.

Peggy Brems serves at Walnut Creek Presbyterian Church in California and has coordinated the Willowcreek Leadership Summit satellite conference at her church for the past two years.

Judy Byford, Administrative Assistant and Facilities Coordinator for BASS (Bay Area Sunday School) in California, has helped plan BASS for twelve years and currently oversees 350 workshops at their conference.

Chuck Caswell is head of the men's ministry at Village Church of Barrington in Illinois. He runs an advertising agency and is one of the most creative people I have ever met.

Pam Chun is one of the co-founders of Hawaiian Island Ministries and coordinates their conferences held in Hawaii and California. She is currently their Vice-President.

Jennifer Cope, Guest Conference Coordinator at Mount Hermon Conference Center in California, works with groups that use their facilities to help them plan their conferences.

Ron Demolar is Program Director at Mount Hermon Conference Center and has had experience in every area of conference planning.

Debbie Dittrich has been speaking for nine years and speaks regularly at women's retreats. She divides her time between her homes in Texas and Colorado.

Jeanne Gregory worked for twenty years with Presbyterians for Renewal, coordinating conferences and camps for youth and has had wide experience helping coordinate conferences for other organizations. She currently lives in Illinois.

Kristen Hilling plans conferences for Crisis Pregnancy Center and helped coordinate Women Aglow area retreats in Washington.

Keith Hirata organizes national conferences for InterVarsity Christian fellowship in Wisconsin and has conference planning experiences from other Christian organizations.

Vicki Hitzges is a professional speaker from Texas who has spoken across the United States and in countries around the world.

Steve Jacobs, CMP, had extensive experience in food and beverage management, catering, convention, and sales departments before becoming a professional meeting planner and starting his own company, reallygreatmeetings.com in Illinois.

Dean Jones, CMP, MTA, is Convention Manager of the National Association of Free Will Baptists, Inc. Their national convention has 7,000 people and three simultaneous conferences.

Rick Leary is both a conference coordinator and speaker. He helped start GLASS (Greater Los Angeles Area Sunday School) and currently helps coordinate CLASS (Class Leadership Service). He is Director of Campus Development and Adult Ministries at Oak Hills Church in California.

Brian Lord works at Premiere Speakers, a bureau in Tennessee that provides Christian speakers.

Dr. Stephen Macchia, President of Vision New England in Massachusetts, has hosted dozens of events, large (up to 12,000) and small, and has covered every area of conference coordinating in his experiences.

Yvette Maher, Vice President of Renewing the Heart Women's Ministries at Focus on the Family in Colorado, has overseen the coordination of a wide range of retreats and conferences, from small intimate settings to conferences that average 16,000 attendees per event.

John Pearson served as the first president of Willow Creek Association, from 1992 to 1994. Since 1994, he's been the president of Christian Management Association.

Ron Sugimoto has had a wide range of conference experiences with parachurch ministries and currently serves as the Director of JEMS Research, Develop and Training Group (Japanese Evangelical Missions) in California.

Terry Toro has worked in the conference industry for fifteen years and was an event manager for a company owned by United Airlines. She oversees the logistical planning of conferences for Willowcreek Association (Illinois).

Vicky Wauterleck was Director of Women's Ministries at Village Church of Barrington, Illinois. She was also interim president for Christian Women United, a women's track of Mission America and coordinated conferences for them.

Brad Weaber, CMP, is Vice President of the Mid-Atlantic Region of Conferon, the nation's leading consultant for meetings and conventions.

Doug Yonamine served as Logistics Coordinator at an Urbana missions conference and helped coordinate logistics for Willowcreek Association's conferences around the world.

✦

This book is dedicated to my wonderful husband, Albert, who has loved me unconditionally, has unwavering faith in me, and spoils me to no end. He has been one of the greatest blessings in my life.

I also dedicate this book in loving memory to my father, who encouraged me in the Lord and was a godly example to me.

Yishan Lin
Dec 1937–Jun 2002

CHAPTER

1 | OVERVIEW

Before you drive to your vacation location, you need a road map to tell you how to get there. This chapter gives you an eagle-eye view of the road you'll be taking to get to your final destination—a successful, effective conference.

WHAT IS A CONFERENCE OR RETREAT?

A conference is a meeting of people, numbering from a handful to thousands, for the purpose of learning or exchanging information. Conferences can take many forms large and small, such as conventions, seminars, workshops, or retreats. To simplify matters, this book will refer to these events as "conferences," although your particular event may be a variation of any of the above events or a combination of different events.

Conferences vary in size, from ten to 10,000 or more. They are held by many Christian organizations—churches, denominations, ministries, professional organizations, and others. The average church in America has fewer than 200 people and does not have an extensive budget to hire a professional conference planner. Christian organizations face the same problem; their conference coordinators often wear many other hats within the organization. Many of the conference planners receive their training by seat-of-the-pants experiences and trial and error. But as you read the pages, you will learn from the experience of conference planners around the country so that you don't have to repeat their mistakes!

WHAT DOES A CONFERENCE LOOK LIKE?

Because no two conferences are the same, there is no such thing as a "typical" conference. Conferences can be one day or multiple days. Those that are one day usually are targeted to people who live in the local area.

The program differs as well. Most conferences have meetings where all the attendees gather in one location. These general sessions may include times for teaching, worship, creative arts, or other activities. The first general session is called the "opening session" and the last one is called the "closing session."

Other times the participants break up into smaller groups and attend meetings led by small group facilitators or workshop leaders. These breakout sessions may involve discussions or teaching times by leaders or teachers.

Exhibitions are areas where people can investigate different resources, products, or services. The exhibit area may also vary in size from a handful of exhibits to hundreds of booths.

In addition, there may be opportunities for individual reflection, recreation, fellowship, sightseeing, and many other activities depending on the nature of the conference.

WHO IS INVOLVED IN A CONFERENCE?

Four groups of people make a conference possible:
- **The organization.** The organization is the group, association, or company that holds the conference.
- **The conference staff team.** The staff team is led by the Conference Director, who coordinates the efforts of the staff to plan and produce the conference. Other names for the staff team may be *committee, board,* or *planning team.*
- **The attendees.** A conference would not be possible if no one attended. People who participate in the conference are also called *delegates, participants, conferees,* or *registrants.*
- **Outside resources.** Vendors who provide services for the conference, and volunteers who help behind the scenes, are other necessary groups of people that makes a conference function smoothly. Whether paid or not, this group of people provides the labor and materials needed for different aspects of the conference: the facility, food and beverage, administration, and other areas.

WHY HAVE CONFERENCES?

Sometimes your goal can be better accomplished through a different format or event. Other times, a conference is an excellent way to meet your goals.

Efficiency

A conference reaches many people at once. An organization that holds a conference can communicate the same message to everyone simultaneously, resulting in time and cost efficiency. At the same time, the program reaches people with different needs by offering a wide variety of workshops or breakout sessions.

Energy

There's something about a large group of people gathering together that generates a kind of energy that you just can't get in a small group. Worshiping, learning, and laughing together with a large mass of people creates an experience worth remembering.

Effectiveness

Many people leave a conference feeling challenged, encouraged, and inspired to put into practice something they have learned. Different program elements such as worship, teaching, and fellowship build on one another to communicate a message that makes an impact.

Encouragement

Through the interaction people experience, they can minister to each other. They aren't the only ones who are encouraged; even the staff benefits by seeing God's work at hand. You'll find great encouragement knowing that God has used your efforts to help others spiritually and practically.

Think of conference planning as being similar to building a house. Turning an empty piece of land into a home is a long and deliberate process; likewise, conference planning is a process involving many details before the actual event. A conference event is broken down into four phases:

1. Commitment
2. Coordination
3. Conference
4. Closure

STEP-BY-STEP

Because every conference is different, it's almost impossible to form a specific order for planning. For many conferences, however, a general order is diagrammed on the next page.

1 Commitment

One day a person decides to move and begins researching the options to see what is best for his needs. If he wants to build a house, he starts investigating sites or talking to an architect to see what needs to be done. The architect draws up an initial plan and then it's time to gather resources to begin the project. Now the commitment has been made to build the house!

Conference planning starts the same way. A person begins with an idea, a concept that needs to be fleshed out: "We should have a conference!" Although he may have an idea of what kind of conference he wants to have, he still has to determine the purpose and audience of the event. Research must be done to find out what needs there are. Concept development involves developing the concept and refining the idea before it can be presented to others. This concept serves as a "blueprint" for the conference planning process. The purpose of the blueprint serves as a foundation for the major decisions that must be made along the way.

Once the concept has been approved, it's time to find others who are willing to commit to the conference. It's very difficult for one person to handle an entire conference by himself. He'll need to find the finances to support the event and recruit others to help him. Only with a commitment of financial resources and people can he proceed with the conference planning.

2 Coordination

The blueprint has been drawn; permits have been approved. Now a flurry of activity sets in as the building process actually begins. The contractor, site preparation crew, framing crew, and others are scheduled and coordinated. At the end, the builder inspects the house and if the final punch list is finished, the house is completed! The owner makes preparations to move in: packing, finding movers, change of address postcards, and other details. Moving involves a big coordinating job in and of itself!

In a conference, once resources and team members have committed to making the conference a reality, their efforts must be coordinated to make sure that every detail is covered. The team members work together to develop a plan for every area of the conference. Advance preparation will make all the difference whether the conference runs smoothly or not. Everything is assembled into a final plan for the conference day. When it's time to go on-site, the team prepares by packing up all the materials needed and it's off to the site!

3 Conference

Now comes the big day: moving in. The owner is busy moving everything into the house. It's an exciting day, the result of many months of work. He can enjoy the final product and see the results of so many people's hard work and a good return for his investment.

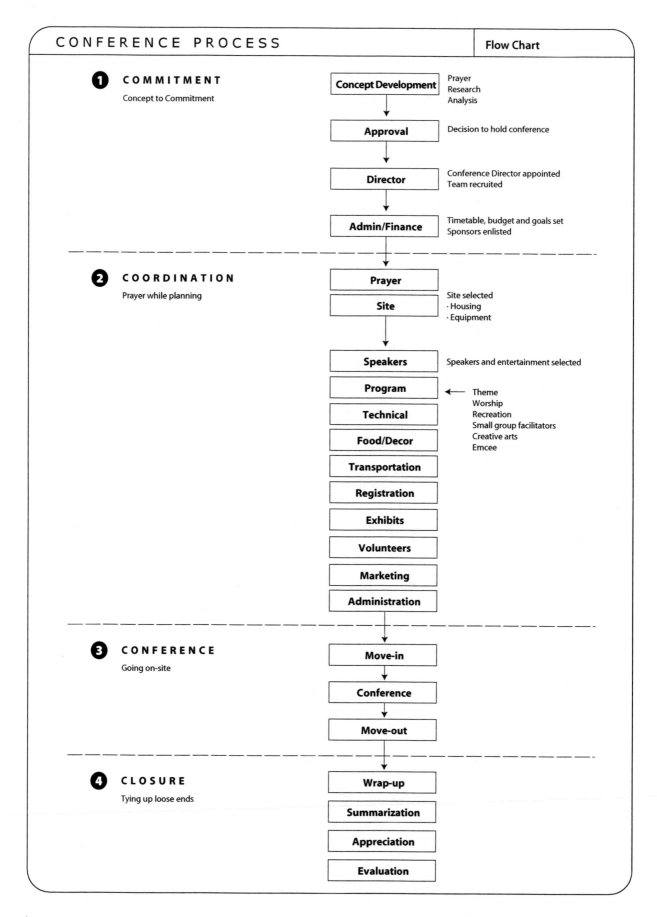

1 COMMITMENT
Concept to Commitment

Concept Development — Prayer / Research / Analysis

Approval — Decision to hold conference

Director — Conference Director appointed / Team recruited

Admin/Finance — Timetable, budget and goals set / Sponsors enlisted

2 COORDINATION
Prayer while planning

Prayer

Site — Site selected / · Housing / · Equipment

Speakers — Speakers and entertainment selected

Program — Theme / Worship / Recreation / Small group facilitators / Creative arts / Emcee

Technical

Food/Decor

Transportation

Registration

Exhibits

Volunteers

Marketing

Administration

3 CONFERENCE
Going on-site

Move-in

Conference

Move-out

4 CLOSURE
Tying up loose ends

Wrap-up

Summarization

Appreciation

Evaluation

With conferences, all the advance coordinated effort culminates on the actual conference day. After moving in and setting up everything, the coordinators oversee every aspect of the conference and make sure that everything runs smoothly. Then when the conference is over, everything is packed up.

4 Closure

It's time for celebration—the owner is finally moved in! It takes a while to unpack everything, but he now can enjoy his new home.

After the conference, the work continues. The important tasks of wrapping up, evaluating, summarizing the conference, and appreciation must be done. These tasks help ensure that the groundwork is laid for the next year's conference to be even more effective.

Now that you have an understanding of the conference planning process (and the house-building process), it's time to begin with the first stage: commitment.

PART 1 | COMMITMENT
FIRST STAGE

Every great product starts with a great idea. The concept of a conference might begin in different ways. Maybe it's just a spark of the imagination, a vague idea of, "Wouldn't it be great to have a conference!" Perhaps a person attends another conference and is inspired to hold a similar conference in her area. Or maybe it's a regular event at your church that has been held every year and this year you are in charge.

Before any planning must be done, the concept must be prayed over, thought through, and weighed. Is this a good idea? What is God's leading? If it passes the initial feasibility tests, then it's time to refine the idea a little farther and flesh out the concept so that it can be developed. Here are the steps to forming the conference concept:

STEP-BY-STEP

1. Prayer
2. Research/analysis
3. Concept refinement
4. Concept approval

PRAYER

Before you even begin a single step in planning the conference, pray! Unfortunately, sometimes prayer is just an extra task to be checked off. Or we forget to pray and only turn to prayer when things get difficult. Prayer is often relegated to the back burner because it's more exciting to start planning and making decisions.

> I can't say enough about prayer. If you're doing a retreat, remember that this is not *our* retreat, these are not women in *our* programs, or people in *our* sessions. This is the Lord's. That is the heart and foundation we should have. Sometimes we think, "What can I do to make this thing great?" instead of just realizing that it's God. We want to give our women refreshment and to have God speak to us and change our hearts. That's only accomplished through prayer and seeking God's will, not mine. ◆ *Debbie Dittrich*

> Bathe everything in prayer. Prayerfully enter into the reason why you are doing the event because the last thing that people need is just another activity to put on the calendar. Is this something that you truly feel the Lord is leading you to do? If He is, all the pieces will fall into place. ◆ *Yvette Maher*

TIPS FOR SUCCESS

So, stop before you start! Before you begin working, pray for God's wisdom and direction. Through prayer He will help you make wise decisions and discern His leading.

TIPS FOR SUCCESS

Sometimes people go ahead with planning a conference without even stopping to examine whether this is a good decision or not; the conference is planned because that's what has always been done. Or, people assume that a conference is the best option without looking at other alternatives. Taking the time to think through some key decisions will save you the agony of an unnecessary, unsuccessful, or mediocre conference.

Is a conference the best option?

Analyze your situation—is a conference the best way to accomplish the goals of your organization? What's the purpose of the conference and how does it align with organizational goals? After reviewing the goals, you might find that having a Sunday School class would be a better way of meeting your goals for fellowship and teaching. Just because your organization has always held this conference is not a good reason to hold another one. Be sure that there's a specific purpose for this event.

> Make sure that you have a solid understanding of the objectives prior to doing anything. There were some meetings that large church organizations wanted to do and we counseled them out of doing them because they didn't achieve the objectives of the church; they could do it in more cost-effective ways. Be honest. What are you trying to achieve? What is the best way to achieve it? Maybe it's not all 2,000 members together; it might be communicating that message through the small group system. ✦ *Steve Jacobs*

Are people interested?

What kind of interest is there for your conference? Survey people from your target audience. Does this event sound worthwhile to them? Would they participate?

> We were having a conference for women's ministry leaders. We sent out a survey to four different regions. We wanted to make sure they were not the opinions of women in only one region. The survey asked, "What are your biggest needs? What issues are you facing right now? What lessons are you doing? What programs are you involved in? What are the demographics of your church?" Study your audience on the front end. ✦ *Yvette Maher*

If your conference extends beyond your church and involves others in the community, gather the community leaders to discuss what interest there is in having the conference. Meeting with the key leaders and asking them their feedback, prayer, and ideas helps develop a sense of ownership in the conference.

> One of the most important things you do when you bring a conference to the community connecting with other leaders in the community. You may check with some of the key pastors in the community. Meet with them and get their approval. Any conference that goes beyond a church needs to find out who the key players are in the community. Bring them in early on in the decision making. ✦ *Vicky Wauterleck*

Networking with the other churches in the areas also provides support, encouragement, as well as a source of resources you can turn to for volunteers, finances, or equipment.

Do you have a passion or burden?

No house building project ever goes smoothly; there are always unexpected expenses and things that go wrong. Likewise, every conference has its moments of difficulty; what carries you through the hardships is knowing that this is what God wants you to do. A passion for the conference also is contagious and motivates others to participate and bring success to the event.

Take the time to think through these issues before you even begin. If you find that it is a good decision and worth going forward, then it's time to begin refining the concept!

CONCEPT REFINEMENT

A homebuilder doesn't wander around randomly and then decide to build a house for no particular reason. Much thought goes into planning and building a home. As you begin, first lay a "blueprint" for the conference. A builder refers to a blueprint over and over. In a conference, those who plan will refer to the conference blueprint as well. This blueprint answers some fundamental questions before proceeding with the planning.

The organization

First, look at the organization that will be holding the conference. What are its missions and goals: How does the conference fit into the organization's plans? How does this conference accomplish the goals of the organization and why you are you having this conference?

The audience

One of the first things to consider is which audience the conference is targeting. Is it for seniors? Women? Men? Couples? A special interest group? What kind of needs do these people have?

- Define your audience: who is this conference for?
- What do you want the event to accomplish?
- What do you want people to remember?

Have the right understanding of your audience. Know what motivates them to go. Men work hard; they're gone all week. They are busy and the last thing they want is to spend a weekend away. They need spiritual input but that's not what will motivate them to go; what motivates men is fun. We fill them to the brim with spiritual input once they're there. But that's not what motivates them to go.

We promoted the event as something that was fun; we made the spiritual aspect kind of secondary. What got to them was having a golf tournament; we came up with a theme that was attractive to men.

We make it fun. If it can't be fun, don't do it! ✦ *Chuck Caswell*

The purpose

Why should this conference be held? What purpose will it serve? Conferences are held for different reasons. You might have a conference for any of the following purposes:

- Teaching/training
- Prayer
- Encouragement
- Inspiration
- Planning
- Fellowship
- Worship
- Discussion
- Entertainment/Recreation

TIPS FOR SUCCESS

The purpose of the conference is the foundation of all the planning that is done. The purpose will vary according to your audience and organization, but a conference should always fill a need of some kind. Effective conferences find the needs and meet them.

Our goal and prayer is that the Lord would speak individually and uniquely to each woman in her heart. We've met the goal if she comes here and has been encouraged, has drawn closer in her individual walk, and her heart has been renewed with the Lord.
✦ *Yvette Maher*

The values

Values are principles that are foundational to how a conference is conducted. Values describe what is important to the event and what makes the conference distinctive. They dictate behavior, decisions and the direction of the conference. Conference values do not have to be stated to the attendees, but should be communicated to the conference staff so that they can work together in agreement of how tasks will be conducted.

- What are the values that this conference or organization holds dearly?
- How do we want people to interact with each other?
- What kind of attitudes are valued?
- What beliefs are important?

For our conferences, we had written value statements:

> *We want to have an atmosphere of:*
> *Celebration: uplifting, rejoicing atmosphere of excitement.*
> *Punctuality: keeping on schedule during meetings, rehearsals, and at the conference.*
> *Quality: displaying professionalism and a high standard in all aspects.*
> *Enjoyment: helping people to have fun, relax, and enjoy time there.*
> *Fellowship: building unity and relationships among attendees.*
> *Encouragement: uplifting the spirits of the women, helping their relationship with God.*
> *Welcome: helping people to feel at home, comfortable, like they are wanted.*
> *Cooperation: volunteers working together in a spirit of Christ's love.*

Other examples of value statements might be:

- Each participant should be encouraged to grow in relationship with God through Bible study.
- The event should allow people to support each other in sharing and prayer.
- We value reaching out to nonbelievers through relevant and creative communication.

CONCEPT APPROVAL

Approval structures

Once the concept has been developed, it needs to be approved by the organization's leadership. Whether the decision maker is an individual or a committee, someone from the organization will have to make the final decision to proceed with the conference. Approval of the concept can take a number of forms. Here are some of the approval structures:

- **Recurring local events.** If your church or organization regularly holds the conference, usually the event is automatically included in the annual budget. A pastor or organizational leader/committee handles the approval of such events.
- **Regional event.** Some events are sponsored by organizations that hold the same conference in a number of different regions. They look for local churches or organizations to co-sponsor the event. In these cases, the local church signs a contract to have the conference and the conference leaders are directed by the sponsoring organization. In other cases, organizations sponsor an annual conference that is held in a different location each year.
- **Brand new event.** When the conference is a new idea, consensus must be built before the approval is in place. If the conference is a first-time event with no past history, the approval process might be submitting a proposal for the event to the organization that will sponsor the event. Page 22 shows an example of a proposal for a first-time retreat that was

EXAMPLES

submitted to the church leadership. (Please note that although a facility was suggested, the church ended up using another facility. The initial suggestion was for reference only).

The proposal

Whether your event is a brand new one or a recurring one, if you need to get approval, submit a proposal for the event. The proposal provides information for the decision makers to make an informed decision whether to have the conference or not. It might explain the conference concept and include a written statement of the purpose and audience of the conference. You can also add any additional information of how you picture this conference, such as how long you think it might be, estimated costs, or other information you have uncovered in your research. Ask for a decision by a certain date so that the planning can start moving. Some churches require events, such as retreats, to be approved by the church leadership board, so be sure to allow plenty of time for the process!

Once approval has been granted, it's time to appoint the Conference Director, who will coordinate the whole event.

To: Pastor and Council Members

From:

Date:

Re: Proposal for church conference retreat

The objective of this proposal is to organize a first-time church conference retreat for ten to eighteen months from now. This idea is submitted respectfully to the pastor and council members to open discussion and request consideration of this large undertaking. The following outlines goals, general structure, planning and scheduling, and finances.

Goals

The church is experiencing gradual changes and growth as a whole and within. New families, young Christians, and visitors are entering into our church. A church conference retreat, planned for [year] would benefit our church in the following areas:

- to nurture growth in all attendees with respect to the Bible and the Christian life.

- to encourage individual relationships with God, in new and older Christians.

- to nurture relationships in a more intimate setting among different peer groups in the church.

- to provide time and space away from distractions for families, couples, and singles to enjoy themselves.

- to promote the church's identity and further church unity.

General Structure

The general structure of the conference retreat involves a two-night/three-day allotment of time. A speaker will be invited to give four general sessions and church members solicited to lead single session workshops. For example, general sessions take place Friday night, Saturday morning and evening, and Sunday morning. Attendees have a choice of two workshops from a selection of approximately five to six, based on eight to ten people per workshop. The workshops may be scheduled Saturday and Sunday late mornings, directly before lunch.

Mealtimes and lodging will be sources of accountability and sharing. Meals may be arranged with random seating to encourage mixing among family members. Younger children of course will stay with at least one of their parents. Men and women will be divided into small groups of three to four same-sex groups, with lodging locale considered, for evening devotions and sharing. Quiet time or individual devotional material may be provided and time scheduled during early mornings.

Based on the previous example, free time is scheduled in blocks on Saturday and Sunday afternoons of three to four hours in length. If desired, a variety/talent show may be scheduled for Saturday night. Music worship will be scheduled to precede the general sessions. Sunday morning's general session will take place of the Sunday sermon and communion shared at this time.

The described structure is designed to meet the goals listed above for church, family unit, and individual needs.

Planning and scheduling

The proposal is being made at this time due to the need for advanced planning and engagement of an appropriate guest speaker. Most conference sites have been reserved through [year] already. After approval from the pastor and the council, the second step would be to form a committee of about four to five people, holding the positions of chair (maintaining timetable/big picture); and secretary (recordkeeper); and additionally, five main areas of 1) general sessions (music, speaker); 2) workshops; 3) fellowship (mealtimes, free times, other activities); 4) devotionals (small group, individual); and 5) liaison (lodging accommodations, registration, finances). It is assumed that other individuals will be recruited for major participation; however, the committee members are responsible for seeing that items are accomplished on schedule. The committee will work in conjunction with the pastor and council to engage an appropriate guest speaker for the conference.

Finances

A proposed site for our first retreat is [city], approximately 1.5 hours from our church. There is a conference location called the [name] Conference Center in [town]. The Center consists of numerous lodges with in-house and separate conference rooms. Three meals per day are included with lodging fees. The Center is within a five-minute walk to the beach and a short drive to major sightseeing attractions.

[Year] rates are $64 per person per night. Children, ages three to seventeen, are charged a rate of $42. It is proposed that the committee design a fee schedule to make fair allowances for families with children. For example, singles and couples pay full price. Parents pay full price for their first child. The church subsidizes half the cost for the second child, three-quarters for the third, etc. The intention is to avoid penalizing singles or couples who do not have children. Additionally, financial aid may be considered on an individual case-by-case basis for those who request it.

Costs for the conference will stem from possible subsidization of lodging fees, speaker fees, and miscellaneous items such as workshop and devotional materials.

In conclusion, the conference retreat is intended to follow along the lines of our church's mission statement to reinforce and boost church unity and growth. Should there be any further questions, I would be happy to speak with you all.

Thank you for your attention and consideration.

Survey Results

1. Maximally, how much would you be willing to spend per person (children under 12 are free) for a sleeping room, meals, and meeting space, for two days and two nights?

$75 - $100	X
$100	XX
$120 - $150	XXXXXXXX
$150 - $200	XXXX
$300	X

2. What type of accommodations would you be willing to live and meet in?

Camping	XXXXXX
Hotel/Motel	XXXXXXXXXXXXXX
Exec. Conf. Center	XXXXXXX
Beachfront	XXXXXXXXXXX
Golf/v-ball/pool	XXXXXXXXX
House at Lake	X

3. When would you most likely be able to commit to attending? A weekend in:?

This year:

Easter	X
Memorial Day	X
July 4-6	XXXXX
July 10-12	XXXXXXX
August	X
Labor Day	X
early Nov	XXXXXX

Next year:

January	XXXX
February	XXXX
July	XXX

CHAPTER

3 | # CONFERENCE DIRECTOR

Some people are not detail-oriented.

"Please fill out this form," says the salesclerk, giving my husband a form. My husband slides the paper to me. He hates paperwork.

To my friend I say, "I plan out all my vacations. Details are important!"

"Who cares," she says. She never plans her vacations.

"Don't forget our meeting tomorrow," I tell a person I work with.

"What meeting?" he says. He had written it on his to-do list. He lost the list.

As much as I appreciate these dear people, they are not the types of people that would enjoy being a Conference Director. It's just a matter of fact that Directors deal with details!

A Director oversees the entire conference from the beginning to the end. Directors are often the people with the initial vision or burden for an event. They are motivated to see the planning carried out so that people can be positively influenced at the conference. They are able to juggle multiple things at once and harness the energy of the staff together. Above all, a Director must pray for guidance and wisdom in direction and leadership.

APPOINTING THE DIRECTOR

The Director may be someone who originally had the vision for the conference. In this case, she already has a passion and burden to see the conference through as she was the one who first thought of the idea.

In other cases, the Director is appointed by the sponsoring organization's leadership. She may be someone who has volunteered for the job, or either paid staff or a volunteer who is asked to oversee the conference.

If you are the Director, you have responded to an important and exciting calling. Just like the contractor of a house coordinates the different subcontractors who actually build a house, the Director oversees the team of coordinators. Each coordinator is responsible for his particular area but the Director organizes the efforts so that as a whole, everyone can be more effective.

OVERVIEW

Initially, the Director develops commitment by planning and recruiting others:

STEP-BY-STEP

1. Setting a planning timetable
2. Securing financial support for the event, or appointing a Finances Coordinator to do it (*Chapter Four: Finances*)
3. Recruiting conference staff members to oversee the different functional areas of the conference (*Chapter Five: Conference Staff*)

The Conference Director oversees coordination of the planning and execution of the conference, including leading the planning team.

Recommended Skills/Qualities

- Has time and passion to lead event
- Leadership abilities
- Administrative/organizational skills
- Attention to detail
- Team builder and good people skills
- Able to delegate responsibilities and follow up on task delegation
- Good communication skills
- Prayerful
- Responsible and dependable
- Able to function under pressure and make decisions; good problem-solver

Job Description

Before the conference

- Set and maintain timetable/big picture
- Develop budget
- Develop master timeline and keep key tasks on schedule
- Record and communicate information, meetings, decisions
- Provide spiritual and organizational leadership
- Communicate vision of event
- Recruit conference staff
- Coordinate and lead planning meetings
- Pray for staff and event

During the conference

- Oversee staff team and implementation of conference
- Make sure conference runs on schedule

After the conference

- Compile summary report
- Express appreciation to staff and celebrate together
- Evaluate conference and suggest improvements for next time

Time Commitment

This position's time commitment is:

Once the conference planning begins, the Director coordinates the efforts of the conference staff team (*Chapter 18: The Conference*).

When the conference is over, the Director evaluates, summarizes, and expresses appreciation to the team (*Chapter 19: Wrapping Up*).

THE PLANNING TIMETABLE

To help your conference succeed, begin as early as possible. You can never start too early! Many conferences begin planning two or more years in advance. Facilities and speakers are booked early so don't wait until the last minute to do everything. Get things done as early as possible. The more you try to get things done before their due date on the schedule, the more you will be glad that you did. The earlier you start, the easier your job will be later on. Build lag time into the schedule too. Allow yourself plenty of time if something unexpected should come up.

Your timetable will depend on the complexity of your event. The major factor that often determines how much time you have for your conference is the site. The larger your event, the earlier you will have to book a site. Most conferences require at least a year to prepare because many sites are booked a year or more in advance. But a small one-day seminar might only need a few months to pull together.

Speaker availability and enough time for marketing are other factors that might determine your planning schedule.

> Book speakers two years out; look at your budget two years out. Think four years out for speakers and musicians. The best speakers and even the middle-road speakers get booked up quickly. ◆ *Jeanne Gregory*

A general planning timetable can be found starting on page 27 for a large, medium, or small event. It lists key responsibilities and suggested dates when they should be accomplished. The actual timetable of your conference will vary depending on the size of your conference and the scope of your program. If you're booking one speaker for a one-day event, you'll be able to pull the program together in less time than a three-day conference with one hundred workshops. Adjust the timing according to the complexity and size of the event. As you schedule, work backwards and set milestones and goals and when they should be accomplished. Distribute this schedule to your team so that everyone will know when their tasks need to be completed.

HELPFUL TIPS

As you head into the planning process, you'll face challenges along the way. Here are some points to keep in mind—they'll help smooth the bumps ahead.

Pray

I already noted this in the beginning of the previous chapter, but it's worth repeating. Pray about anything and everything, from beginning to end! Seek God to guide you throughout the process, and ask for a heart that follows after His own.

> First and foremost is to let God lead you. Don't have retreats or conferences just for the sake of doing something. You have to make sure it's God-led. God will lead you. It's amazing if you ask God and persist. He will give you a vision if He has called you to lead His people. The job of a leader is to find out what God wants. ◆ *Vicky Wauterleck*

PLANNING TIMETABLE

| Type of Conference | | | Area of Coordination | | | |
Small	Medium	Large	Director and Admin	Program	Logistics	Marketing and Prayer
9+ mos	13+mos	2+ yr	Get event approved by organization leadership; Begin securing financial resources			
9 mos	13 mos	1.5+ yrs	Set budget; Recruit planning team; Define purpose and audience; Set goals and determine format; Set theme; Set preliminary date of event	**Program/Speaker:** Discuss possible speakers, workshop teachers, and topics	**Site:** Begin researching sites (call and visit); **Exhibits:** List exhibitors to invite	
9 mos	12 mos	1.5+ yrs (5–10 yrs for very large conference)	Visit site; Investigate conference insurance; **Finance:** Open bank account	**All:** Visit site; **Speaker:** Begin calling speakers and entertainment sources	**All:** Visit site; **Site:** Negotiate, select, and book site; **Transportation:** Investigate airlines and other transportation vendors; **Exhibits:** Ask vendors for bids	**All:** Visit site
7-9 mos	11 mos	1+ yr		**Program:** set preliminary schedule; Recruit worship leader; **Speaker:** Book speakers and entertainment	**Transportation:** Book transportation companies; **Site:** Obtain map/floor plan of site and housing forms; **Exhibits:** Draw floor plan, assemble exhibitor's packets; **Hospitality:** Determine meals and breaks needed; **Technical:** Investigate AV options	**Marketing:** Set marketing strategy and begin implementing; Select photographer and copywriter; Put event announcement on Web site
7-8 mos	10 mos	1+ yr	Reserve P.O. box	**Speaker:** Confirm dates with site before confirming dates with speakers; Book speakers and entertainment	**Exhibits:** Contact exhibitors; **Registration:** Plan registration system; **Hospitality:** Research caterers and vendors (linens, equipment, chairs and tables)	**Marketing:** Take photo of site and/or local area
6-7 mos	9 mos		Plan site office setup	**Speaker:** Send speakers forms	**Exhibits:** Confirm exhibitors	**Marketing:** Get printing bids
6 mos	8 mos		Arrange for site office equipment	**Speaker:** Receive speaker bio info; Give biographies to Marketing for brochure	**Exhibits:** Make arrangements for exhibitors/assign booths; **Registration:** Set up reg. system; Give registration form info to Mktg; **Site:** Give map/driving direction to Marketing	**Prayer:** Begin recruiting prayer team; Begin sending monthly e-mail prayer requests; **Marketing:** Receive info for brochure
6 mos	7 mos					**Marketing:** Design and print brochure; **Prayer:** Make arrangements with Site and Program

Page 2

| Type of Conference | | | Area of Coordination | | | |
Small	Medium	Large	Director and Other	Program	Logistics	Marketing/Prayer
6 mos	6 mos	6+ mos		**Program:** Develop small group materials **Speaker:** Receive equipment list from speakers; give to Technical	**Site:** Give preliminary schedule to site to reserve rooms **Volunteers:** List volunteer needs **Hospitality:** Select caterer and menu Sign contract with caterer	**Marketing:** Distribute brochures Order banners **Prayer:** Begin sending out monthly e-mail requests
5 mos	5 mos	5+ mos		**Speaker:** Arrange transportation for speakers Receive message outlines from speakers and give to Marketing	**Volunteers:** Begin recruiting volunteers **Hospitality:** Arrange for rented/borrowed items **Technical:** Receive list of equipment from speakers **Registration:** Begin receiving registrations, discuss ideas for registration packets **Transportation:** Arrange parking **Site:** Reserve housing for staff **Exhibit:** Send housing forms to exhibitors and floor plan to Marketg	
4 mos	4 mos	4+ mos			**Site:** Make room assignments and setup plans **Hospitality:** Plan decor scheme Give food signage list to Marketing **Volunteer:** Arrange volunteer registration and training materials **Registration:** Plan on-site registration process **Exhibits:** Confirm booths with exhibitors, plan exhibitor program	**Marketing:** Design conference handbook Review signage needs
3 mos	3 mos	3+ mos		**Program:** Finalize program schedule Receive worship list from worship leader	**Technical:** Arrange for equipment **Volunteer:** Assign responsibilities **Registration:** Order badge supplies **Exhibits:** Order signage, make arrangements	**Marketing:** Order or make signage Arrange for bulletin/verbal announcements
2 mos	2 mos	2+ mos	Order office supplies	**Program:** Submit stage setup diagram to Site/Technical Begin cue sheet Song and lyrics order to Marketing for PowerPoint	**Transportation:** Arrange parking **All:** Make appreciation plans for after the conference (gifts, notes) **Registration:** begin assembling materials for registration packets **Exhibits:** Make arrangements for storage of exhibitor materials	

Type of Conference			Area of Coordination			
Small	Medium	Large	Director and Other	Program	Logistics	Marketing/Prayer
1 mo	1 mo	1+ mo	**Director:** Form crisis management plans, finalize program details with planning team	**Speakers:** Send out final confirmation letter Arrange for speaker hosts with Volunteer Coordinator **Program:** Finalize cue sheet	**Equipment:** Arrange security **Volunteer:** Confirm volunteers, assign volunteers to job positions **Exhibits:** Confirm arrangements **Registration:** early registration deadline, assemble registration packets	**Marketing:** Send out news release **Prayer:** Finalize arrangements with Site and Program Begin sending out weekly prayer requests
3 wks	3 wk	3 wks	Pack items for shipping Prepare evaluation form	**All:** Pack items for shipping **Speakers:** Give final equipment list to Technical	**All:** Pack items for shipping **Transportation:** Confirm arrangemts **Hospitality:** Decorations finished **Equipment:** Finalize equipment list **Volunteer:** Finalize thank you gifts for volunteers	**All:** Pack items for shipping
2 wks	2 wks	2 wks	**Director:** Run final planning meeting **Finances:** Prepare honorarium checks	**Program:** Finalize speaker intros **Speaker:** Prepare speaker packets	**Transportation:** Arrange carpools **Site:** Submit final setup diagrams, assign housing, confirm arrangements **Hospitality:** Confirm rentals, food Order flowers **Volunteer:** Assemble job description sheets for volunteers	**Prayer:** Confirm arrangements with prayer intercessors and Program
1 wk	1 wk	1 wk	**All:** Check that materials have arrived		**Registration:** Give final registration count to staff and food outlet, make last-minute badges	**Prayer:** On-site prayer meeting Begin sending out daily prayer requests via e-mail
Day before	Day before	3 or 4 days before	**Director:** Review assignments with conference and site staff Set up office at site	**Speaker:** Welcome speakers Coor. rehearsals with speakers Take speakers to dinner **Program:** Run rehearsal schedule	**Volunteer:** Run orientation and training for volunteers **Exhibits:** Welcome exhibitors **All:** Set up site	
Conference	Conference	Conference	**Director:** Oversee entire conference	**Program:** Run program part of conference **Speaker:** Oversee speaker needs	**All:** Oversee own areas	**Marketing:** Post signage
After	After	After	**All:** Write thank you notes, evaluate conference	**All:** Write thank you notes, evaluate conference	**All:** Write thank you notes, evaluate conference	**All:** Write thank you notes, evaluate conference

Have realistic expectations

If you had a conference of fifty people last year, don't expect 500 to come this year. If God does provide the numbers, that's a wonderful praise, but estimate conservatively and be pleasantly surprised!

> Even the very best conferences grow about two to four percent. ✦ *Jeanne Gregory*

Communicate

An informed team is an effective team. Communicate with your team frequently. Let them know what is happening. Ask their opinion. It's better to communicate too much than too little.

COMPUTER HELPS

A great way to keep everyone informed is to set up an e-mail list where everyone receives the information. Web sites such as www.yahoogroups.com allow you to set up such lists. Or, if you know a computer guru with a server, they can create one for you. All you have to do is set up a group alias name, such as "ABCconferenceteam@yahoogroups.com." Then when you send e-mail, type in the alias and the message will automatically be sent to the whole group. If a person replies to that message, it is sent to the rest of the group.

Follow up frequently

It's an unfortunate fact of life that people are forgetful. Mail gets lost; phone messages aren't returned. Keep a running list of people who need to get back to you and then follow up! It will save you trouble in the long run and even though it's a little extra effort on your part, you won't regret it.

Know your priorities

Keep your focus on your role and the important aspects of the conference. If you've delegated a task to someone, let her handle it!

> A lot of meeting planners get stuck on some of the little details, neglecting the big pieces. For example, you might get into a marketing situation where you try to promote an event and you may fiddle with some elements of a print piece *ad nauseum* when the fact of the matter is that it's good enough. ✦ *Andrew Accardy*

Be flexible

The prime law of conference planning is, "Nothing will go exactly the way you planned it." Conferences are composed of thousands of little details and something is sure to go a way that wasn't planned. The best thing you can do is to be on your toes, ready to make adjustments along the way.

> At our last conference, we were broadcasting live. Dr. Dobson was supposed to be there to speak at eleven o'clock sharp. The cameras went on, I was introducing him—and he was stuck in traffic. For fifteen minutes I basically did a little song and dance and talking. I did an infomercial on several books and resources and acted like this was all supposed to be happening. But I was having a cow and wondering when he was going to get there! ✦ *Yvette Maher*

Although your conference may not be broadcast, every conference is a "live" event and you can't redo the mistakes. A director who is flexible, quick thinking, and reliant on God in prayer will help the conference proceed smoothly. Most participants will never know that anything unexpected has happened! Just accept that God has a hand in all the surprises. Then relax and enjoy yourself and see what God does!

> Plan the best conference or ministry you can and then be prepared to change the whole thing if that's the way God is leading. ✦ *Ron Sugimoto*

Be positive

Since you know nothing will go the way you expect it, be positive and look at the good things that are happening.

> One of the speakers at our last conference went way over her allotted time. Our conference was tightly packed from minute to minute during the program sessions. We told her clearly beforehand, "Thirty-five minutes." She went forty minutes ... forty-five minutes. ...Her husband typed in big bright letters on his laptop computer, "HURRY UP!" and then held it up from the back of the auditorium. She looked up, saw the message—and smiled and went on. But after her message seven people accepted Christ (the most we had ever had at previous conferences was one person). We later shortened our break and the worship but we were still able to end on time. Later I was glad that she was more in tune with what God was doing than with my own plans to keep according to schedule!

Evaluate

Throughout the process, get feedback from the staff on how things are going. Listen to their concerns and make adjustments where necessary. Evaluation is an important part of follow-up after the conference too (page 231).

Encourage and appreciate others

Take the time to encourage your staff and recognize what they are doing. At the planning meetings, talk about successes, what they did right, and thank people publicly. Your staff will receive valuable positive feedback and a sense of purpose in what they are doing.

Celebrate!

Don't wait until the conference is over to celebrate. Celebrate along the way. Celebrate little victories. Pop out the Martinelli's at every opportunity! Throw a party for finalizing the program or confirming all your speakers. It brings a great positive atmosphere to the whole process and the team has a fun time together. Even bringing food to the planning meetings adds an air of celebration to a normally mundane task.

Now that you have an understanding of the Director's task, it's time to turn to establishing the financial foundation of the event.

4 | FINANCES

When it comes to my checkbook, I am "numerically-challenged." No matter how hard I try, the balance is wrong in the end. My husband finally took pity on my pathetic efforts and bought me a software program so that now I can do it all on the computer. Now, if only I could figure out how to get someone to make my mortgage payments for me . . . .

Fortunately, God has blessed some people, unlike me, with the ability to handle financial tasks with ease. These people not only are able to balance any kind of financial statement, they think it's fun! Every conference team should have one of these people on the team. These people are able to keep a sharp eye on the finances and determine the wisest use of money.

In the corporate world, nobody bats an eye at spending tens of thousands of dollars on a speaker, reserving a five-star resort, or renting state-of-the-art equipment. But the non-profit world is a different matter; putting on a quality conference with a limited amount of finances is a major challenge for Christian organizations.

Although finances aren't the most exciting subject for most people, they are a crucial part of conference planning. Your financial situation will impact major decisions such as where the event will be held or how much you can compensate speakers.

TIPS FOR SUCCESS

It's easy to worry about finances and obsess over costs, particularly if finances are tight. You may wonder if you will have the finances to carry the event through. As you begin, make Philippians 4:19 your key verse: "And my God will meet all your needs according to his glorious riches in Christ Jesus." There may be times when you'll wonder if you will have enough to see the event through. But remember that God is always faithful. If he wants this event to happen, he will provide the financial resources that you need!

If you have a complex conference, you may need a person whose sole responsibility is handling financial matters. This Finance Coordinator works with the other members of the team to handle any transactions or financial issues. If your event is simple or small, you may choose to include the financial responsibilities as part of another coordinator's duties (such as the Registration Coordinator).

Because the Director usually gets approval from the organization's leadership before the Finance Coordinator is recruited, the initial steps in this chapter may actually be carried out by the Director.

The Finance Coordinator oversees the financial procedures of the conference, including the budget, finances and finding sponsors for financial support.

Recommended Skills/Qualities

- Experience working with finances
- Good "business sense"
- Trustworthy, responsible
- Attention to detail
- Administrative/organizational skills
- Good record-keeper
- Responsible and dependable
- Good communication skills

Job Description

Before the conference

- Attend planning meetings
- Set budget
- Open and manage bank account
- Establish a record-keeping system
- Track records and receipts
- Disburse payments
- Help solicit and find sponsors

During the conference

- Pay bills
- Distribute honorariums

After the conference

- Close bank account
- Submit final financial report
- Send notes of appreciation to co-sponsors
- Evaluate conference and suggest improvements for next time

Time Commitment

This position's time commitment is:

OVERVIEW

STEP-BY-STEP

The Finance Coordinator (or Director, whoever is handling finances at this point) establishes the financial procedures according to the purpose of the conference by:

1. Setting the budget (including determining registration fees)
2. Establishing a record-keeping system
3. Finding co-sponsors for the event

At the conference, the Finance Coordinator pays bills and invoices, and deposits money from on-site registrations (*Chapter 18: The Conference*).

After the conference, the Finance Coordinator pays final bills and summarizes the records from the conference (*Chapter 19: Wrapping Up*).

THE BUDGET

The Finance Coordinator's first task is to establish a budget. A budget sets down a financial plan for the event. A budget can provide a number of benefits. It:

- provides a basis for wise financial decisions
- directs expenditures of different areas
- helps prioritize what is important
- ensures wise stewardship of God's resources

Once the purpose and goals of the conference have been established, you can begin planning the budget. If you have financial statements from previous conferences, you can review them to see what may be expected. First-time conferences will have to estimate amounts as there is no past history to rely on.

TIPS FOR SUCCESS

Help your conference succeed financially by planning your budget as far in advance as possible. Be detailed in your budget planning and, if possible, set a healthy cushion it so that you won't run out of money later. It's always better to have money and not spend it, than to run short and find that your program's effectiveness is reduced because of insufficient funds.

If your organization is tax-exempt, find out the laws for non-profits so they can help you budget wisely.

Determining who is financing the event

Although after the conference you'll hopefully break even or make a profit, initially you'll need funds to pay the expenses. Find out who provides the initial funds, whether it is your church, organization, or sponsors that support the ministry. Where will you get the money to pay for the site deposit and other bills that must be paid before the income begins flowing in?

Setting financial goals

Before you can set financial goals, you'll need to review the purpose of the conference. Maybe your conference is for students. Most students don't have a regular income and are not able to afford a high registration fee. Therefore, a realistic financial goal for your conference might be trying to break even. Since you know that the student registration prices will be low, you'll need to find an outside source to help subsidize your event. Maybe your church will provide a fund, or maybe you can get outside sponsors or fundraising.

> At Urbana, we figure out how much students can afford and what is okay for them to pay. The rest is shortfall and we fundraise for it—it costs significantly more per delegate to go to Urbana than a student is charged. For fundraising, there are foundations that give money away, so we write proposals for grants. Individuals donate too. People go to Urbana as Stewards; Stewards pay their own way and they go there to work.
> ✦ *Keith Hirata*

What kind of financial goal do you want for your conference? Do you want to make a profit? Break even? Your goal will impact how you calculate the amounts. If you want to break even but the income is looking thin, you'll need to find a source to make up the difference.

Financial goals help prioritize your decisions: Is it more important to save money or is it acceptable to spend a little more money to improve the experience? What does your audience value more—a nice place to sleep, or a great meal? Looking at the goals helps prioritize the decisions that need to be made.

Although saving money is important to nonprofits, be aware that being too limited with finances works against you. Sometimes it's worth paying more for a better conference experience.

> Sometimes people cancel little things to save money but they harm their own conference. When people arrive, it looks like a nice hotel but there is a small breakfast and they don't get drinks or cookies; there's not much extra and it's not much fun. People, like businessmen, go to nice hotels and pay for nice experiences. They won't come to a retreat and forget all that. Our church used to do a low-cost men's retreat and had fifty men going. Now they don't mince the price; they show the men that they are important, and they feed them great. They now have 102 men. If you're not careful planning financially, you can sacrifice your own goal. ◆ *Jeanne Gregory*

Estimating income and expenses

EXAMPLES

1. Fill out the *Budget* worksheet on pages 36 and 37.
2. Estimate to the best of your ability how much income you'll receive.
3. List the expenses.
4. Work with the numbers until you find that the income total (A) and the expenses (D) are equal (or, if you want to make a profit, the income is more than the expenses).

In some cases, your organization will give you money. Other times, you may estimate an initial amount and then the financial people will give feedback on how that number needs to be adjusted. Go through the worksheet on the next page and put down ballpark amounts to figure out a rough budget.

> We use benchmarks: 20% of the expected gross revenue is spent on marketing. We try to spend no more than 60% on other direct expenses. ◆ *Andrew Accardy*

If you don't know yet what your registration fee will be, skip the first line "Registrations" for now.

Setting registration fees

EXAMPLES

If you don't know how much to charge for registration, then use the worksheet on page 39, *Registration Fee Calculation*. There are a few different ways to calculate registration fees.

1. First begin by asking yourself some background questions:
   - What is the anticipated attendance?
   - What is the reasonable amount for people to pay? You can find out the reasonable amount by looking at what other similar events charge. Be aware that amounts may also vary by geographical location.

BUDGET PLANNER	Worksheet

ESTIMATED INCOME

Registrations: # of registrants (_____) x amt. each ($_____) = ...$ _____
Sponsors: # of sponsors (_____) x amt. each ($_____) = ...$ _____
Exhibitors: # of exhibitors (_____) x amt. each ($_____) = ...$ _____
Carryover from previous conference ....$ _____
Funds from your organization ....$ _____
Donations (merchandise or monetary gifts) ....$ _____
Fundraising ....$ _____
Advertising revenue ....$ _____
Sales of promotional items (t-shirts, etc.) ....$ _____

A. TOTAL INCOME (add amounts) ....$ _____

ESTIMATED EXPENSES

Administration

Stationery, envelopes ....$ _____
Telephone ....$ _____
Office supplies (paper, printer ink cartridges) ....$ _____
Postage ....$ _____
Planning expenses (food for planning meetings, childcare) ....$ _____
Insurance ....$ _____
Staff expenses (travel, meals, supplies) ....$ _____
Legal consultations (contracts) ....$ _____

Program

Speakers: # of speakers (_____) x fee each ($_____) = ...$ _____
Workshops: # of speakers (_____) x fee each ($_____) = ...$ _____
   Travel, hotel, meals for speakers ....$ _____
   Workshop supplies (overhead pens, transparencies, etc.) ....$ _____
   Speaker packets ....$ _____
   Thank you gifts for speakers ....$ _____
Entertainment ....$ _____
Worship:
   CCLI Fee ....$ _____
   Sheet music ....$ _____
   Equipment (CDs, cables, etc.) ....$ _____
Creative arts:
   Drama scripts ....$ _____
   Video production ....$ _____
   PowerPoint production ....$ _____
Translators/translation fees ....$ _____
Small group materials ....$ _____
Recreation equipment ....$ _____
Prizes, awards, doorprizes ....$ _____
Exhibits:
   Setup costs ....$ _____
   Table/furniture rental ....$ _____
   Labor ....$ _____

Site

Room rental ....$ _____
Equipment rental:
   Audiovisual ....$ _____
   Computer ....$ _____
   Lighting ....$ _____
   Chairs/tables ....$ _____

Kitchen equipment . . . . $ _____
Other rentals . . . . $ _____
Labor . . . . $ _____
Staff costs . . . . $ _____
Rehearsal/setup times . . . . $ _____
Housing . . . . $ _____
Insurance . . . . $ _____
Security . . . . $ _____
Gratuities . . . . $ _____

Registration
P.O. Box rental (if expecting many mail-in registrations) . . . . $ _____
Registration supplies (nametags, clipboards, pens) . . . . $ _____
Credit card registration processing fees . . . . $ _____
Ticket printing . . . . $ _____
Handout materials:
Envelopes/folders to hold materials . . . . $ _____
Programs . . . . $ _____
Evaluation forms and other inserts . . . . $ _____
Giveaways (pens, paper) . . . . $ _____
Name badges (including ones for staff and volunteers) . . . . $ _____
Complimentary registrations (and scholarships) . . . . $ _____

Food
Linens . . . . $ _____
Utensils/service items . . . . $ _____
Meals: # of meals   (_____) x cost each ($_____) = . . . $ _____
Snacks: # of snacks   (_____) x cost each ($_____) = . . . $ _____
Beverages . . . . $ _____
Speakers' refreshments/food . . . . $ _____
Food for volunteers . . . . $ _____
Staff and gratuities . . . . $ _____
Cleanup . . . . $ _____

Other Logistics
Volunteer thank you gifts . . . . $ _____
Childcare costs . . . . $ _____
Decor:
Centerpieces . . . . $ _____
Other decorations . . . . $ _____
Transportation:
Airfare . . . . $ _____
Ground transportation . . . . $ _____
Parking . . . . $ _____

Marketing
Design . . . . $ _____
Photography . . . . $ _____
Printing . . . . $ _____
Mailing list rental/postage to mail brochures . . . . $ _____
Web site development . . . . $ _____
Advertising . . . . $ _____
Press kits/news releases . . . . $ _____
Photography . . . . $ _____
Signage . . . . $ _____

B. SUBTOTAL EXPENSES (add amounts) . . . . $ _____
C. Contingency (B x 10%) . . . . $ _____

D. TOTAL EXPENSES (add B + C) . . . . $ _____

REGISTRATION FEE INCOME | Worksheet

First early bird rate: ($_____) x expected no. people (_____) = ...$_____
Offered at the previous conference for people who sign up for the next conference

Second early bird: ($_____) x expected no. people (_____) = ...$_____
For those who register a month or two before the event

Regular rate: ($_____) x expected no. people (_____) = ...$_____

On-site rate: ($_____) x expected no. people (_____) = ...$_____
The regular rate plus an additional charge

Daily rate: ($_____) x expected no. people (_____) = ...$_____

Member rate: ($_____) x expected no. people (_____) = ...$_____
A discounted amount from the regular rate

Non-member rate: ($_____) x expected no. people (_____) = ...$_____

Student rate: ($_____) x expected no. people (_____) = ...$_____

Ministry rate: ($_____) x expected no. people (_____) = ...$_____

Regular rate: ($_____) x expected no. people (_____) = ...$_____

Guest rate: ($_____) x expected no. people (_____) = ...$_____

Total registration income (add all totals above) . . . .$_____

SAMPLE REGISTRATION FEE STRUCTURES

Sample fee structure for a weekend conference.

Rate when registering at the previous conference: $100

Deadline:	1 month before	At the door
Member	$150	$225
Non-member	$200	$275
Ministry	$100	$125
Guest	$80	$105
Student	$75	$95
Daily rate	$80	$100

2. Then follow one of these two methods:

REGISTRATION FEE CALCULATION | Worksheet

Method One
A. Total Expenses ("D" on page 37) .... $ _____
B. Number of expected participants .... _____ people
C. Expenses ÷ expected participants (A÷B) = registration fee for each person .... $ _____

Method Two
A. Total Expenses ("C" on page 37) .... $ _____
B. Reasonable price per person .... $ _____
C. Expenses ÷ reasonable price (A÷B) = # of people needed to break even .... _____ people

---

COMPUTER HELPS

If you work these numbers on a spreadsheet, then you can adjust the amounts until you arrive at a satisfactory amount. Spreadsheets allow you to easily adjust the numbers until the income and expenses are balanced. If you're finding the numbers are too high, then you will need to make up the difference by finding sponsors.

Types of registration fees

Many conferences also offer different rate structures for registrations. See if any of these options might work for your event:

- **Regular rate:** the amount paid for people who register after the "early bird" cutoff date.
- **Early bird rate:** the discounted rate(s) for people who register before a certain date. Early bird rates may be offered in phases. For example, the biggest discount is received when the participant registers for next year's conference at the end of this year's conference. After a few months, this first early bird rate is replaced by another rate which is higher. This second rate is extended until perhaps a month or two before the next event, at which point the regular rate takes effect. Don't have more than two rate changes or people will get confused!
- **On-site rate:** (also called *walk-on rate*) the amount paid by people who arrive and register at the conference. This rate is usually the regular rate plus an additional amount to discourage people from waiting until the last moment to register.
- **Daily rate:** the amount paid by people who are only attending part of a multi-day conference, or who attend but do not stay overnight.
- **Member rate:** the discounted amount paid by a member of the organization hosting the event.
- **Non-member rate:** the rate paid by people who are not members.
- **Student rate:** the discounted rate for students. Some events offer discounts to only full-time students. Other organizations will give students the discount even if they are currently taking a one-hour class.
- **Ministry rate:** the discounted rate for people in vocational ministry.
- **Guest (or spouse) rate:** the amount paid by guests or spouses of attendees who pay the cost of meals, accommodations, and social events.

Looking at the list above, you might feel like you are in an ice cream store with dozens of choices, and your eyes may be boggled by the possibilities. Don't be alarmed. This is just a smorgasbord of the types of fees available and you can select which fee structure works best for your event.

ESTABLISHING A RECORD-KEEPING SYSTEM

Now that your budget is done, distribute it. Give every staff member a copy. Make sure they understand how much they have to spend.

Although your budget is finally complete, it won't do you a bit of good unless you develop a system for tracking the income and expenses. Set up an organized system for payments, receipts, and recording information.

STEP-BY-STEP

1. Decide what payment options will be available and whether you will be accepting credit cards, checks, or cash. Open a checking account for the conference if your organization doesn't have one that you can use for the conference.

2. Decide what record-keeping system you will use, whether handwritten in a ledger, entered in a spreadsheet, or tracked with accounting software. Set up your system so that you can easily enter and find information.

EXAMPLES

3. Make expense report forms for the staff (see the sample *Expense Reimbursement* form on page 42). Educate them on how to fill out the forms and the reimbursement policy. Since your job will be more difficult if you wait until the end to do everything, ask them to turn in their receipts frequently; then pay all bills regularly.

4. Update all income and expenses. Every month check the budget to make sure everything is on track. Prepare a regular financial report for the team. When the conference is over, prepare a final financial report for next year's conference.

FINDING SPONSORS

If you find that your conference doesn't have enough income from registration fees alone, you'll need to find organizations or companies that would be willing to help sponsor your event. Sponsors can give anything from a small donation to being a major underwriter of the event.

Learn sponsorship laws

Check into the federal laws regarding non-profit organizations (and also any state laws). Contributions from corporations may not be subject to taxes as income if they are within certain parameters. Check the laws so you know what is permissible and you can learn how to handle the sponsorship money wisely and legally.

List potential sponsors

Who might be willing to be a financial sponsor for your event?
- Your denomination, church, or organization
- Organizations that may attend your conference
- Foundations
- Community businesses
- Exhibitors at your event
- Individuals

Donation requests do not have to be limited to monetary amounts. You can also ask for donated items, prizes, food, transportation, or services. Look over your budget to see what needs you have and then ask the sponsors if they might be willing to cover one or more items.

Contact sponsors

When approaching sponsors, approach them from their point of view. Ask yourself why the sponsor should support your event. How will the sponsorship benefit them? Businesses look at how opportunities will impact the bottom line, so emphasize the benefits they will receive in sponsoring. Let them know how they will be acknowledged or promoted at the conference. For example, they may receive:

- a linked button from the conference Web site to their Web site
- advertising space in the program booklet
- a free exhibit space
- access to the mailing list
- an opportunity to interact with the delegates.

Before you contact the potential sponsors, write out a list of benefits and advantages to their sponsorship at the conference. This will give you (and them) a clear picture of how sponsors benefit from joining your conference effort. It's also a helpful aid to have on hand if you are on the phone and are asked for details. As you call, don't be afraid to ask what they can contribute—the worst they can do is say no!

> We have a leadership conference for students. The hotel treats them to a poolside hotdog party. It doesn't cost them much, but it's great PR. ◆ *Dean Jones*

As you write the solicitation letters, be specific about an amount that you would like from them and to whom the check should be made. Set a deadline for responses. Keep it brief—one page is adequate and anything longer would not be read anyway.

If you choose to call first to see what interest there is, find out the name of the person to send the letters. Make sure that the name and address are spelled correctly. Within a day of reaching them by phone, send your letter or proposal out as soon as possible. When you do, tell them you will follow up and then two weeks later call them again.

When a sponsor sends in their donation, immediately send a thank you note. After the conference, send them another letter to let them know what the results of the conference were. When they see the success of the event and the effectiveness of their sponsorship, they will be more likely to sponsor your event next year!

EXPENSE REIMBURSEMENT

| Form |

Name _____

Address _____

Phone number _____ Fax # _____

E-mail address _____

Date	Vendor	Description and Purpose	Amount
_____	_____	_____	_____
_____	_____	_____	_____
_____	_____	_____	_____
_____	_____	_____	_____
_____	_____	_____	_____
_____	_____	_____	_____
_____	_____	_____	_____
_____	_____	_____	_____
_____	_____	_____	_____
_____	_____	_____	_____
_____	_____	_____	_____
_____	_____	_____	_____
_____	_____	_____	_____
_____	_____	_____	_____
_____	_____	_____	_____
_____	_____	_____	_____
_____	_____	_____	_____
_____	_____	_____	_____
_____	_____	_____	_____
_____	_____	_____	_____
_____	_____	_____	_____
_____	_____	_____	_____
_____	_____	_____	_____

Total _____

CHAPTER

5 | CONFERENCE STAFF

One of the keys for a successful conference is recruiting an effective conference staff team. This team of people will be working with the Director in the many months ahead in preparing and overseeing every detail of the conference.

OVERVIEW

STEP-BY-STEP

Your key task now is finding and recruiting the people who will commit to planning the conference:
1. Recruit an advisory group
2. Recruit a conference staff team
3. Run the first meeting

RECRUITING AN ADVISORY GROUP

TIPS FOR SUCCESS

If this is a first-time event, it's advantageous to have a group of people you can turn to for guidance and advice. The Advisory Group doesn't have to meet together, but may be a group that who you can turn to for feedback and advice.

People with wisdom and discernment are good choices for advisers. They may be people experienced with events or mature believers such as your pastor, ministry leader, or perhaps a wise friend. It's also helpful to have a person on your team who is familiar with the goals of your organization. Here are some possibilities:

- Mature Christians with biblical wisdom who can help in making decisions.
- People with experience coordinating conferences.
- People who are experienced in the field.
- Leaders in the organization.

If you are coordinating a conference as an extension of another organization (the organization holds conferences in different geographical areas and you oversee the local conference), then you don't have to worry about finding an advisory group because the organization will provide guidelines for you.

This advisory team can help you by being a resource for any questions that might come up when you're planning the conference. It's good to have people provide insight and wisdom for making decisions.

Often a new Director makes the mistake of having everyone report to her; she is the one leader and all 100 volunteers go to her. During the conference, she is stressed out answering the questions of fifty different people at once.

The Director should only manage a handful of people to be truly effective. Delegating allows Directors to divide the tasks so the team carries out the different responsibilities, yet she remains aware of what is happening and can make key decisions. Building up a conference staff team to plan the event is far more effective than doing it alone. It can be a lot more fun too!

The purpose of the staff is to plan and implement the conference according to the goals and purposes of the organization or conference. Having a written statement to distribute to your staff will help them understand their role and keep everyone on the same page.

Recruit staff as soon as possible. They will balance you out and help spread the workload. What's the best way to recruit an effective staff? Here's a step-by-step list:

1. Assess your leadership style.
2. Determine qualities needed for a well-rounded team.
3. Assess planning team position needs.
4. Brainstorm a list of possible people.
5. Ask people.

1 Assess your leadership style

The starting point to putting together an effective staff is understanding your own leadership style. When you know how you best lead, then you can recruit a team that can help compliment your gifts. Conference Directors come in all shapes and sizes. Some will find that their strengths lie in one area; others are a mix of multiple working styles. Here are just three to start with; there are many other types of leaders.

Visionary Leader

The Visionary Leader has the ability to communicate a compelling picture of the future so that people are motivated to make it a reality. Visionary leaders are able to cast an exciting view of the event so that people want to get involved. However, Visionary Leaders, because of their strength in seeing the big picture, often miss details. If you're a Visionary Leader who would rather focus on the overall picture, then enlist people on your staff who will help you cover those details. Visionaries are most successful as Conference Directors when they find people who are good at laying out a plan for their vision and implementing it.

Organizer/Administrative Leader

The Organizer takes the idea (perhaps suggested by a Visionary Leader) and systematically details the multitude of steps needed to accomplish the goal. Organizers excel at pulling plans, resources, and tasks together to finish the job. Often, Organizers need those who are strong on the relational aspect of coordinating. They can become so task-focused that they forget to take care of their team, or they forget that not everyone finds it fun handling details and discussing business all day.

Relational Leader

The Relational Leader helps people feel like part of one big happy family. Relational Leaders are energized by interacting with people. They prefer people over tasks and need to look for team members who can help keep things on track to ensure that everything is completed.

Other leaders

There are countless other leaders who excel in different areas of leadership—strategizing, financial management, creativity. Effective leaders understand their strengths and weaknesses and look for people to balance them out.

2 Determine qualities needed for a well-rounded team

Once you know what your strengths are, list the qualities needed to make your staff effective. Maybe you are great at relating to people but need a creative person to think of great ideas. Or if you are good at accomplishing tasks, maybe you need someone who is a good motivator and encourager to pull people together. As you look for people to fill positions, keep this list in mind so you can find people who can help round out the staff.

> Tom Patterson, former consultant for IBM and Disney, has identified five different types of people.
>
> The first is a grinder: Give them a task and they can do it, but spell out exactly what they need to do. An example of a grinder is a conference registrar. You define a system for them; they grind through all the registrations.
>
> There are Minders: they improve the system once they understand it. They mind their tasks so they have more ability to see the improvements that can be made, but they are capable of doing routine work.
>
> Keepers can see the tactical with the strategic, turning vision into reality. They understand the strategic objectives of where the meeting needs to go and yet also understand the need to facilitate day-to-day work in order to get it done.
>
> Finders are the people who can find other people to work for them. They aren't so good with day-to-day stuff but are more interested in team building.
>
> The last one is the Theorists, the visionaries. They come up with all the great ideas.
>
> Any organization needs all of these: someone who's managing, building the team, creating the vision, managing the systems and improving them, and people who are grinding the work out. ✦ *Andrew Accardy*

You may not be able to find people to cover every area, but these are some helpful qualities to have on every team.

- **Spiritual leader:** shepherds and encourages the team spiritually.
- **Creative thinker:** can think outside of the box; comes up with new ideas and new ways of doing things.
- **Business manager:** has good business sense; can make good financial decisions and determine how to best use resources.
- **Motivator/encourager:** keeps the energy level up on a team; a relational person who is upbeat and optimistic and brings out the best in everyone.
- **Strategist:** good at seeing the right direction to go and laying out goals to get there.
- **Administrator:** keeps on top of details, good at scheduling and recording information.
- **Communicator:** keeps everyone connected, good at communicating information.

3 List staff positions

Now it's time to list the positions and job responsibilities of the staff.

Paid staff or volunteers?

Many conferences are entirely run by volunteers. Others combine both paid staff and volunteers. Some organizations hire people specifically to oversee conferences. What is your situation? If your team will have paid staff, who will they be?

What positions do you need?

What are the different functional areas that will need coordinators? In the first chapter, we discussed an overview of the different areas. If your event is simple and small, you may only have a few coordinators, some who may handle more than one area. More complex events may have a coordinator for each area and they have leaders under them overseeing each sub-area.

A conference can be divided into different functional areas for coordination. Although each area stands alone and may have its own coordinator, they overlap each other and impact the other areas as well. Each area can also be further subdivided into areas of responsibility. The four main functional areas are:

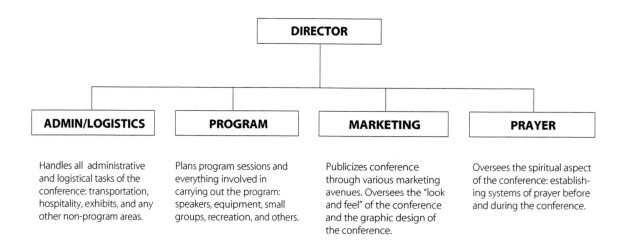

ADMINISTRATIVE/LOGISTICS COORDINATOR: Oversees conference operations and administration:

- **Childcare:** on-site childcare staff and programs.
- **Exhibits:** companies and organizations showcase their products and services to attendees.
- **Finances:** budget establishment and finance tracking.
- **Site:** arrangements for meeting rooms and accommodations.
- **Follow-up:** evaluation of conference as well as following up attendees who have made decisions for Christ.
- **Hospitality/Food:** food, decorations, and special touches to make delegates feel welcome.
- **Registration:** registering delegates.
- **Technical:** equipment selection, setup, and operation.
- **Transportation:** arranging transportation for speakers and attendees. Includes arrival/departure as well as on-site transportation between meeting sites.
- **Volunteer:** volunteers utilized before, during, and after conference.

PROGRAM COORDINATOR: Oversees everything that happens in the meeting rooms. You may also choose to break the Program Coordinator's job into other positions if you have a particularly large or complex conference. For example, one person designated as the Speaker Coordinator handles all the speaker arrangements.

- **Speaker:** general session speakers and workshop teachers. (If you have a large number of workshops, you may want to divide the main session speakers from the workshop speakers.)

- **Worship:** worship arrangements.
- **Entertainment:** musicians, drama, and other entertainment.
- **Small Groups:** small group breakout times and materials.
- **Recreation:** recreational activities that delegates participate in.

MARKETING: Publicizes the conference through print, media, and verbal promotion. Establishes a graphic identity and positive image for the conference.

- **Promotional materials:** brochures, flyers, posters and other literature.
- **Signage:** complete and clear signage.

PRAYER COORDINATOR: Supports the conference through prayer. Oversees prayer times at meetings, recruits prayer intercessors, and handles the prayer ministry time at the conference event.

As you assess which positions are needed, avoid having too large of a staff team. A large staff makes it difficult to find a time that everyone can meet. It's also hard to make decisions with a large, cumbersome team. Instead of having twenty different coordinators for twenty different areas, have just a few key leaders and divide those twenty leaders under them. Your staff then is made up of those five people and they are the ones who attend the planning meetings. After, they update the leaders under their particular area.

Make an organizational chart

Create an organizational chart to show authority and accountability. The organizational chart helps everyone involved in the conference know where they fit in the overall picture and who they are responsible to. The organizational chart can be simple or complex. Its complexity will depend on the scope of the conference. Here's a sample structure for a simple event, where each person oversees multiple functions:

SMALLER CONFERENCE TEAM

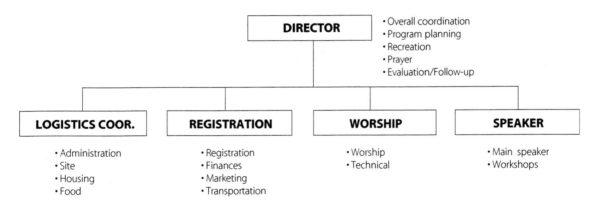

With a smaller conference staff, a few people oversee the areas and recruit volunteers to help them. Since the event is quite small, there is no need for a Volunteer Coordinator.

A more complex event needs more people to oversee the different functions because the event increases in complexity. It might look like this:

MEDIUM CONFERENCE TEAM

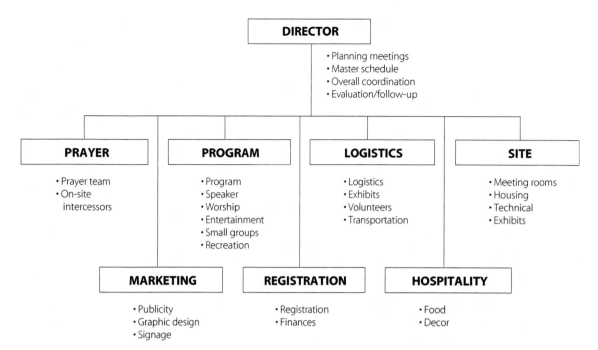

The leaders (in the rectangles) are the coordinators and are the staff who attend the planning meetings. Each one oversees his own responsibilities, usually alone. A very large conference event might involve a number of coordinators with sub-leaders under them (below). Planning meetings could include all the main leaders as well as a number of key sub-leaders

LARGE CONFERENCE TEAM

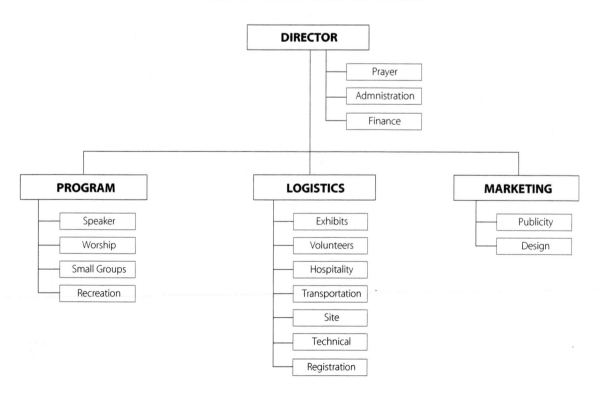

(such as Registration, Finance, and Prayer).

These are just examples of the many ways your staff can be structured. Pray and ask God to guide you in how to structure the team in a way that would efficiently plan for the upcoming conference.

Write job descriptions

Write a sample job description for each staff member. It's up to you how detailed you want to be, but at the very least include:

- Title of position
- What is done before the conference
- What is done during the conference
- What is done after the conference
- How much time is involved

This allows people to know what they are committing to so that there is no misunderstanding later.

The chapters in *Part Two* begin with sample job descriptions for each functional area. Use these descriptions as a starting point for writing the job descriptions for people needed on your team.

3 Brainstorm a list of possible people

Now it's time to draw up the list of potential candidates. Ask yourself what qualities these people should have and what types of people you want on the team.

When he looks for people to join his team, conference coordinator Doug Yonamine has modified a list used by Bill Hybels:

Character: This is the most important quality to have. A person of character will have integrity and the values to make wise decisions. He or she will be dependable and trustworthy. When you have a person of character on your team, you know that everything will be in good hands.

Competency: Does this person have the right skills for the job? Is he qualified? Can he make decisions based on past experience?

Chemistry: How well does this person get along with others? Is he effective working with this team? Is he a team player? Don't be alarmed if at first impression it seems this person has a little bit of difficulty fitting in. It may be a matter of time to adjust to each other's personalities. But if the person has poor social skills and has a history of conflicts with other people, then it's time to re-examine if he is the best choice.

Composure: How does he handle stress and change? Conferences sprout problems and challenges like mushrooms. Every conference leader must be flexible and remain calm. Can he adjust on the spot? Does he take a responsibility and run with it? People who have to be told exactly what to do are probably not the best candidates for a leadership position.

4 Ask people

Now it's time ask other people to join you in the fun! The best way is to ask people you know and that you have worked with before to join you. This way you know what they are capable of and that you can work together. If you can't fill all the positions in this way, then ask people you know for recommendations. This is a great way to put together a very effective team of qualified people.

If you're new to the organization or don't have an extensive network of people you know, you'll have to take another route. Put out a general announcement about the upcoming event and ask interested people to attend a meeting. Those who attend discuss what their interests are and then positions can be assigned based on their interests. The advantage of using this method is that more people can get involved. Sometimes people unknown to you step forward and do a fantastic job.

As you talk to people, find out their working styles. Is this person a detail-oriented or a big picture person? Does he like to be structured or prefer spontaneity? Does he like to be on the phone? Try to match the position with one that will fit his personality best. *Chapter 16: Volunteer Coordinator* includes more information about recruiting and managing volunteers. Look over the chapter to find ideas for managing your team.

YOUR ROLE ON THE TEAM

Directors are the glue that holds the staff together. Besides leadership, their main responsibilities are:
- Vision casting
- Coordination and accountability
- Shepherding

Vision casting

One of the most important things the Director can do in the beginning is to communicate the vision of the conference. It's especially important for you to remind the staff that this event is God's ministry, not yours or theirs. Giving this kind of reminder helps set a proper perspective on the entire event. If minor details fall through the cracks (or even some major ones) they won't seem like major disasters if people remember that God ultimately is in control and that His plans and His purposes are beyond our own. Looking at the conference from a spiritually-centered heart gives a balanced focus to every task.

The staff needs to understand what this conference is all about as a part of God's purpose. They also need to understand why the event is being held and who they will be serving: the conference is to meet the needs of the people attending. Then they will have a Christ-centered focus.

Directors also help the staff to see a picture of what the conference will be like. Share with them how you see things happening, then show them how they fit into the overall scheme of things. This encourages the staff to look beyond themselves and their responsibilities and have a sense of how everything works together.

Coordination and accountability

Another key responsibility of the Director is to make sure everything gets done on schedule. You handle the overall coordination, scheduling who is doing what and holding staff accountable to getting everything done. Hold team members accountable to accomplishing their tasks on time.

You also run the meetings. Plan ahead of time—preparation makes the meetings more effective and efficient. Have an agenda and a purpose to the meeting.

Shepherding

Jesus is the best example of a leader who cared for his team of disciples. Take care of your staff. Pray for them. Encourage them. Acknowledge people publicly for their efforts. Give them the credit. Take the blame. Be a peacemaker if your team members need to work out a conflict. Care for them as Jesus cared for his disciples.

As soon as people decide they want to join the staff, schedule the first meeting. Here's the agenda for your first meeting. If your conference will not be held for a couple years, you might only touch on each of these areas. If the timetable you have for planning the conference is short, you might need an extended meeting to go over each item in detail. Although this list might seem intimidating, it's important to go over each area briefly so people know what to expect. The goal for the meeting is to help people get an overview of the conference.

1. Welcoming activity
2. Open in prayer
3. Discuss planning process
4. Discuss goals/audience
5. Review job descriptions
6. Discuss conference format
7. Discuss possible sites
8. Brainstorm theme
9. Discuss possible speakers
10. Discuss food requirements
11. Determine children's needs
12. Discuss technical needs
13. Discuss exhibits
14. Discuss follow-up plans
15. Discuss preliminary budget
16. Discuss planning timetable
17. Schedule all meetings
18. Build relationships
19. Pray

1 Welcoming activity

Start your meeting with an icebreaker or welcoming activity to help the people on your staff get to know one another and be comfortable with each other. If it's a new team where people don't know each other, they'll appreciate the opportunity to be familiarized with each other.

2 Open in prayer

Begin by asking for wisdom and direction as you plan. Seek after what God would like you to do.

3 Discuss planning process

Establishing ground rules for decisions will prevent miscommunication and headaches in the future. Discuss issues such as:

- **Ground rules.** Many of these will be obvious, but it's still helpful to go over them so that everyone is on the same page. Examples of guidelines that can be used are: starting and ending meetings on time, not criticizing others' ideas, and staying on the topic.
- **Decision process.** How will decisions be made? How much time is there to make decisions? Does other input need to be gathered first? What authority does each person have to make decisions in his area? As a group, who makes the final decision?
- **Meeting roles.** It's helpful to have someone in the group to be the facilitator (leading the discussion), recording the meeting, and distributing follow-up information. Find someone who will take care of each of these roles.

4 Discuss purpose/audience

Before planning is started, your first task is to help the staff understand the big picture of the conference. Back in *Chapter 2: Concept Development,* you created a blueprint that included the purpose and goals of the conference. It's time to share that blueprint with the others so that they can develop ownership of the plan.

Organization, audience, purpose, and values

Give them background information about the organization (if they are not from your organization) and its mission. Help them to understand how this conference accomplishes the goals of the organization and why you are having a conference.

Then discuss the audience. Who is this conference for? Why would this group attend this conference?

The purpose of the conference is the foundation of all the planning that is done. Share the purpose of the conference and refine these purposes into clear statements. It's also a good time to go over the value statements and develop those as well.

Goals

Goals are another important part of the blueprint that must be laid before any planning is done. With goals, decisions can be prioritized. Goals serve as a structured framework for the entire planning process of the conference.

> Stephen Macchia approaches conference planning from a macro view and a micro view. Macro issues ask the overall questions: Why hold a conference? Who do you want to come? When is it? Where will it be? After looking at the macro issues, they are broken down into micro issues with details. Even goals should be approached with a macro view and a micro view: have an overall goal and then smaller goals. For example, one of Vision New England's macro goals is having a certain number of churches attend with an average of two teams per church. A micro goal would break that down by describing the type of group that attends.

The type of goals you set will depend on your audience. If you are holding a conference for youth, a goal based on action and activity is more effective than giving them time to rest and be pampered.

> "SMART" goals are Specific, Measurable, Achievable, and Results-oriented. We created a goal to have 10,000 people at the conference. We asked, "Is 10,000 specific?" Yes, it was time-specific because of the definitive date we had. "Is it feasible and realistic? Is it results-oriented?" Yes, because we were impacting the bottom line of the organization. ◆ *Andrew Accardy*

> When we get the team together for the retreat plan, we begin with the end. We create a profile of what we want our attendee to be at the end of the event. What do they leave with? How they should be different when they leave? One time our profile said we wanted them to be pleasantly exhausted. If they just sat there and didn't break a sweat during the week then it didn't seem worth it! ◆ *Ron Sugimoto*

> The goals depend on the type of retreat. A youth retreat's goal might be to get new people to come to the retreat. Or maybe a retreat for first time believers would provide discipleship and leadership for those who have accepted the Lord and want to grow more. A women's retreat might want to remove them from the daily situation of children, work, job, stress; it should be more of an emotional retreat than a time of activity. A men's retreat might be to remove them from business and stress and provide a good environment for fellowship. Family retreats normally are designed around spending time with the family. ◆ *Jennifer Cope*

TIPS FOR SUCCESS

What kind of measurable results do you want to achieve by the end of the event, or after the event? Keep the goals in mind when discussing all aspects of the conference. They will serve as a clear guide for you in your planning.

5 Review job descriptions

Pass out to the team the job descriptions that you put together earlier. It's also helpful to pass out a list of contact information of the other team members too, so people know how to reach each other.

If people do not know what area they will oversee, take some time to go around and ask people what areas look interesting and where their strengths lie. Then assign positions to those who are willing to oversee the areas.

Review the responsibilities of each person so that people know who is responsible for what. Clearly outline the accountability structure so people know who they are responsible to report to. If you have put together an organizational chart, giving a copy will help people understand the structure.

> As a leader, one of the key things you have to do is make sure that the people you are giving responsibility to are well-suited for the job. You never give the responsibility without the authority. ◆ *Vicky Wauterleck*

Encourage people to recruit teams to work with them. Having a team of at least three people ensures that even if one person drops out, there is at least one other person to help. It also allows other people to be trained. An added plus is that having three people provides opportunities to get to know others and fellowship together. You can't do that if you are doing the job yourself!

6 Discuss conference design

The design of the conference refers to what will be happening at the event. This is not the time to begin planning out the schedule specifics, but instead a chance to brainstorm ideas and discuss how the conference will look. Interact with each other on what types of program elements might accomplish the goal. Try to establish a "big picture" of what the event will look like.

Length of program

How long should the program be? Is it a small seminar, or multiple days with multiple sessions? The goals you have set determine what format the program should take.

Is the conference one day? A weekend? During the week? When should it start or end? If it is to be held during the week, traffic or people's work schedules might cause them to be late. Will this be an issue?

For a retreat, an event of at least two nights' stay allows more opportunities for group interaction and relationship building. But be aware that if the conference is more than a day, some people will leave early or not stay for the entire day. Encourage people to stay for the whole weekend for maximum benefit; but remember that not everyone will listen!

What kind of ideas are there for what will happen at the conference? Brainstorm ideas and weed through them for a rough outline of what the conference will look like.

Size of event

How many people do you think will attend? If you have never held the conference before, look at similar events in the area. Take your best guess. The estimated size of the event helps you narrow down facilities and estimate the budget needed.

7 Discuss possible sites

What kind of location would be best suited for this event? Discuss ideas. See *Chapter 7: Site* for ideas and information about sites.

8 Brainstorm theme

A theme serves as a unifying factor for every aspect of an event. Using a theme reinforces the message in people's minds. People have a difficult time remembering the fifty different things they learned at the conference. But if they are able to remember one main theme, they are more likely to remember the other things that are related to the theme. Repeat the theme in the messages, the drama, the music, and as many different ways as you can to reinforce the message.

Repetition is important. People are inundated with so much today; you have to give it to them several times in different ways. ◆ Vicky Wauterleck

Begin determining the theme by starting in prayer. Sometimes the theme is quickly decided—just like that, everyone agrees unanimously what the theme is. Other times it involves many discussions and long periods of prayer. If you have the evaluation forms from the previous event, they can provide valuable information about needs or desires of the audience you are targeting.

Ask yourself these questions:
- Who is the audience? Who is this event for? What age is the audience? What is the gender? What stage of life is the audience? What are their special interests?
- What needs or issues are occurring in their lives?
- How can their needs/issues be best addressed?
- What is the goal of this event and what kind of theme would reflect this purpose?

Use a short slogan or phrase as a theme. "Discover How You Can Experience Freedom That Gives Meaningful Purpose to Your Life," is almost impossible to remember; "Freedom With A Purpose" is better.

9 Discuss possible speakers

Who are speakers that would fit the audience and purpose of the conference? Toss around some initial ideas. Check out *Chapter 9: Speakers* for more details on speakers.

10 Discuss food requirements

Based on the program and schedule, what meals will be needed? What kind of food suits the audience and purpose of the conference?

11 Determine children's needs

Will childcare or a children's program be needed at the conference? If so, how will it be provided? For some conferences, childcare is not an option due to liability issues. If you would like to provide childcare, check with your organization first to see if it is a feasible option.

If you would like to provide a program for children, decide what ages and what the scope of the program will be—full time, only during general sessions, or only at certain times. What is the purpose of the program—to entertain them, let them play, or to teach them? Each purpose leads to a significant difference in how time will be spent.

Although this book has tips about providing children's programs, it will not cover the detailed specifics of developing them because there are many other excellent resources available on the subject. If you would like to provide childcare, recruit a qualified person to oversee this area.

12 Discuss technical needs

What kind of equipment or technology will be needed at the conference? Possible areas of technology include:
- computer systems for registration
- audiovisual equipment in main sessions
- audiovisual equipment for individual workshops
- Web site development

Discuss what kind of technology is cost-effective for the type of event you are holding.

13 Discuss exhibits

Will your conference have exhibits? What is the purpose of having an exhibit area? What is the extent of the exhibit area? Will you have tabletop or booth exhibits? What kind of exhibitors will be solicited?

14 Discuss follow-up plans

Take some time to discuss what will happen after the conference is over. A lot of effort, time, and finances go into conducting a conference, so further your investment by planning a follow-up strategy.

> A lot of people look at an event as an isolated experience—it's a huge mistake to do so. If you know why your organization exists, you need to do things other than the event. Develop a strategy that continues after the event. After the great experience, what is the next step? Don't just do events for the sake of doing the event. ◆ *Andrew Accardy*

15 Discuss preliminary budget

Pass out copies of the preliminary budget that you put together (pages 36-37). If there is a Finance Coordinator on the team, you may want her to review the budget with the team and explain procedures for spending and reimbursement. As the budget is reviewed, point out:

- Who is financing the event.
- What the financial goal of the conference is.
- Preliminary registration fee prices.
- Ballpark figures for the individual areas. Each coordinator will need to break down the budget into specific line items. They may need to do some research to find out what the exact figures should be.
- Clarify how the expenses are handled.

16 Discuss planning timetable

SCHEDULING

Set a date

Set an approximate time for the event. What time of year will it be? Consider major holidays, sports events, school events, long weekends, weather factors, or any other local events that may conflict with your event. If you know of Christian organizations that hold major events in your area, make a note to call them or search their Web sites to see when their next event in your area is scheduled. If your event is to be held in your church, check that there are no conflicts with other church events. Scheduling a conference during a holiday or in conflict with another major event is a sure recipe for low attendance.

What day(s) during the week will the conference be held? Is a weekend or a weekday better? What time of day will the event start and end?

Set the schedule so that you will have enough time to accomplish everything, especially tasks that require a long lead time such as finding a site or booking a well-known speaker. Will there be enough time to book the site or find a speaker?

You might find it helpful to run the dates by some potential attendees to get their feedback.

Keep in mind that hotels offer discounts at certain times of the year. Hotels price according to "peak" seasons (periods of high demand), "value" (low demand), and "shoulder" (variable demand).

It's difficult to finalize the date until the site and speaker are found. So keep your dates flexible and choose a few alternate dates in case the first choice doesn't work out.

Once you know what the date will be (it may be an approximate date until you are able to confirm the site), then you can begin drawing up the planning timetable.

SCHEDULING

17 Schedule all your meetings

Set all your meetings for the rest of the planning process when you get every-one together in one location. The frequency of meetings will vary depending on the size of your event and how long you have to plan it, but a general rule of thumb is to have meetings every other month until about six months before the even. Then meet every month until the month or two before and then meet every other week or so. If you find you don't need to meet, just cancel it and everyone will be grateful for the extra time.

It's important for everyone on the team to be updated on each other's areas because everyone should know a little of what is going on in the rest of the conference.

18 Build relationships

When I first stated planning conferences, I wanted to end every meeting on time. As a result, I really pushed the meetings to get through the agenda items. One day after a meeting, one of the team members told me, "Did you know Diana found out she was pregnant? She wanted to tell the team but she didn't have a chance to." I felt terrible and learned to make time for sharing what was going on in our lives so that we could encourage and pray with one another.

Jesus modeled that relationship was the basis for ministry. Conference plan-ning can easily be all task and no relationship unless you make a priority of establishing relationships on the team. Take some time to share with each other and pray for each other. Schedule an occasional social event. Have fun!

Understanding where a person is spiritually, looking out for them spiritually, and not put-ting them in a place where they're going to fail, is important. ◆ *Vicky Wauterleck*

19 Pray

Since prayer is an important part of laying the foundation of the conference, spend some time praying together. Pray for each other's personal requests, as well as for the upcoming planning process and conference. If your team has a Prayer Coordinator, have him decided how to best close out the first staff meeting.

THE NEXT STEP

Now that the initial meeting is over, the next phase begins. It's time to coordi-nate the efforts of the staff into an efficient and effective result!

COORDINATION
SECOND STAGE

FOR THE DIRECTOR

Have you ever seen a millipede?

Now, I am not a bug lover, but even I have to admit that a millipede it is a work of art. Its ability to coordinate the seemingly hundreds of legs is amazing. It never trips over itself or gets confused trying to make its legs work together. It's a good thing that people don't have as many legs as millipedes. Imaging trying to coordinate the tasks of dozens of people *and* their legs!

At times, planning a conference feels like you are trying to coordinate a herd of millipedes. Every conference has many areas to oversee and it's a major undertaking to make sure that they are synchronized.

This section details the different areas of coordination until the time of the conference (the conference is covered in the *Part Three*). Even if you are a coordinator of only one area, skim over the sections of the others to have an idea of what the others are doing.

To make sure that everyone is working together, communicate frequently. Every team is different. Some teams require face-to-face contact. Others work great on e-mail.

> The conference that we planned took a year and had almost 1000 attendees. But we only had three or four face-to-face meetings total with the team. Ninety percent of the work was done over e-mail. Since the team members lived a distance from each other, e-mail was a lifesaver for us! We only set meetings for times when the group had to make decisions as a whole. Otherwise, the e-mail list served as the hub of communication for the entire team. By the end we were getting tons of e-mails each day about the conference. It was crazy but it worked great.

TIPS FOR SUCCESS

Communication is key because often things break down when there is miscommunication. Keep everyone up-to-date on what is going on. Use e-mail, telephone, face-to-face meetings. Repeat yourself often, even though you may feel like you are being redundant. It's amazing how little people remember!

When the program has been set, your job is overseeing the tasks of the team members and holding them accountable to getting their tasks done. Keep team members enthusiastic and excited by giving them updates of what is happening. Involve them as much as possible to increase their sense of ownership and responsibility in the event.

At meetings, pass out updated schedules, contact sheets, and other pertinent information about the conference. Even though everyone is overseeing their particular area, it is helpful for all the team members to know what is going on other people's areas so they can see how their role fits in.

Now, on to the different areas!

CHAPTER

6 | PRAYER

Like many other conference planners, I'm prone to "Martha-ness." Martha's stressed-out busyness in the Bible has been compared to her sister Mary's quiet contemplation of Christ. It's sad but true that given my natural inclination, I would rather "do" than "be." Often we conference planners are Type A personalities who rush around from activity to activity. We're busy and we like to get things done. We are efficient . . . although admittedly there are occasional lapses.

Case in point—this morning our family prepared to go out of town. I spent the whole morning cleaning the house, packing, and getting things ready for the trip. It wasn't until we arrived at the airport that I realized an error. I remembered my husband's bag. I remembered my son's bag. I remembered my daughter's bag. But my bag was missing: I had forgotten it.

But I didn't forget to pray! I prayed for my mom, who had graciously offered to drive home to pick up my bag. I prayed that she would get back in time so that I wouldn't miss my flight! (And she did, although I was reprimanded by the airport staff for holding up the plane!)

Unfortunately, sometimes conference coordinating is like that too. We are so busy rushing around that it isn't until things go wrong that we remember to pray. Like Martha, we are so busy preparing that we forget the focus of why we are doing the conference.

TIPS FOR SUCCESS

The foundation of every event is prayer. We may put every effort into putting on the best event that we possibly can, but unless we pray and rely on God's strength, it will just fall flat. For there to be true effectiveness and lasting results, praying for the Holy Spirit's work is a must. God's plans are intricately woven, and no matter how much we try, we can't fully understand what He is up to; all we can do is trust in Him. Every person involved in the planning team needs to nurture that attitude of trust and dependence on God in prayer—not an easy thing to do!

WHY PRAY?

1 Thessalonians 5:17 tells us to pray without ceasing. Besides the fact that we are commanded to pray, there are many practical reasons and benefits to do so. When we pray:

- We are reminded of our reliance on God.
- It gives protection over the event.
- It gives us wisdom in guidance as we plan.
- It helps the event be more effective in people's lives.
- It builds our faith as we see prayer answered!

The Prayer Coordinator oversees prayer coverage of the entire conference from beginning to end, including coordinating prayer meetings and teams of prayer intercessors.

Recommended Skills/Qualities

- A heart for prayer
- Encouraging and supportive
- Creativity
- Able to coordinate meetings and tasks

Job Description

Before the conference

- Attend planning meetings and lead prayer times
- Decide how to include prayer in program
- Recruit prayer team before conference to pray for requests
- Send out prayer requests via e-mail network before conference
- Support planning team with prayer
- Lead prayer meeting the night before the conference
- Lead additional prayer meetings as needed
- Recruit prayer intercessors to pray together during conference and to pray with participants during and after the conference

During the conference

- Serve as contact person for prayer intercessors during event
- Oversee prayer sign-up list

After the conference

- Compose summary report
- Send out praise report of answered prayer and thank you notes to prayer partners and intercessors
- Evaluate conference and suggest improvements for next time

Time Commitment

This position's time commitment is:

We are reminded of our reliance on God

It's so easy to try to rely on our own strength. When we pray, it's a reminder for us to depend on God. It's humbling when things don't go right, and we pray desperate prayers and God comes through. When amazing things happen, we know it's all God's doing and He gets the credit, not us!

One of the most encouraging things after a conference is when I review all the prayer requests that went out before the conference. Seeing all these prayers answered is a visual reminder of God's faithfulness!

It gives protection over the event

Though we can't see it and often are not aware of it, spiritual warfare is a reality. When we are doing God's will, we will face opposition. Prayer builds up protection around us and the event. Sometimes the opposition is subtle; other times it is obvious. If we build an awareness of the battle going on, we can prepare for it by praying and asking for God's protection.

> Another time, the night before the conference, one of our main speakers was suddenly ill with a fever and could not get out of bed. Our prayer team prayed for her healing and protection at nine p.m. The next day, she came to the conference and said, "At nine o'clock last night I suddenly felt better, got out of bed and was able to do housework and felt fine!" She gave an excellent talk.

The conference must be backed by prayer. This will only happen if intentional steps are taken to cover every aspect of the conference in prayer.

It gives us wisdom in guidance as we plan

Have you ever tried to drive somewhere without knowing the directions? Chances are you spent some time going in circles and trying to find your way around. You probably took some wrong turns and may have even had to ask for directions.

It's the same way with conference planning. We can try our best to plan and prepare, but only God ultimately knows what is best since He knows what will happen. If we pray for wisdom and guidance, He will lead us. All we have to do is ask. Why not turn to the ultimate Guide?

> When we first began planning the Asian American Women's Conference, we had no idea how many people would show up. We found a very nice church that seated a maximum of 500 people. As I prayed, I felt uncomfortable because I thought, "What if we have more than 500 people?" Although the idea of getting more than 500 people to attend seemed incredible, I trusted that God would guide us. We decided to proceed with booking the facility. But after we went ahead, we found out that the facility was not available at the date we needed. We ended up finding another church that could hold more than 1000 people, but I wondered if it would feel too empty if only a few hundred showed up.
>
> The month before the conference, our planning team struggled with discouragement. Only forty-two people had registered. Then the early bird deadline passed and suddenly 800 registrations appeared in one week. The day of the conference, over 900 women showed up. God knew best!

It helps the event be more effective in people's lives

After people attend the event, they say, "That was an awesome event!" Then, after a month of facing everyday struggles and the daily grind of life, that inspiration is gone. But when we pray, God is able to use this event to bring lasting impact in ways we can't imagine. Only the Holy Spirit can bring about permanent change in the lives of those who attend.

> We've always had a prayer team. They pray us through the whole year. They meet monthly. We have a prayer team on-site too. The team comes the night before and

prays over every room. They pray for delegates as well as speakers. The prayer team is also available during the conference. People sign up for prayer slots and they pray during the sessions. We have prayer coordinators who train people in praying. We have seventy denominations and hundreds of churches who attend and barriers between churches are falling down. As we see more of that happen, it fulfills our vision! ✦ *Pam Chun*

It builds our faith as we see prayer answered

There's nothing that builds your faith as much as seeing the visible work of God, through answered prayer and through the change in people's lives.

OVERVIEW

TIPS FOR SUCCESS

STEP-BY-STEP

Prayer can easily be forgotten unless someone on the team takes ownership of this important area. If the team has a person interested in being the Prayer Coordinator, assign her the responsibility of developing the area of prayer, and of coordinating prayer coverage of the entire conference from beginning to end. If the team doesn't have such a person, find someone who loves to pray and who wants to see other people have the chance to pray.

The pre-conference responsibilities of the Prayer Coordinator include:
1. Listing areas of prayer
2. Integrating prayer into the program
3. Recruiting prayer partners
4. Praying for the planning team
5. Scheduling prayer meetings
6. Making conference plans

At the conference, the Prayer Coordinator handles the on-site coordination of the prayer intercessors and prayer ministry times (see *Chapter 18: The Conference.*)

After the conference, the Prayer Coordinator expresses appreciation to those involved and summarizes the results to the team (see *Chapter 19: Wrapping Up*).

LISTING AREAS OF PRAYER

The Prayer Coordinator begins by drawing up a list of all the different areas of the conference. Your list may be long or short, depending on the complexity of the event. Here's an A-Z list of areas of prayer that can be included on the list:

- **Attendees:** that those who come would be impacted for Christ
- **Balance:** balance in busy lives
- **Coordination:** meetings, guidance, team members
- **Divine appointments**: that God would orchestrate the meetings of people in order to build relationships, and bring healing and encouragement
- **Equipment:** cost-effective, finding good quality equipment, smooth operation, people to set up and operate equipment
- **Finances:** that God would provide the finances needed, wisdom in being good stewards financially; sponsors, fund-raising
- **God's protection:** safety and security, spiritual protection from the enemy's attacks
- **Holy Spirit:** protection, Holy Spirit working, open hearts, timing in attendees' lives
- **Intercessors:** people to come forward to pray for the conference
- **Jesus-focus:** eyes would be kept on the Lord and not on selves
- **Knowledge:** guidance, wisdom for decisions
- **Love for each other:** conference staff would be unified and would love each other

- **Marketing:** mailings, word of mouth, churches would partner to promote event
- **New Christians:** for people to accept Christ and for those who are new believers to grow
- **Outreach:** an opportunity to reach out to those who don't know Christ
- **Post-conference tasks and follow-up:** guidance in the process and good closure to the conference
- **Quiet hearts:** people's hearts receptive to hear what God is saying
- **Registration:** people register quickly and that process would go smoothly
- **Speakers:** finding speakers, guidance in preparation, authority in teaching, changed lives
- **Time:** people would be able to find time for meetings and to get their work done
- **Undivided attention:** no distractions so that people can concentrate
- **Volunteers:** finding good volunteers and enough of them
- **Worship:** worship leader, team members, worship experience
- **X-tra energy:** so that everything could get done
- **Yes to God:** people would respond to God
- **Zeal for God:** God would renew waning hearts and inspire people to follow him

Tailor the list to fit your particular event and be as specific as you want. This will serve as a master list of ongoing prayer requests.

INTEGRATING PRAYER INTO THE PROGRAM

Discuss with the Program Coordinator and the conference staff how prayer can be integrated into the program. If an extended prayer time is not appropriate for your program, there are many other ways that prayer can be used effectively at an event:
- Have an on-site prayer intercession team to pray during the entire event.
- Offer a prayer ministry time for the participants after the general session. Have the speaker make an announcement that people can go to the front to be prayed over by the intercessors.
- Put out a sign-up list for people to sign up to pray with intercessors. Or make the prayer room available for anyone who would like to drop in.
- During small group time, give people a chance to pray for each other.
- In workshops, ask workshop teachers to use a few minutes at the end for people to respond in prayer.

RECRUITING PRAYER PARTNERS

As you begin recruiting, set a goal for how many people you'd like to join. Do you want one person to pray each day of the week? Or do you want a group to pray any time? Pray for the Lord to bring people forward and keep actively recruiting people until you reach your goal.

How can you find prayer partners? Write an announcement that you are looking for prayer partners. Be creative in distributing this announcement:
- Put the announcement in the church bulletin.
- Send it via e-mail.
- Ask people on the planning team to forward it to people they know.
- Include it in your organization's newsletter.
- Add a button to your Web site for people to sign up

COMPUTER HELPS

As people begin joining, decide what is the best way to communicate prayer requests to these people.

We've found e-mail lists to be effective in getting timely prayer requests out. We set up a listserv on yahoogroups.com and sent out prayer requests to the alias so that it automatically went to all the people at once. When we sent out prayer requests, we also sent out answers to prayer so that people could be encouraged to see how their prayer efforts were helping.

Send out regular prayer requests to the people on the list. Rotate through the list you made on pages 63-64, concentrating on one area every week. Initially, you can send requests out monthly as things get started. Then a few months before the conference, start sending out requests every week.

Provide people practical reminders how to pray:

- Attach the prayer time to a regular routine you do every day: brushing your teeth, eating breakfast, getting in the car.
- Pray immediately when you receive the e-mail so you don't forget to do it later.
- Put a daily reminder on your calendar (if you have an electronic organizer, you can program it to repeat daily).
- Set your watch alarm at the same time every day to remind you to pray.

Some of the prayer partners may also be interested in being on-site prayer intercessors during the event. If you plan to have prayer intercessors at the event, be sure to make an announcement early so that people can begin planning.

Ask the Registration Coordinator to put an announcement in the confirmation letter asking participants to pray and prepare their hearts for what God will be doing at the event. You can even ask those interested in praying for the conference to contact you.

PRAYING FOR THE PLANNING TEAM

Another area of prayer that Prayer Coordinator oversees is leading the prayer times at the planning meetings. Try to devote some time each meeting to pray for the conference and the team members.

> We usually reserved the last half our of the meeting to prayer. We tried to have variety in our prayer time. Sometimes, we would go in a circle and pray for each person and the area she was coordinating. Other times we pulled out our Bibles and prayed over Bible verses. One time the Prayer Coordinator went around and blessed each woman and her ministry—it encouraged everyone on the team.

SCHEDULING PRAYER MEETINGS

TIPS FOR SUCCESS

If you will be having prayer meetings for the upcoming event, invite the planning team as well as other prayer intercessors to attend. The meetings may be held right after a planning meeting or at a separate time.

One important prayer meeting is held the night before the conference or the night before the setup begins. Bring the prayer partners through the facility and pray over the entire location.

- Do a prayer walk through the facility.
- Pray over the chairs where people will be sitting.
- Pray for the speakers on the stage.
- Go into the workshop rooms and pray for the speakers and participants there.
- Walk around the exhibits area and pray for the exhibitors.
- Pray in the dining room, that significant ministry will be accomplished over the fellowship time.

- Pray in the tech booth that the equipment will function properly.
- Walk through the hallways and pray for significant conversations and God's love to be shown.

MAKING CONFERENCE PLANS

STEP-BY-STEP

If you are having prayer intercessors at your conference, you'll need a system for how the intercessors will pray for the attendees.

1. Send out invitations.
2. Let them know the expectations and responsibilities.
3. Compile a list of who is attending.
4. Register the prayer intercessors.
5. Set up a schedule with breaks.
6. Send confirmation information and directions.

When the intercessors arrive, they can be given a packet of information similar to what attendees receive. Packets can contain:

- nametags/badges
- maps
- schedule
- directions

Prepare for moving to the conference site by putting together a list of things to bring:

- sign-up list
- pens
- clipboards
- conference schedule
- prayer intercessor schedule
- tissue boxes

As you drive to the site, pray for safe travel for everyone!

7 | SITE

When our family arrived at the hotel for a conference, we were looking forward to staying in the posh downtown historic hotel. But when we checked in, they told us there were no rooms available that could hold our family.

"Don't worry," said the receptionist. "We can put you in the parlor room. It's a nice big room, more expensive than the usual room—but I will give you the regular room rate." When we got to the room, we discovered that the room was huge. It had an exercise bicycle, a desk, a conference table, and a bar.

But the only bed was a sagging sofabed. The kids jumped into the bed and claimed it, leaving my husband and me to fend for ourselves. "Wait a minute!" I protested to the kids, but they snuggled into the blankets and made themselves permanent fixtures.

We made a phone call to the front desk and the hotel staff brought up two rollaway beds. As I lay in the bed that night trying to sleep, I couldn't help but think, "I can't believe we are staying in a room worth $525 a night and sleeping in rollaways and a sofabed!"

Our family has not had the best of luck with the housing accommodations—going from a low-cost, insect-infested facility to a top-of-the-line hotel with no beds. Maybe we should rethink going to conferences!

Every aspect of a conference impacts the experience a person has at a conference, and one area is the condition of the facility. A participant who doesn't get a good night's rest just doesn't have the energy to benefit from the program; a poor facility can ruin the conference experience.

Overseeing housing accommodations is only one part of a Site Coordinator's responsibilities. The Site Coordinator handles all aspects of site management before, during, and after the event. Sometimes the site may be only one building. Other times it may be a large group of buildings close together, such as group of hotels, a college, or church campus. Conferences that are city-wide may be located at multiple locations throughout the city, requiring ground transportation to move people from one site to another.

OVERVIEW

One of the first tasks of the Site Coordinator is to find a place to hold the conference. Usually the date of your event will be determined by when the site is available. The sooner you begin, the better options you will have. Large conferences sometimes book years in advance! The smaller your audience, the easier it will be to find a location. Your job will involve:

The Site Coordinator secures a site for the conference and coordinates all arrangements between the conference staff and the site staff.

Recommended Skills/Qualities

- Administrative/organizational skills
- Attention to detail
- Good people skills
- Good leader
- Good at problem solving
- Able to negotiate prices
- Clear communication skills

Job Description

Before the conference

- Attend planning team meetings
- Investigate and select site(s)
- Coordinate planning team requests with facility contact
- Make site arrangements as needed

During the conference

- Handle arrangements for conference staff

After the conference

- Compile summary report
- Send notes of appreciation to site staff
- Evaluate conference and suggest improvements for next time

Time Commitment

This position's time commitment is:

STEP-BY-STEP

1. Determining site requirements
2. Researching site possibilities
3. Contacting potential sites
4. Compiling information
5. Visiting top choices
6. Negotiating with the site
7. Selecting a site
8. Signing the contract
9. Making arrangements

At the event, the Site Coordinator checks the setup of different areas and coordinates any special needs (*Chapter 18: The Conference*).

After the conference, send notes of appreciation to those who helped you and put together a summary report of the event (*Chapter 19: Wrapping Up*).

DETERMINING SITE REQUIREMENTS

In order to make a wise choice for the site, you will need some information about your conference.

Purpose
The purpose of the conference will help you decide what site is best suited for accomplishing your goals. If you are planning to do intensive teaching, don't look at a location near a golf course or a beach! If you are giving families a chance to spend time together, going to a site with recreation nearby is a must.

Audience
What kind of expectations will your audience have? What kind of message do you want to communicate to them? What kind of needs do they have?

If you're planning a conference for youth, you'll need a safe place with recreation available. A youth retreat doesn't need to stay at a five-star hotel; it's just not appropriate for the audience and the type of activities they would enjoy (and the hotel wouldn't appreciate it either). Likewise, seniors would not want to stay in a camp that only has bunkbeds! The audience determines many other factors, such as food, speaker, and the type of program you will be holding.

A conference for families with children puts a need for child-friendly facilities—safe and clean rooms, children-sized furniture, and equipment, such as playgrounds or playing areas.

Budget
How much can you afford to pay for a site? Select your site after you settle the budget so you know what price range to look for.

Dates
Select a few alternative dates in case your first choice site is not available.

Location
How far will people be traveling? What site is centrally located for the attendees? What is a reasonable length of time to ask people to drive? If you are holding a one-day or weekend event, don't book a site that takes more than three hours driving to get there, or people will feel like they are spending more time in the car than at the conference.

If your conference has a national audience and people are arriving from around the country, there are similar considerations. What is a site that is centrally located for those who are coming? Major convention cities usually have higher rates. Smaller cities have lower rates in order to attract business. However, some of these cities may be harder to access if people are flying in because there might not be a major airport.

Estimated number of people attending

How large does the site need to be? Look for a place that has a meeting room large enough to hold your group and with enough accommodations if people are staying overnight.

General idea of programs or activities

The program will determine what types of rooms you will need. Will you have large group sessions, small groups, or breakouts? Both require different room arrangements. Will people need to write and take notes? If so, you might need a classroom setup. How about recreational activities or other program plans? How many will you need? What size? What kind? Try to plan the site around the program instead of the other way around. Make a list of areas that are needed (see *Site Inspection* checklist starting on page 79 for specific information about each of these areas):

EXAMPLES

- **Meeting rooms.** The rooms needed will depend on the types of programs you will be holding and the expected attendance. Rooms for general sessions and breakout sessions vary in purpose and size. How large do the rooms need to be? How many rooms do you need?
- **Registration area.** Where will people be checking in and registering when they arrive on site? Calculate enough area needed for registration tables, storage, and traffic passing through.
- **Dining area.** If people will be eating on site, the area should hold enough tables and chairs for people to eat comfortably. Consider whether you would like the food to be provided on-site or if going off-site is an option—ask the Hospitality Coordinator's opinion.
- **Exhibits area.** Exhibits need space for booths, storage, and aisles for traffic. How many exhibitors do you expect and how closely can you locate them next to the meeting areas?
- **Accommodations/housing.** What kind of housing do you need? List the rooms needed either on-site, off-site, or a combination of both.
- **Additional rooms.** What other rooms are needed? Possible rooms are ones for staff, volunteers, speakers to rest and rehearse, prayer, storage (for equipment and supplies), and a command office center.
- **Recreational areas.** Some conferences provide recreational activities for attendees. These may be activities on-site (such as indoor sports or outdoor recreation), or nearby facilities (such as parks or sightseeing locations). It's sometimes a challenge to find that balance between maintaining a focus on the conference and allowing for recreation.

RESEARCHING SITE POSSIBILITIES

Where to look

What type of site would best accommodate your program and purpose? Begin laying some initial groundwork by checking around to see what types of facilities are available. Look at:

RESOURCE TOOLS

- **Retreat center directories.** Some denominations have their own conference centers and can provide some names for you. Other campground or retreat site organizations list their members facilities:
  - Christian Camping International, http://cci.gospelcom.net/ccihome/, 719-260-9400. Lists directory of over 1,000 camps and conference centers.
  - Church 2000, Inc., www.church2000.org/Links/conference/, 305-861-3670. Lists conference centers located primarily in the United States.

- **Web sites.** Web sites that list a selection of available facilities are available. Many conference centers and hotels also have their own Web sites. Check a search engine such as www.google.com to find out what kind of sites are available. Try a search for "conference center" or "retreat". A number of Web sites are great resources for finding sites. www.mpoint.com has a comprehensive database of facilities and suppliers. It serves as a great resource for information too. If you're looking for a place that has "hot dates" (dates where hotels offer lower rates to fill empty rooms), check out www.hotdateshotrates.com or hotmeeting dates.com. These sites allow you to generate a Request for Proposal (page 74) to find facilities that fit your needs.
- **Word of mouth.** Ask around. Conference staff or people in your church might have attended conferences at different sites. Call other churches too. They may have something available or know of another location.

What kind of sites to consider

A wide variety of sites are available. Here are some possibilities:

- **University/College/School.** School campuses are well suited for conferences. They are a good choice since they have classrooms for breakout sessions, dormitories for accommodations, and large areas to do recreational activities. Colleges also come in different sizes, are reasonably priced, and have cafeterias for food. Many colleges are booked years in advance because of their advantageous facilities for holding conferences.
- **Convention Center.** When a conference outgrows a large church or hotel, convention centers are the next step for large conferences. They have multiple rooms for meetings but no housing accommodations or recreational areas.
- **Cruise/ship.** Cruises provide every imaginable amenity in one location. Ships can provide conference facilities and specifically work with clients who hold conferences. One example is Cruises for Causes, www.cruisesforcauses.com, 704-861-8437.
- **Resort.** Resorts offer all-inclusive packages and have numerous recreational facilities on site.
- **Hotel.** Hotels are frequently used for conferences and have the advantage of housing and meeting rooms in the same facility as well as food services. Hotels have a person on staff dedicated to coordinating conferences with clients. Large chain hotels may have directories listing their locations and facilities.
- **Public buildings.** Halls, government buildings, libraries, and other public locations have rooms that are suited for conference meetings.
- **Church.** Churches provide suitable rooms for meetings but housing needs to be found elsewhere.
- **Conference center.** These sites vary in size from a single meeting room for smaller groups to multiple facilities. Conference centers provide one-stop shopping, including meeting areas, housing, audiovisual equipment, and food. Their primary business is hosting conferences so they are experienced and convenient. Many are in the midst of nature, a plus for outdoor enthusiasts. International Association of Conference Centers' Web site, www.iacconline.com, has a searchable list of their members.

RESOURCE TOOLS

- **Camp or retreat center.** These include sites that have rustic cabins, as well as higher quality locations that have accommodations that look like hotels and have dining facilities. The range is wide so visit the location to get a firsthand look. Campsites where people bring tents is a low-cost option for families or groups willing to camp.

- **Facilities for 100 participants or less**
    - **Restaurants.** Many restaurants have large banquet rooms that can be used for meetings. Of course, you will have to purchase their food to use their room!
    - **Rental homes.** If you are holding a small retreat, rental homes with multiple rooms might be a good option. Multiple rental homes located in the same area allow larger groups to stay together.
    - **Bed and breakfasts/inns.** Some have conference meeting rooms and an added plus of built-in accommodations.

- **Unusual sites**
    Be creative and have your conference in an unusual place, such as:
    - Theaters
    - Art galleries
    - Movie theaters
    - Historical sites
    - Train tours
    - On an island
    - Ranches
    - Monasteries
    - Malls/shopping centers
    - Zoos/parks/gardens
    - Clubhouses
    - Museums
    - Boats/yachts

RESOURCE TOOLS

Look at www.uniquevenues.com, which lists an extensive offering of unusual sites.

Different sites have their own advantages and disadvantages. Some are more cost-efficient than others, but on the flip side, they may only provide minimal services.

> There's a big difference between convention centers and churches. The biggest one is that when you're in a convention center, you can snap your fingers and people will do things for you. In a church you have to manage relationships, and you usually have volunteers. Expect to do more physical work in a church than in a convention center.
> ◆ *Andrew Accardy*

Convention centers and churches also differ in how much control you have over an event. If you hold the conference at your church or your own facility, you're the boss and everything is under your control. But when you hold the event at a place such as a conference center or hotel, you're only able to control certain areas such as program and volunteers, for example. Other areas, such as the facility itself, are controlled by the hotel.

As you investigate sites, keep your program and purpose foremost. A site should help move forward the program, not hinder it.

What is your audience and what do they like? What kind of environment are you looking for?

> Know your group of people. Ours are mostly women and they want to go somewhere shopping. We've held our conferences at Leavenworth, Washington, a quaint Bavarian village. Women loved it! ◆ *Kristen Hilling*

Recurring events sometimes will use the same location year after year. This is especially true of conference or retreat centers where your group is given the first chance to rebook the site for the following year. If you've used the same site repeatedly and suddenly decide to change locations, some might not return because people are creatures of habit and don't like change. But don't let that discourage you; others will love the change. Just make sure that the advantages of changing your site outweigh the disadvantages.

CONTACTING POTENTIAL SITES

After you have drawn up a list of possible sites, begin contacting them to gather information. The two most common ways are submitting a Request for Proposal or making a phone call.

Request For Proposal

EXAMPLES

The first way is to submit a *Request For Proposal* (RFP) or a written fact sheet (pages 74-75), which saves you the trouble of repeating your information every time you contact a new location. Mail or fax this information directly to the site office, or use a Convention and Visitor's Bureau (CVB) that will find sites for you. Some CVBs and hotels have online RFPs that you can fill out and submit immediately. RFPs may contain information such as:

- Your organization and goals
- Preferred and alternate dates
- Expected attendance
- Number of hotels needed (meeting rooms and accommodations)
- Program activities
- Schedule (arrival/departure)
- Setup times
- Expected number of exhibitors

After you put everything in writing, submit this information yourself, or send it to a Convention and Visitor's Bureau (page 76).

Phone calls

Another way to contact a site is to call them directly. Usually facilities have a guest services/conference coordinator whose sole purpose is to coordinate site arrangements with the groups using the site. Remember to get all agreements in writing!

In your initial phone call, find out more information about:

- Available dates
- Size of site: Will it hold the estimated number of attendees?
- Accommodations arrangements and availability
- Programming options
- Rates and fees: Are there special conference rates?
- Policies: What are the policies for minimum guarantees, deposits, cancellations and insurance?

Call a variety of sites in the same geographical area to see what is available. If it suits your purpose, you may find it's more cost-effective to use a variety of sites (such as different hotels) in the same location.

Professional Meeting Planner

If you are in over your head or if your lazy streak is taking over, use a professional meeting planner to do the initial scouting and contracting the site: Meeting planners know what to look for and how to assess the options. Because of their experience and relationships in the industry, they are able to work with the site to secure a good deal for you.

Find a meeting planner used to working with church groups. When I call a hotel I usually use, the person there knows me. He's willing to work with me because I bring him other business. Another meeting planner I know does many events; when he called with a church group they were willing to help because he had just sent them a big conference with a secular company. The meeting planner has a relationship with the site and the

Prefix: (Mr, Ms.) _____ Name _____

Title _____

Organization _____

Address _____

City _____ State _____ Zip code _____

Country _____

Telephone _____ Fax _____

E-mail _____

Meeting name _____

Type of meeting (conference/retreat/seminar/workshop, etc.) _____

Expected total attendance _____

Preferred cities and/or states

Preference #1 _____ Preference #3 _____

Preference #2 _____ Preference #4 _____

Meeting Dates

Start date _____ End date _____

Alternate dates _____

Arrival/departure dates _____

Housing

Preferred types: ❏ Hotel or similar   ❏ Residence halls   ❏ Suite style/apartment   ❏ Other

Total number of rooms blocked _____

% of Singles _____ % of Quads _____

% of Doubles _____ % of Suites _____

% of Triples _____ % of Any combo _____

-- OR --

Room by Date	Single	Double	Triple	Quad	Suite	Total

Total number of rooms _____

Meetings

General session: ❑ Theatre ❑ Classroom ❑ Other setup

Number of people attending _____

Days needed: ❑ Mon ❑ Tues ❑ Wed ❑ Thu ❑ Fri ❑ Sat ❑ Sun

Meeting room requirements: _____

_____

_____

Breakout rooms? ❑ Yes ❑ No

Exhibit space (sq ft) _____

Number of booths _____

Move-in day _____

Move-out day _____

First show day _____

Last show day _____

Number of food/beverage functions (include details such as meals required, breaks, times, meal attendance, etc.):

_____

_____

_____

_____

_____

Number of off-site food and beverage functions _____

_____

Breakfast type: ❑ Buffet ❑ Continental ❑ Plated

Largest meal period _____

Suggested budget including meals, AV, lodging: (total per person) _____

Facilities contact us via: ❑ Phone ❑ Fax ❑ E-mail

Response to RFP needed by (date) _____

Decision date: _____

Group history: (list previous facilities used and dates) _____

_____

_____

_____

_____

site is willing to give a discount or a good deal. It's helpful to have someone on the inside helping you. Some churches have a person like this and don't even know it. If such a person is not in your church, ask other churches if they use meeting planners.
◆ *Jeanne Gregory*

Convention and Visitors Bureaus

Convention and Visitors Bureaus are a great resource if you are planning a larger conference and are planning to use facilities within their city. They are familiar with the available facilities, and they even know which sites are in need of business and offer the best deal. Some CVBs are private (businesses pay for membership); others are public (part of the government).

Ask CVBs up front which services are free. Many CVBs provide their services for free because they want you to bring your business to the city, stay there, and spend your money there. All you have to do is tell them your requirements for a site and they will do the legwork for you.

CVBs will provide information but won't make recommendations or negotiate for you. They also provide information such as maps, visitor's guides, event information, brochures, and ticket sales. You can even order this information for the people attending the conference (but sometimes there is a small charge).

Housing Bureaus

Convention and Visitors Bureaus have a department called a housing bureau that specializes in handling accommodations for large groups. Housing bureaus help you select hotels, assign the rooms and send the hotel a confirmation without charging you a fee. If you negotiate a discount rate with the site by yourself, you receive the discount that the housing bureau would have received. The down side is that it's more effort on your part.

COMPILING INFORMATION

As you call, keep all the information together. A sample *Comparison Chart* of the features and advantages of using each area is on page 77.

EXAMPLES

VISITING TOP CHOICES

After you have sifted through all the information, narrow down your choices to the top two or three based on your program, purpose, and requirements. If you don't plan to use some sites, don't visit them; it's a waste of your time and the site staff's time.

Then visit your top choices. Never book a place without checking it first.

One time we were doing a small group training experience for camp directors. We wanted to do it in the Washington, DC area. Someone said, "I have a friend in DC who knows the places all the senators go to, a little Christian retreat center where they go for a break—it's so quaint." The price was so cheap we thought it was unbelievable. We didn't have much of a budget so we took her word for it and didn't fly from Chicago to check it out. When we got there for the event, we found out the place was totally vegetarian and didn't believe in serving meat. It was a week-long event with no bacon, no eggs, and no meat. The workshop tables were tables that kids had used for crafts. They had built a new log cabin with real logs but the pitch had never dried and you could see through the logs into the room next to you. Fortunately, it was all men. Always do the site inspection before you book the place. ◆ *John Pearson*

If you used the site a few years back but haven't been there recently, visit again to be see if anything has changed.

Although large conferences with multiple sites may need a number of

SITE COMPARISON CHART

	Forest Retreat Center			Lakeside Center		
Name	Santa Maria			Countrytown		
Location						
Lodging level	Economy	Moderate	Deluxe	Cabins	Lodge	Main Hall
Number of rooms	20	15	10	16	30	20
Beds per room	8 bunk	4 twin	2 queen	4	2	2
Total beds at site	160	60	20	64	60	40
Bathrooms	shared	private	private	outdoors	shared	private
Adult price total	$70	$80	$90	$90	$110	$120
Children's price	$50	$60	$70	75% adult price		
Children's ages		6-11			0-4	
Meals/snacks		6/0			5/2	
Childcare	nursery facility			use side rooms		
Deposit	10% or $300, whichever is greater			20% guaranteed minimum		
Cancellation	25% or $500, whichever is greater			before 90 days		
Dates available	Nov 20-22, Dec 4-6			Nov 2-23, Oct 23-25, Nov 6-8		
Notes	clean and well-lit			little park, playground		
Decision	First choice but booked for a year			too expensive		

days to inspect all the sites, most conference centers and hotels can easily be covered in a day.

When you do your site inspection, include the Conference Director. Bring along the *Site Inspection Checklist* on page 79 and find the answers to your questions.

EXAMPLES

NEGOTIATING WITH THE SITE

Sometimes people seem to be born with negotiation in their blood. As children, they bargain their way out of chores and punishments. These are the people you want on your side—and on your team—especially as you negotiate with the site.

MONEY SAVERS

Negotiation depends on the type of site you are using. Some Christian conference centers have set prices and are unable to negotiate. But sites such as hotels are able to negotiate. They'll often negotiate their rates depending on the dates, season, or the size of the group. To negotiate effectively, know what competitive prices are, what your budget is, and what you want. Let them know you are considering other sites as well; they'll be more willing to work with you. Check to see if the site will allow late arrival or early departure; some sites have preferred arrival or departure times. Don't be afraid to negotiate: ask if they will provide plants, linens, or other decorations to save you the cost of renting. The worst thing that can happen is that they say no.

> I've had hotels that will give their Saturday ballroom free if we are out by three o'clock because they didn't have business on Saturday but had a wedding Saturday night. Ask questions. Is there a possibility to get a certain room? How do I get the ballroom free? Some say you can if you book 200 rooms and pay the deposit. Others, if you have 200 people in a sit-down meal, they will give you a room free. Be aware what industry standards are. For example, convention centers charge for every additional chair that you want. ✦ *Jeanne Gregory*

Watch out for any extra charges! Check any information or contract carefully to make sure that you are aware of additional fees or charges. This will avoid any unpleasant surprises later.

> Beware of hidden costs. When you use a convention center, you may rent a room for $10,000 but it doesn't include staging, electricity, labor, and security, all of which are required. When you are dealing with unions, make sure they pay for their own lunches. You'd be surprised how many times it's slipped on a bill. Even if they were taking a break and not working, they would bill me for it. If you've never done a convention center, get some hired help. Hire a consultant on the front end so they can identify the issues for you. It's well worth it to spend money on a consultant versus spending money on a convention center. ✦ *Andrew Accardy*

If you're booking a convention center, ask someone who is experienced in working with convention centers to help you. They will know the ins and outs of working with convention centers, which seem intimidating because of the scale of the facility.

Be creative in thinking of win-win situations both for your group as well as the site.

> Ron Sugimoto tells of a retreat that was held in a hotel. Since the bar would not be used, they made arrangements with the hotel not to staff a bartender but to instead turn the area into an ice cream fountain. It was a win-win situation because the hotel made money in an area that they would normally have not with a Christian group. The group also had a great fellowship opportunity.

HELPFUL TIPS FOR A SITE INSPECTION

- Before you visit the site, go through this checklist and cross out any items that are not pertinent to the site or to your event. This will streamline your time so that you can spend your time on the important questions without having to sift through a lot of information. Write down many notes because if you visit multiples sites, after a while the sites will all start looking the same.
- Ask many questions. Don't think a question is "dumb" if you don't know the answer.
- Take notes. Don't trust your memory to recall everything.
- Bring a camera and take videos or photographs.
- Look for a meeting that is in progress. It will give you a preview of what your group will be experiencing.

LOCATION

Driving

❏ **Distance:** How far is the site located from where people live or where your church or organization is located?

❏ **Traffic:** What are the traffic patterns and when are the commuting hours?

> *Try driving to the site and see how long it takes you to get there. Try driving during the time that people will be driving to your event.*

Airport

❏ **Distance:** How far is the site from the airport? What kind of transportation is available from the airport to the site? How long does it take to get to the site from the airport? Are there other routes in case of traffic?

❏ **Flights:** What are the flight schedules? Do they vary according to season? Are there enough connections for those coming? What kind of upgrade opportunities are there?

> *Be cautious about using a site near an airport that has inconvenient flight schedules.*

❏ **Shuttle:** Is there a shuttle service that people can take from the airport? Is there a fee for the shuttle service or is it complimentary?

Local information

❏ **Recreation:** What local attractions are there for people to attend during recreational times? What local entertainment venues are there?

❏ **Dining:** What restaurants or dining facilities are nearby?

❏ **Shopping:** What kind of shopping is available?

❏ **Office:** Where are nearby office supply or copy vendors in case you need to take care of last minute items? Does the facility have on-site copying capabilities?

❏ **Streets:** Are there any street repairs or road closures scheduled? Any one-way streets the participants should be aware of?

GENERAL FACILITY QUESTIONS

❏ **Age:** What year was the facility constructed?

❏ **Ownership:** Who owns the facility?

❏ **Strengths/weaknesses:** What are the strengths and weaknesses of the site?

❏ **Condition:** What is the overall condition of the facility? Is it clean and well maintained?

❏ **Lighting:** Is there adequate lighting at night?

❏ **Entrances:** How many main entrances are there? How convenient is it to reach them?

❏ **Floor plan:** Is there a scaled floor plan available?

❑ **Decor:** What is the décor of the site? Color of carpet, walls, or furniture? Condition of furniture? What kind of limitations do you have on decorations?

Watch out for a visually-distracting environment.

❑ **Meeting rooms:** How many meeting rooms are available? How near are breakout rooms to the main meeting room and to each other?

A facility with a limited number of meeting rooms may limit how many workshops can be held simultaneously.

❑ **Sound issues:** What other events will be going on in adjacent areas? Are the rooms soundproof? Is the meeting room near a dining area (which tends to be noisier)? Will sound from the meeting disturb other groups meeting or nearby neighbors?

If you have a group that is small in number, see if it can be placed farther away from the noisier large groups.

❑ **Environment:** Is ventilation adequate? Is there air conditioning—window units or central air? Heating? Where are the controls? How easy is it to operate them? Do the vents blow directly on people? How loud is the system? What is the average temperature of the rooms during the time we will be holding our conference?

Some sites, such as convention centers, may not operate air conditioning or heating during move-in and move-out periods. If your group will need heating or cooling, ask the site what additional charges are for those periods.

❑ **Meeting room access:** What kind of access is available to the meeting rooms? Are there elevators? Stairs? Ramps?

❑ **Elevators:** Where are the elevators and are there enough for the size of the group? Are they easy to find?

❑ **Hallways:** Are hallways large enough for traffic flow?

❑ **Shared rooms:** What group uses the facility before us? Can we share their setup or equipment in order to reduce fees? Will rooms be shared with other groups who are not part of our conference? If another group is using the room, how much time will we need in order to reset it?

❑ **Furniture:** Are we allowed to move furniture?

❑ **Emergencies:** What kind of emergency procedures do you have in place?

❑ **Americans with Disabilities Act compliance:** Does the site comply to ADA regulations?

❑ **Restrooms:** How many restrooms? Where are they located? How close are they to the meeting area? How often are they cleaned and restocked?

If your event has more than 75% of one sex, change the signs of 75% of the restrooms to accommodate that sex (if the facility allows it).

❑ **Coatroom:** Is there a coatroom (for areas with cold weather)?

❑ **Shielded areas:** Are there areas where two-way radios or cellular phones do not work?

❑ **Telephones:** Are there public telephones available? Where are they?

❑ **Permits:** Are any permits needed?

❑ **Experience:** What size is the average group you work with?

If you have a large group, ask the facility how experienced they are working with a group your size.

Renovations

❑ **Extent:** When was the site last renovated? What areas were renovated?

❑ **Future renovations:** Do you have another renovation scheduled? When is it?

Avoid scheduling your event during a major renovation period.

MEETING ROOM(S)   *(See Chapter 8: Program for more information)*

❑ **Exits:** How many exits are there? Is it easy to enter and exit the room? Where are the emergency exits? Are the doors squeaky? Do they close or open automatically?

❏ **Size:** What is the square footage?

❏ **Shape:** What is the shape of the room?

> *The ideal proportion is a ratio of 2:3 (width to length). Avoid rooms that are long and narrow, because people have a difficult time seeing the speaker or the screen.*

❏ **Color:** What color is the room? What is the decor?

❏ **Capacity:** What is the seating or dining capacity?

> *Seating depends on your layout arrangement but sites should be able to tell you estimated seating based on different arrangements.*

❏ **Overflow:** Do you have an overflow area if the room is filled to capacity?

❏ **Furniture:** Are the chairs comfortable? Is the furniture in good condition?

❏ **Map:** Do you have a scaled map of the room?

> *Draw a rough map of the room and locate doors, windows, blank walls, electrical outlets and wall jacks (telephone/computer). If there are telephones, make a note to disconnect them or turn off the ringer during sessions.*

❏ **Line of sight:** Are there items blocking the sight lines to the speaker?

> *Look for pillars, hanging lights, mirrors, exit, or fire signs.*

❏ **Ceiling height:** How high is the ceiling?

> *If you are using screens and people will be standing during singing, will they be able to see the words on the screen? If you have larger groups, look for rooms with higher ceilings. Also, if the ceiling is too low, the worship leader or speaker will have to stand to the side in order not to block people's view of the screen.*

❏ **Screens:** What is the size and location of screens? Are they front or rear projection screens (the picture is projected from the front of the screen or the rear)?

> *Front projection gives a brighter, clearer picture, but the projector may be noisy. Rear projection is clearer in a room with brighter lighting. If you need to install your own rear projection screen, allow at least twenty feet behind the screen for the projector.*

❏ **Walls:** Are the walls movable? How quickly can they be opened or closed for changes between sessions?

> *Close the walls and check how soundproof they are.*

❏ **Sound:** Is the room soundproofed? Will we be able to hear events going on next door? What are the room acoustics like? Will sound be reflected off hard surfaces, or are there floor or wall coverings to absorb sound?

❏ **Stage:** Is the stage permanent or portable? How large is the stage? How high is the stage?

> *In a large room, a recommended height is forty inches above the ground.*

Where is the entrance in relationship to the stage?

> *You don't want the seated people to see people using the door while the meeting is going on!*

❏ **Storage:** Does the room have a storage area for workshop materials?

❏ **Tech booth:** Where is the sound or projection booth?

Lighting

❏ **Stage:** Does the stage or speaker area have enough lights?

❏ **Screen:** Does the screen area have lights that need to be dimmed?

❏ **Windows:** Can windows be covered or darkened during AV presentations?

❏ **Controls:** Where are the lighting controls? Is there a master switch for all rooms? For rooms that are divided by movable walls, which sections are controlled together? If we turn off one section, will the other sections be dark also?

❏ **Types:** What type of lighting is in the room? Natural, florescent, or incandescent? Can lighting be dimmed?

❑ **Labor:** If we need to rig lights, who handles it?

❑ **Power capacity:** What power capabilities or limitations do you have?

❑ **Glare:** Is there any glare in the room from reflective surfaces or the sun shining in?

Equipment *(See Chapter Ten: Technical for more information)*

❑ **Speaker:** What equipment do you provide for speakers? What can you provide at an additional charge? What items do we need to return, and what items can we keep? Can you provide:

- Easels/flipcharts   • Pens/pencils/markers   • Whiteboards   • Notepads

❑ **Audiovisual:** What audiovisual equipment do you have? Do you provide extra bulbs or extension cords?

- Microphones: lavaliere, handheld, wireless, table, floor, hanging, lectern
- Stage TV monitors
- Stage sound monitors
- Stands for microphones

❑ **Additional equipment:** Do you also provide:

- Easels: how many and in what condition are they?
- Skirting: do you have skirting for tables and for the stage?
- Stages/platforms: how many and in which rooms?

❑ **Quality:** What is the quality of your equipment? Where is it located? How is it controlled?

❑ **Guarantee:** Do you guarantee that equipment will be there or that you will have a replacement if it fails?

Consider renting from an outside source (if the site allows it) as in some cases it may be more cost-effective.

❑ **Setup time:** How much time is required to set up your equipment?

❑ **Labor:** Are there labor charges? Do you provide a technician to operate the equipment?

❑ **Deposits:** Are there deposits on equipment?

EATING AREA *(See Chapter 11: Hospitality for more information)*

❑ **Areas:** What eating areas are available? Banquet room? Outside eating areas?

❑ **Capacity:** How many people does the eating area hold?

❑ **Shared areas:** Are the dining areas shared with other groups?

❑ **On-site food services:** Do you have an on-site caterer? Do you have restaurants on-site? What are the hours and prices? What is the menu?

❑ **Room service:** Do you provide room service? What hours and what are the prices?

❑ **Quality:** What is the quality of the food? Is it possible to sample the food in advance?

❑ **Decorations:** May we decorate the tables?

Check page 138-140 for more questions.

BREAK AREA *(See Chapter 11: Hospitality for more information)*

❑ **Space:** Is there enough room to serve refreshments and allow people to mingle? Are there any areas for informal gatherings?

❑ **Staff room:** Where will the staff break room (greenroom) be located?

❑ **Distance:** What is the distance of the break area from the meeting rooms? Will people have enough time to take a break? How long will it take them to get to the break area?

REGISTRATION AREA *(See Chapter 13: Registration for more information)*

❑ **Location:** Where is your registration area?

❑ **Lighting and ventilation:** Is there adequate lighting and ventilation?

❑ **Space:** Is there enough room?

❑ **Check in time:** What is the check-in time? How long is the check-in process?

❑ **Storage:** Is there a location to store luggage before people check in and after they check out?

EXHIBIT AREA *(See Chapter 14: Exhibits for more information)*

❑ **Space:** Is there adequate room for exhibits? What are the room dimensions, including ceiling height?

❑ **Fees:** What do you provide and what kind of charges are there?

❑ **Requirements:** Are there any labor/legal requirements?

STORAGE

❑ **Centerpieces:** Is there a location for storing centerpieces overnight?

❑ **Equipment:** Is there a location for storing equipment overnight?

❑ **Size:** How large is the storage area?

❑ **Accessibility:** How accessible is the storage area? Is the storage area accessible by vehicles? Trucks?

❑ **Security:** How secure is the storage area?

❑ **Shipping:** Do you store items that are shipped in advance? What space limitations do you have? Do you charge additional fees for this service?

LOADING AREA

❑ **Meeting area:** What is the proximity of the loading area to the meeting area? Exhibit area?

❑ **Hours:** What hours is the loading dock available?

❑ **Restrictions:** What restrictions are there?

❑ **Elevator:** How close by is the freight elevator? What hours does the freight elevator operate?

HOUSING

❑ **Distance:** How far is the housing from the meeting rooms. If multiple hotels, how far apart are the hotels from each other?

> *Hotels should be located no more than ten to twelve minutes via shuttle bus from the meeting location or from other hotels (to reduce transportation cost). The best location is within walking distance.*

❑ **Rates:** Do you have group rates? Rates for additional people? Do you have reduced rates for staff/speakers?

> *Check that the rates and quality of the housing are suitable for your audience (business professionals will expect something very different than teenagers going to a youth camp) and that you offer a variety of rates for different housing options.*

❑ **Types of rooms:** What types of rooms are available: suites (one or two bedroom), cabins? dormitory style? What are the different rates?

❑ **Types of beds:** What types of beds are available? How many: singles, twins, doubles, queens, kings, sofa beds, rollout beds?

❑ **Bathroom:** Is the bathroom attached or in a separate facility?

❑ **Capacity:** How many people does a room hold?

❑ **Special needs:** Do you have rooms for people who are physically challenged?

❑ **Smoking:** Are the rooms for smokers or non-smokers?

❑ **Sound:** How soundproof are rooms from adjacent rooms and outside noise?

❑ **Amenities:** What types of amenities are available in the room? Telephone, television, radio, refrigerator (empty or stocked), hair dryer, ironing board, toiletries, desks?

❑ **Services:** What services are included with the rate? What housekeeping services are there?

❑ **Dates:** What is the cut-off date for reservations? What is the cancellation date?

❑ **Holds:** Do you allow holds on rooms? Is there an extra charge for holding rooms?

> *Hotels: Hotels allow you to reserve a number of rooms for your group. This is called a "room block." When you block rooms, block conservatively so you don't have additional rooms to pay for.*

OFFICE/ADMINISTRATIVE AREA *(page 210)*

❑ **Location:** Is there an area that can be used for administration?

❑ **Negotiating:** If we get two free rooms for booking 100 rooms, can we exchange them for a suite to be used as an office area? If we designate your hotel as the headquarters, can you reduce our rates or provide complimentary rooms?

OUTDOOR

❑ **Location:** Is there an outdoor area that can be used for overflow, breaks, or dining?

❑ **Bad weather:** What is the backup plan in case of bad weather?

❑ **Equipment:** Are there space heaters available? Do you have tents?

❑ **Permits:** Are permits needed to set up the outdoor areas?

> *Some localities require permits for setting up tents and other outdoor venues.*

RECREATION

❑ **Facilities:** What types of recreational facilities are available? What hours are they open? What are the usage fees?

PARKING

❑ **Types:** What kind of parking is available—free, hourly, daily, valet, parking garage, off-site, or validation?

❑ **Discounts:** Are there parking discounts for people who are registered at the conference?

❑ **Capacity:** What is the parking capacity?

❑ **Streets:** Are there any one way or narrow streets close to the parking area?

SIGNAGE *(see Chapter Fifteen: Marketing for more information)*

❑ **Available signage:** What signage is already in place at the facility?

❑ **Clarity:** Is the signage clear?

❑ **Adequacy:** Are there enough signs? What areas need signage? Is there a place to hang banners or signage? Where and what signage does the facility provide?

- • Parking   • Registration   • Activities
- • Directional—check end of hallways, in lobbies, and ends of stairways.
- • In doorways of all sessions—workshop number, title, presenter name, workshop time

❑ **Limitation:** Are there limitations to where signage can be placed? Is there a size limitation on signage?

SERVICES PROVIDED

❑ **Hours:** What hours is the staff available?

❑ **Available:** Do you provide:

- Water for speakers/head tables?
- Setup?
- Cleanup and trash removal?
- Table skirting?

- Easels for signage or flip charts?
- Are there public phones?
- Do you have laundry service?
- Internal communications equipment (such as two-way radios or headsets)?

PHYSICALLY CHALLENGED

❑ **Facility:** How is your facility suited for mobility-, sight-, or hearing-impaired? Are there special rooms with wide doorways, raised sinks or large bathrooms? Are there low curbs or parking for vehicles? Are elevators large enough and do they have wide openings?

❑ **Staff:** Is staff informed of the special needs so that they are aware and can help when needed?

SECURITY

❑ **Lighting:** Does the area have adequate lighting for night, especially areas where people will be walking? Are parking areas well lit?

❑ **Emergency/safety aids:** Do the meeting areas and housing have smoke alarms? Sprinkler system? Emergency lights? Surveillance cameras? Manual fire alarms? Emergency speakers in the rooms? First aid kits? How close is the nearest medical facility?

❑ **Exits:** Are fire exits clearly marked? Are evacuation procedures posted? Are there fire doors?

❑ **Services:** Do you provide security? Is it in-house or contracted from an outside source?

❑ **Staff:** Is your staff trained to deal with security issues? Do you have security staff?

❑ **Plans:** Do you have contingency plans or safety programs for emergencies? What do we do in case of a crisis?

❑ **Brochures:** Do you have brochures for fire or emergency procedures? Can you provide enough for our attendees and can we include them in our registration packet?

STAFF

❑ **Hours:** What are your office hours? How do I contact someone before or after office hours?

❑ **Main contact:** Who is the main contact person? How easy is it to contact him or her?

In your conversations with the contact person, evaluate if the person is helpful.

❑ **Room assignments:** Who assigns rooms?

Be sure one person handles this responsibility so there isn't any confusion later.

❑ **Relations:** Is the staff professional in its conduct? Do they have positive attitudes and seem to enjoy serving the guests?

❑ **On-site contact:** Who will be the person on site during the event? Who opens and locks doors, darkens the room, operates the ventilation controls and sound equipment? Does the staff carry pagers or two-way radios?

❑ **Contact information:** What are emergency phone numbers?

❑ **Union:** Are there unionized employees? What are the fees and regulations for using unionized employees?

SCHEDULING

❑ **Move-in/move-out:** When will rooms be available, doors unlocked, temperature set, lights and equipment turned on? Do you set up the rooms the night before or early in the day? Does your staff begin dismantling the room promptly at the ending time?

❑ **Vacancy:** When do the premises need to be vacated?

❑ **Cut-off dates:** What are the cut-off dates for when the held rooms will be released??

REFERENCES

❑ Could we have references of people who have events similar to ours? What rates did they pay?

Be sure that references are recent!

FINANCES

❑ **Lower room rates:** Do you have any dates when you can offer lower rates?

Many hotels price their rates according to the season. They usually have "peak" seasons (periods of high demand), "value" (low demand), and "shoulder" (variable demand).

❑ **Packages:** Do you have any special packages or discounts?

❑ **Free rooms:** Do we receive free rooms after a certain number are booked? Free meeting room or hospitality suite for a certain number of rooms reserved?

Hotels usually offer a free meeting after a number of rooms are booked, usually one complimentary room for every fifty or 100 rooms booked. These rooms may be used for staff or suppliers. Other hotels will price their rates on a sliding scale based on the number of rooms booked.

❑ **Minimum guarantees:** Do you require us to base our payment upon a minimum number of people?

❑ **Price guarantee:** Do you guarantee room or menu prices?

❑ **Payment:** What payment methods do you accept?

❑ **Deposits:** What is your deposit policy? Is the deposit refundable? When is final payment due?

❑ **Cancellation:** What is your cancellation policy? What about no-shows?

❑ **Additional charges:** Will there be overtime or setup charges? Labor charges? Utilities charges? Are there any other fees or gratuities that we should be aware of?

Many convention centers require an electrical charge. Other places may charge you if you are using equipment for a period of time.

The hotel industry has a lot of turnover so keep clear who the lines of communication or authority are. Establish your authority from the beginning so that there is no misunderstanding later.

As you are deciding which site to use, discuss with them how reservations and room assignments will be handled. One way is to reserve a block of rooms, and you assign the attendees to their rooms. The attendee pays you directly and you pay the hotel or site one lump sum. You are given all the keys and people check in directly with you. If you are using a hotel, you can send people to the front desk to pay for their incidental charges. They may ask you to have one person from each room submit a credit card upon registration. Clarify with the hotel up front so that you aren't liable for their incidental charges. Be clear with your registrants also, letting them know what you will cover and what they are responsible for paying.

The other way of handling reservations is for people to go to the hotel directly. The site assigns the rooms and you charge a registration fee for the program. Attendees make their own arrangements for housing. This is the easiest way!

SELECTING A SITE

Don't just select a site based on the price, location, and available dates; consider all aspects to make a well-informed decision. Does the site suit the purpose of the conference? Are the services offered a good fit for the audience and type of conference that will be held?

SIGNING THE CONTRACT

TIPS FOR SUCCESS

Before signing, review the contract with the Program Coordinator to make sure that everything is in order. Some contracts are simple; others may seem like doctorate dissertations. If in doubt, find a legal adviser or experienced meeting planner to help you wade through the details.

Check the contract to make sure all details are correct: the dates and times (including late arrival or early departure), check-in and check-out times, room rates and rooms used, rates for food and equipment used, payment methods, deposit requirements, cancellation policies, security requirements and complimentary items, and that all charges are noted up front. Check the ending of the event too, to make sure that all the elements involved are in place.

> One conference planner tells of an error he made reading a contract. The event was supposed to be out of the convention center by midnight, but everyone had already left. They had another show coming in at six a.m. that morning and he had to take the whole stage down. He literally broke every union regulation and tore everything down himself, including thirty-foot high screens. He got the decorating company to bring a forklift to bring the Steinway off the stage, knowing that if it had fallen, he would been in serious trouble. They stayed up until four in the morning tearing everything down. He learned: read your contract!

> Another conference planner makes it a habit to review her contract three different times. Every time she takes a new look, she sees something she missed before.

Hotels include an "attrition" clause in their contracts. They give you an attrition rate—a rate schedule showing how much money is refunded if you cancel. For example, at 120 days out the rate is zero percent which means that you receive all your money back if you cancel before then. At sixty days you may pay ten percent and after thirty days out you pay 100%. Allow plenty of time for your attendees to return their reservations so you don't have to pay for any empty rooms that you have reserved and are unable to cancel because it is too late! In fact, it's wise to have a cancellation clause in the contract stating up to what date you can cancel, and how much you owe if you cancel. This way you aren't stuck with a huge bill if you need to cancel.

Check the contract to see if there is a clause that says that you are not liable for unused rooms that the site is able to rebook; ask if there is a way to check your room block afterwards to see if the rooms are rebooked.

Find out what the site's policy is for transferring registrations or changing names. Cut-off dates for booking rooms (afterwards the hotel is free to sell the remaining rooms) are another area to examine; industry standard is thirty to twenty-one days for the cut-off date.

Make sure the contract is as specific as possible. For example, note specific rooms to be used so the facility doesn't do a last-minute switch on you. Or, write down what happens if the hotel is full and they must send a confirmed attendee to another location.

> One person got $1200 back from the facility because she had detailed penalties on her contract. If the site booked the facility to another group she would receive a refund. Sure enough, they booked another group, and she got some money back.

> Jeanne Gregory always books two or three rooms that only she and the hotel know about. It's helpful to have the extra rooms in case they are needed in an emergency.

Don't sign the contract unless you agree with all of it. Cross out parts and initial it, or add addendum pages. The changes need to be signed both by you and the site contact person.

And last of all, never rely on a verbal commitment; get everything in writing.

MAKING ARRANGEMENTS

As the Site Coordinator, your tasks will primarily be:
- communicating and arranging needs with the site
- assigning locations for programs, housing, and and other areas
- making arrangements for other site needs

In your mind, walk through the program from beginning to end. Imagine you are a participant. Where will you go and what will you do? Try to anticipate where the people will be and what needs they will have.

> Terry Toro considers the logistical aspects of releasing 4500 people for a break. They cannot release them simultaneously because there is no place to put 4500 muffins in one place. They even need to consider that all the bathrooms in one side of the building do not all flush at once! Terry's solution is to have people take breaks in different areas of the facility.

Many of you probably will not have to deal with the challenge of figuring out where to put 4500 muffins, but find out if your site does have limitations for crowds of people. If so, figure out how you can distribute people more evenly throughout the site, or stagger their break times.

Another area of coordinating the site is working with the city if you are holding your conference in a metropolitan area or expecting crowds. Establish a police liaison if you will need officers on duty to help direct traffic.

Meeting rooms

Assigning rooms

If you have multiple meeting rooms, begin assigning sessions to the rooms. Make your best estimate for the number of people who will be attending and assign the rooms to each session.

After checking with the Speaker and Program Coordinator to see what the requirements are of the people involved in the program, draw up a schedule for each room, including times needed for setup and rehearsal. Some worship teams need a full rehearsal, or some speakers want to walk the stage and try out their message to get comfortable. Even if a speaker does not think that is necessary, allow time for a microphone sound check. Find out what equipment is needed for rehearsals and ask the Technical Coordinator to provide it.

The Program Coordinator will also have a list of workshops that will need to be assigned rooms. If you are having groups of workshops with similar topics, assign these workshops to the same room or area of rooms. People who are attending by topic can stay in the same area for the workshops.

> Judy Byford, Facilities Coordinator, and Wilma Pickrell, Program Committee Chairperson, assign the rooms by area. The youth workshops are held at a neighboring church location. At the main convention site, sets of rooms are designated for the various tracks such as the children's workshop track and the pastors' track. One room is set aside for a track for women.

How do you know which rooms to assign to which speakers? Looking at past conference history is one way to make an educated guess on what attendance will be for workshops. If you have no past history, make an educated guess based on the speaker or topic. When rooms are assigned, put together a chart of room usage.

Assign housing a week or two before the conference because people change their minds at the last minute and it will save you the trouble of having to redo the assignments.

Laying out room setups

How each meeting room is set up will depend on the program. Different configurations of the seating may be more effective for different programs. While you review the program, ask what kind of seating is appropriate for what is being accomplished. If you are going to have your participants break into small groups during the session, putting long rows of tables and chairs in a classroom seating arrangement makes it difficult for people to turn to talk to one another.

As you are drawing the setup, look at the shape of the room. Ideally, the room shape should be betweeen a square to a ratio of 2:3. This gives you the most flexibility in setup. Rooms that are long and narrow are difficult to arrange, unless you want your participants to feel like they are in a tunnel. Look at where the speaker will be placed, as well as any stage sets that you may be using.

The room shape will also impact the placement of the speaker and the seating setup. If you have a long, narrow room, it's more of a challenge to put your speaker in a location so that the people sitting farthest away don't feel like they are in Sibera. A room with a bank of windows along one wall would benefit from having speakers on the opposite side so that the audience doesn't just see their silhouettes because of the backlighting.

To reduce cost, try to use the same setup for multiple sessions. Or find out if the site will allow your volunteers to handle setting up the rooms.

MONEY SAVERS

Facilities have a deadline to submit room setups so find out when that date is. Most of the time, a rough drawing of the room is adequate, so don't worry if you think your artistic skills aren't the best!

Page 91 has examples of different types of room layouts.

Overseeing equipment needs

Work closely with the Speaker Coordinator to find out what speakers will need for their sessions.

Begin writing down a list of equipment to check when the site is available. If the site does not provide all the equipment, make a list of what other items must be brought:

- Whiteboard erasers, markers
- Overhead transparencies, markers
- Easels
- Flipcharts

Work with the Technical Coordinator to assign equipment to the different locations. If possible, work with audiovisual companies or equipment suppliers directly. This makes communication easier and avoids excessive charges by the site.

Housing

The complexity of the housing arrangements depends on the requirements of the event. If your small retreat is using a small house, the arrangements may simply be figuring out who is sleeping in one room and separating the snorers from the non-snorers.

A very large conference that involves multiple hotels would benefit from using a housing bureau or asking attendees to make their own arrangements with hotels.

If you are in charge of assigning rooms, create housing forms for the attendees to fill out. These forms show the types of rooms and rates available and asks people to select a range of rooms they would like. See page 92 for a sample *Housing Request* form. These forms can be included in the registration brochure. Or, if you are working with a Housing Bureau, the attendee sends the form to the housing bureau after they have registered.

Review check-in times with the site. If people are arriving early, be sure staff will be on hand to register them. Remember to arrange for late check-in (or check-out) for staff who need to pack up things before they arrive.

Food

Ask the Hospitality Coordinator to draw up diagrams needed for the dining and serving areas. Communicate to the site any food preparation or serving equipment needed.

Break

If refreshments are being served, the Hospitality Coordinator can also work with you to determine what area would best be suited for breaks. Additional arrangements for the break area might include making sure there are enough chairs for people to rest.

Registration

Check with the Registration Coordinator as to what kind of furniture, equipment, or room setup is needed.

Signage

Develop signage for the sessions and site with the Marketing Coordinator (page 189).

Theater
Rows of chairs facing speaker

Chevron
Rows angled in a chevron-shape.
Tables may be placed also.
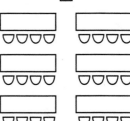

Classroom
Rows of rectangular tables
with chairs facing speaker

U-Shaped
Tables placed in a horseshoe
shape around speaker
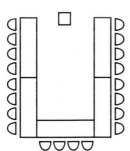

Hollow/Closed Square/Rectangle
Tables in a square formation
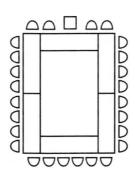

Theater in the round
Stage centrally located among
tables (round or rectangular)
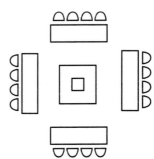

Panel
Rows of chairs facing a panel
with a moderator

Roundtable
Seating at round tables.
Chairs may be placed in clusters.

Mixed seating
Combination of any of the above

| HOUSING REQUEST | Form |

Conference Name: _____

Instructions

1. Use one form per room.
2. Fill out personal information for the contact person of the group.
3. List your hotel preference. Rooms are assigned by a first-come, first-served basis.
4. List room preferences, names of occupants, and arrival/departure dates and times of contact person.
5. Complete payment information.
6. Reservation deadline is (date). Reservations after this date are subject to availability. Contact hotel directly for cancellations or changes.
7. Mail or fax form to: (Name and address info, fax number)

Personal information

Prefix: (Mr, Ms.) _____ Name _____

Title _____

Organization _____

Address _____

City _____ State _____ Zip code _____

Telephone _____ Fax _____

E-mail _____

Hotel choices (Please rank by preference: 1st, 2nd, 3rd, 4th)

_____	Hotel 1:	Price: $
_____	Hotel 2:	Price: $
_____	Hotel 3:	Price $:
_____	Hotel 4:	Price $:

Room ❑ Single (1 bed/1 person) ❑ Double (2 beds/2 people) ❑ Triple (2 beds/3 people)

❑ Double (1 bed/2 people) ❑ Quad (2 beds/4 people)

Room Occupants (List each person)

1. _____   3. _____

2. _____   4. _____

Special Requests: ❑ Nonsmoking ❑ Wheelchair access ❑ Rollaway bed ❑ Crib ❑ Other: _____

Arrival and departure date, times _____

Payment Information

Deposit policy: _____

Payment: ❑ Check attached (make payable to: _____

❑ Credit card: Name on card _____ Number _____ Signature _____

Other areas

Talk to the site staff about the areas being used to make sure that all arrangements have been handled: storage rooms, office/command center, parking, and other areas you will be using.

FINAL COMMUNICATIONS

Communicate precisely with the site staff the arrival and departure times for conference staff, speakers, and attendees. Give them an estimate of how many people are expected to use the food outlets and rooms so that they can be prepared with adequate staff.

When the schedule has been finalized, give a copy to the site, especially if meetings are at another location like a convention center. Then they will know when to expect attendees to return.

Right before the move-in, inspect the site with the site contact person. Draw on the floor plan any damage so that you aren't liable for it later. After the event, walk through the site to see what damage has been done and what you are liable for. For example, sometimes convention centers will charge for removing tape residue from exhibits.

TIPS

TIPS FOR SUCCESS

One person on your team should be the main contact person for the site (probably yourself!). This will help reduce confusion and conflicting requests. Ask to work with one main person at the site.

Keep records of all your conversations. Date your notes and write down who you talked to. If a misunderstanding comes up later, these notes will be invaluable.

C H A P T E R

8 | PROGRAM

Designing the program of your conference is like designing a room in a house. Depending on the purpose of the room, you plan what kind of furniture will be needed and where it will be placed. Colors, fabrics, and accessories are coordinated to evoke an atmosphere that suits the function of the room. The different elements work together to create a room that is functional and beautiful.

Likewise, in program design, you may have different elements such as the speakers, worship, and small groups. Combining these elements in an order that flows smoothly and matches the purpose of the conference creates a finished product that is far more effective together than alone. Just having a speaker might be somewhat effective, but a speaker's effectiveness can be greatly enhanced by an awesome worship time and then a small group discussion that will reinforce the speakers' message.

OVERVIEW

The Program Coordinator oversees the planning of the conference program. Just because you are the Program Coordinator doesn't mean that you should plan the whole program by yourself! If the conference will be large or complicated, you may want to delegate the separate areas to different people who will oversee the arrangements for each area. For example, you can have a different person over each of these areas:

- Speaker
- Workshops
- Worship
- Creative arts
- Entertainment
- Small groups
- Recreation

You can have one person over each area, or have someone take a few of the areas. One person could oversee the speaker as well as the workshop area and she would coordinate the speakers for the entire conference.

The pre-conference responsibilities of the Program Coordinator involve planning the program and coordinating all the arrangements.

At the conference, you will be the one directing and giving cues so that people know when to go on stage or when to change the lighting (*Chapter 18: The Conference*).

After the conference, your main tasks are evaluation, summarization, and appreciation of those who were involved in helping (*Chapter 19: Wrapping Up*).

PROGRAM COORDINATOR	Job Description

The Program Coordinator oversees all aspects of planning the program of events for the conference and runs the program at the conference.

Recommended skills/qualities

- Creativity
- Administrative/organizational skills
- Attention to detail
- Able to function under pressure and make decisions

Job Description

Before the conference

- Attend planning meetings
- Set and schedule program
- Work with Speaker Coordinator to secure speakers and entertainment
- Contract entertainment
- Plan small group discussion logistics and materials
- Recruit worship leader to oversee worship times
- Plan fellowship and recreational activities

Night before conference

- Oversee staff responsibilities in preparing program areas

During the conference

- Call cues for the program

After the conference

- Compile summary report
- Send notes of appreciation to program staff
- Evaluate conference and suggest improvements for next time

Time Commitment

This position's time commitment is:

DESIGNING THE PROGRAM

The purpose of the conference serves as a filter for decisions. As you decide what to include and what not to, ask yourself one main question: does this contribute to meeting the purpose and goals of this conference? Keep these questions in mind as you plan:

- When people leave this event, what do we want people to walk away with?
- What do we want to accomplish? What is the outcome?
- Unplanned events happen too (bad weather, equipment breaking down, tiredness). Even if such disappointments occur, what kind of memories will people have?
- What kinds of needs do people have that are unmet? What would motivate them to come? Target as many of the unmet needs as possible. The more needs that are targeted, the more likely the person will consider going.

Here is the general order of designing a program for your conference:

1. Finalize theme and purpose of conference.
2. Determine conference events to include (general sessions, breakouts, small groups, etc.).
3. Brainstorm what elements to use (speakers, creative arts, etc.).
4. Find speakers/talent/people resources (speakers, worship team).
5. Arrange program order and schedule. Create cue sheet.
6. Arrange logistics for program (equipment, materials, room setups).
7. Communicate logistics and schedules to everyone involved.

STEP-BY-STEP

1 THEME AND PURPOSE OF CONFERENCE

TIPS FOR SUCCESS

A theme can be an effective way of building the conference so that the program is consistent and focused. Creativity with the theme helps people remember the message and retain what they learned at the event. Discuss with others on the team different ways the theme can be communicated. Use a short, catchy phrase so that the theme can easily be remembered.

> We come up with a theme and take that theme out as many different directions as it can go. This year the theme was Home Builders. At our church, we had a promotional table that looked like a construction site. We signed men up for the event on a piece of plywood. On the table was a blueprint of the men's ministry. At the event, in the hotel driveway there was a sign that said, "Home Builders 2002." Towards the lobby there was a construction sign that said, "Men Under Construction" with blinking yellow lights. We had Tyvek all around. When they signed in, they got a toolbelt that said "Home Builders 2002." In their rooms we gave them a twenty-five foot long tape measure in a bag that said, "The measure of a man is not by his width or his length, not by his might or his strength. The Lord looks to see Christ in your heart." At the last session they brought their tape measures and the person with a number on his measuring tape won—but it was written at the twenty-five foot mark. We always do more than you would expect to add value to what the person pays to be there.
> ✦ *Chuck Caswell*

2 CONFERENCE EVENTS

To help decide what to include in the program, ask:

- What kind of events would best the suit the purpose and goals of this conference?
- What is the audience like? What are effective ways of relating to them? What is their gender, age, or culture?
- What will the program look like? How many sessions will we have? What kinds of activities will be going on?

Below is a list of events that might be included:
- Registration
- Orientation
- General sessions
- Breakout sessions/workshops
- Small group discussions
- Devotional time
- Special events/tours
- Recreation/socializing opportunities
- Breaks
- Sleep
- Meals

Program elements:
- Speakers/teachers
- Worship
- Entertainment
- Creative arts: drama, video
- Awards/prizes

Resource people
- Translation/sign language interpreters—are they needed?
- Children's program/childcare—will it be needed?

As you go through the events, brainstorm which ones you might use and how they might help meet the purpose and goals. Then list a preliminary order.

SCHEDULING

Registration

When planning the starting time, don't forget to account for people's work schedules and travel times. If there will be traffic, start later.

Are people arriving when it is dark or light? If it will be dark, what are ways you can help direct people? I've attended retreats where entrance signs were practically invisible and people with flashlights stood by the roadside to flag down those arriving.

As people arrive, how can the transition be made smoothly? If you are able, have people escort them to their living quarters. If it is dark outside and housing is walking distance away, have them register and keep their luggage in one place. Assist them with their luggage after the program and escort them to their rooms.

Schedule time between arrival and the first session so that people will have an opportunity to register and check into their rooms. Then work with the Registration Coordinator to develop a streamlined on-site registration process (page 161).

Orientation

The orientation for the participants may be very simple or more detailed. Explain the facility and any rules that people should be aware of. Go over the schedule and any other information people should know.

General Sessions

General program sessions come in different structures such as:
- Lecture format
- Talk show/interview format
- Panel discussion
- Interactive discussion/question and answer

The general sessions are where the entire group gathers for teaching or some kind of input. If possible, avoid sessions after lunch where people will be sitting the majority of the time, because most people might be tired and have difficulty concentrating. Instead, schedule a free hour after lunch. If time does not allow a long break, then try to make the after-lunch session interactive or stimulating to help people stay away. This applies to after dinner too; include activity in the program.

> Never give information after dinner. People are tapped out after dinner and can't learn anything. Have a storyteller or something more entertaining. A general rule of thumb is to have 75% content and 25% entertainment in the morning. Afternoon is fifty-fifty and go with 100% entertainment after dinner. ◆ *Brian Lord*

Between sessions, allow time for people to travel to the next session; at least fifteen minutes if possible. Pad the schedule between sessions in case the program runs late and allow time for people to travel from the lodging to the meeting area.

Opening Session
The first session of the conference is usually called the opening session. Start and end with a bang. If the size and purpose of your group allows it, begin with a welcoming activity or icebreaker to set a positive mood. Some groups like to begin retreats by introducing the team coordinators and any small group facilitators so that attendees can feel more at ease. Others are more formal, with a dramatic opening program. If you are holding a conference, surprise your audience with a special element: a video, special music, a drama, something out of the ordinary. Place a speaker that will be a draw in the first session so that people will have incentive to attend. A memorable opening session starts the event off with a positive, upbeat impression.

Closing session
The last session is called the closing session. Plan your closing session carefully in order to have the most impact. Make it memorable, schedule an inspiring speaker, or add something creative and different. Don't forget closure for small groups too.

> What our final session looks like depends on the conference and where people are and how the week went. More often than not it's a celebratory event where we pump them up and send them out. Other times we get a sense that the people were slacking all week and need a kick before we send them out the door. Other times we want to be very reflective. Most of the time we want them to be very challenged to go back and do something specific, and in the final session we affirm their decision. ◆ *Ron Sugimoto*

Breakout Sessions/Workshops
Offering multiple alternatives gives people the freedom to choose because a wide variety of workshops allows more people to attend a session that interests them. Effective workshops draw on the theme in some way to tie in the teaching to what is being taught in the main sessions.

> We try to pick people who are ministering in a particular area. So if we want to do a men's track, we find someone who is ministering to men to put together the program. For the children's track, we find a children's pastor. The women's track uses someone in women's ministry. The key is finding people who serve in that capacity. ◆ *Rick Leary*

See *Chapter 9: Speakers* for more information about finding workshop speakers.

Small Groups
Breakout sessions may be workshops or small group discussion groups for people to reflect upon the material.

Effective retreats have small group activities to discuss the sessions. They build on the message and help people internalize it. They also build rapport with new people. Most groups put you with people you don't know. They separate groups of friends who hang out so people meet new people. A lot of women will really open up. We get feedback saying, "I didn't want to go to the new group, but when I did I made new friends."
✦ *Debbie Dittrich*

Planning small group sessions includes planning for the discussion questions as well as recruiting facilitators to lead the discussion time.

Recruit Small Group Facilitators
If you'll be including small group sessions in your program, enlist small group facilitators who will lead these discussion times. Look for people who have:
- experience leading group discussions
- good listening skills
- good facilitating skills
- knowledge of the topic being discussed
- discernment and wisdom on where the group is and what direction to take it
- respect from those they lead
- a shepherding heart to care for those they are leading

Small groups can be led by one facilitator or even a pair of facilitators. Pair a more experienced person with one who has less experience. This provides a good mentoring situation and the development of future small group facilitators. Also, people might be more willing to facilitate if they don't feel like they have to do it alone.

SCHEDULING

Schedule timing
Figure out the timing of the small group sessions: when in the program the groups will gather and how long the meeting time should be. The larger the group is, the more time you should allow in small group sessions so that everyone has an opportunity to speak. Groups ideally should be no more than twelve people; more than twelve means fewer chances for everyone to talk.

The facilitators will need material and direction on how to lead their group. Work with the Speaker Coordinator to find material that reinforces what the speaker is teaching. Or, write questions that will stimulate discussion.

Assign small groups
How will people be divided into their small groups? Will it be random (where people just meet with whoever they are sitting with at the session) or pre-assigned? Because people will naturally congregate with their friends, having pre-assigned small groups is an effective way for people to build new relationships during the event. However, if time is an issue, or if your group is too large, having a quick discussion with those around you is a better choice.

Assign locations
As you are preparing for the small group sessions, assign each group facilitator to a location to save time and minimize confusion at the event. Make a list of each group with the leaders and where the meeting location will be. Distribute this information to your leaders so they know where they should meet. A copy of the list included in the registration packet will help people remember where to go to meet their group.

Run training session
Two weeks before the conference, set a training session for the small group facilitators. Training ensures consistency among the groups and helps everyone understand their responsibilities and how to carry them out. At the training session:

- Pass out all materials, including schedule, map of facility, and any discussion material.
- Review the program and explain how their session fits into the overall purpose of the conference.
- Teach facilitation and listening skills.
- Help people get to know each other.

Make it a requirement that everyone attends, even the experienced facilitators, so that everyone is on the same page. It's also a good opportunity for the facilitators to get to know one another, so toss in a get-to-know-each-other activity.

Worship

Determine worship needs
What style of worship best suits the target audience? What would be meaningful and help them worship? If your audience is varied, use a mix of hymns and contemporary music. Size may impact the style also: if it is a small retreat group, perhaps an intimate acoustic guitar-led or keyboard-led worship would be appropriate.

Recruit worship leader and team
Ask a person who is experienced in leading worship to oversee the worship for the conference. His tasks will be to recruit a team, select the songs, and put together any overheads or video projection slides.

List equipment needs
Check what equipment is needed, such as:
- Microphones
- Microphone stands
- Music stands
- Instrument stands
- Monitors
- Sound system
- Direct boxes
- Cables
- Extension cords
- Mixing equipment
- Computer with projection software
- Video projector
- Overhead screen

Draw up a stage diagram where the team members and equipment will be placed. This will be helpful for the technical crew to know where everything needs to be placed.

As you plan the worship, plan the transitions between worship and the speaker. Don't put in announcements right after the worship and before the speaker since it disrupts the flow of the program. How can you have worship flow smoothly between the other elements? Long gaps of silence are uncomfortable for the audience unless it is intentional silence.

Music reproduction

The worship leader may also be in charge of securing a license for the rights to reproduce the music. Christian Copyright Licensing International (CCLI) offers licenses for one-time events that are shorter than seven days. Their fees vary depending on the size of the event. Call them or check their Web site for rates and information: www.ccli.com, 800-234-2446.

Conferences are increasingly using PowerPoint or other video graphics to project lyrics. The Worship Leader can oversee this, or ask someone else who has had experience in this area.

Devotional time

At a conference, people are bombarded in all directions with information, emotions, and experiences. Unless there is some time for people to process what they are learning, they can easily leave the event without any lasting impact or change happening.

A one-day intensive conference doesn't have extensive time for devotionals or private reflection. Processing time can be scheduled in the few minutes at the end of a session, letting people fill out a commitment card or jotting reminders in their notebook.

Longer conferences have the advantage of having more time for people to process what they are learning. People can have morning quiet times, prayer walks, retreats of silence, or other opportunities to pray and reflect on what they are experiencing.

Putting one person in charge of any devotional or small group materials is helpful when there are multiple sessions because it may be task-intensive to compile the information for the different devotional times.

Devotional materials may take many different forms:
- **Personal devotional materials.** Write your own or look for material that fits the theme. There are countless books out on the market that are good sources for personal devotions.
- **Group devotions.** Sometimes before or after breakfast, a teacher gives a devotional talk to the group. Find a teacher who can teach spiritual insight that is applicable to the audience.
- **Cabin devotions.** At night before going to sleep, cabins have a group time together. The easiest way is to assign the cabin leader the task of either giving the devotions or finding a person in the cabin to give the devotions. You provide all the cabins the same material or ask each leader to come up with her own devotions.

Recreation/socializing opportunities

Recreational or fellowship activities are some of the most fun and memorable experiences at a conference.

The types of activities run the gamut:
- Competitive games
- Icebreakers
- Talent shows
- Campfires
- Hiking or outdoor activities
- Sports activities
- Crafts
- Board games

Welcome activities or icebreakers are great ways to help people adjust to the new event. Make them fun, with the goal of helping people get to know one another and be more comfortable.

Ideas:
- Have icebreakers at meals, mixing people up with different groups of people as a way to meet other people.
- Do icebreakers on a long bus ride to make the time pass by quicker.
- Start out a small group session with an ice breaker.

Special events/Tours

Sometimes exhibitors or sponsors will sponsor a special event to a local attraction: an event, a sightseeing trip, or an activity related to the purpose of the conference. These trips can be for the whole group, for only spouses of the members, or for the children while the parents are in session.

> Offer a tour. You can hire a company or tour bus. There are all sorts of museums in the downtown area. Do a cruise—a lot of cities are near water. You can cruise in a riverboat, private yacht, or sailboat. There are discount tickets to area attractions. Six Flags has a commission program. You sell tickets for them and you keep a cut—you can offer a discount. If you want an educational program, consider your resources downtown. Last year we hired the Memphis Zoo to do a project for us; it was $100 for two hours. We divided it into four thirty-minute programs. Some museums have traveling exhibits . . . you will eliminate the expense of transportation. You may even have children at the museum, spouses at the shopping mall, and teenagers at the amusement park [simultaneously].
> ◆ Dean Jones

Meals

It seems like giving people time to eat is just a necessity in the program—let's get it over with and get back to the real program! But often people don't realize that meal times are important for fellowship. People are able to minister to each other over a meal or during a quiet conversation together.

> One of the things that we have come to realize is that people minister to each other a lot, so even things like your meals and breaks are strategic times at a conference. There's a lot of ministry that takes place as people interact. We even include the meals as part of our program. It's not separate because at the meals you want good ambience so people can interact. We have circular tables so people are facing each other. Don't over-program because when you do, you take these kinds of events away. For a lot of people, just getting away is a chance to replenish. If you run a really tight schedule, it doesn't help them do that, it just wipes them out and they have to go back to rest. Have balance in your programming. ◆ Ron Demolar

Meals present excellent opportunities for fellowship and ministry to each other. Round tables work better than rectangular tables for people to see each other and talk. You can even throw out a question each meal for people to discuss:
- Why did you come to this conference?
- What statement did the speaker make that impacted you the most?
- What have you enjoyed most about this conference?

You can also use other questions that are not related to conferences—be creative! Maximize those meal times!

Some conferences hold their sessions during meal times. If you do this, be sure the majority of the people are done eating before starting, or the speaker will have to be heard over the clank of silverware.

Breaks

Schedule frequent breaks. A conference day can be more tiring than a workday as people are assimilating information all day in an intensive situation. Providing food during breaks makes for a change of scene and a chance to rest the mind.

Sleep

The longer your conference or retreat is, as the days elapse people will be more tired and will need more sleep. Schedule less and allow people more time to sleep.

Speakers/Teachers

Since speakers are a large part of every conference, an entire chapter is devoted to this area. See the next chapter for information on speakers.

Entertainment/Talent

Entertainment—musicians, comedians, dramatists, and other entertainment—is another element that can be used effectively in a program. Like other vendors you may use, be sure to review all their services and references before you book them. Even if someone from your organization is doing the entertainment, it's a good idea to preview them just to be sure that the performance is in good taste.

Effective entertainment is entertainment with a purpose. Don't book entertainment with the sole purpose of entertaining people, but have it serve dual purposes.

> Never use just entertainment. Use entertainment with a purpose. One evening we didn't have a speaker or worship and we only had a musician. He did a concert but it was a unique style, using music to teach and preach as well. ✦ *Keith Hirata*

See page 114 for a listing of sources to find entertainment.

Creative Arts

Using creative arts in the program allows people to open their minds to the message by looking at the topic in a new way. Creative arts pieces may be effective lead-ins to the message but will require coordinating with the speaker ahead of time what the direction of the message will be.

If you will be using creative arts, find a creative arts coordinator, a video coordinator, or a drama coordinator. Ideas for creative lead-ins to the message include:

- video interviews on the topic
- a reading of a story, acted out
- a drama on the topic
- a song about the topic, with still photographs shown on the video projector

What kind of elements can enhance the experience for people?

Your use of creative arts, such as drama, will be impacted by how much space is available in the room. Drama is also affected by available lighting, sound equipment, acoustics, and room for placement of scenery or props.

Some organizations that offer creative arts resources include:

RESOURCE TOOLS

- Willowcreek Association, www.willowcreek.com (look under "Resources"), 847-765-0070. Offers a wide variety of drama scripts and books.
- Lillenas Drama, www.lillenasdrama.com, 800-877-0700. Dramas for children and adults ranging from short sketches to full length productions.
- Contemporary Drama Service, www.contemporarydrama.com, 800-937-5297. Wide variety of plays, comedy scripts, theatrical books, and musical comedies.
- Drama Ministry, www.dramaministry.com, 866-859-7622 (toll free). Offers individual drama scripts that pertain to real life situations, as well as a drama subscription service.

Awards/Prizes

Offering doorprizes at the beginning of each session is a good way to help people to arrive on time. Offering a prize is also an excellent incentive for people to turn in their evaluations at the end of the conference!

Ask exhibitors or sponsors if they would be willing to provide complimentary prizes; this gives them good publicity as well!

Transitions

If you were to ask a participant what made a program effective, they would probably mention the speakers or the worship or the drama or any of the elements. Very few people would say, "Great transitions!"

So why are transitions an important part of effective programming?

Transitions are only noticed when they are bad ones. Have you ever sat through a program when the speaker stopped talking, walked off the stage and you were wondering what would happen next? Then what seemed like an eternity later, another person walked on to say a prayer. That was an example of a bad transition, only noticed when it was not done well. A good transition will not be noticed because it will not bring attention to itself. Instead, the audience's attention is kept on what is happening in the program.

How do you have great transitions? Try to reduce any "dead space" between program elements. This might be done by doing changes during prayer, asking the speaker to come up before the end of the song, or playing "transition music" on a piano or keyboard as people move around the stage. You've worked hard to bring people to a certain place mentally and emotionally. Don't drop the bottom out and distract them by an awkward transition!

4 RESOURCE PEOPLE

Emcee

The emcee ties the program together and sets the tone for the conference. The choice of emcee is an important one as he or she will take care of transitions and introductions. People look to the emcee for direction because the emcee will know best what should be happening and what changes will need to be made. Look for an emcee who is comfortable in front of groups, speaks clearly, and helps make people at ease. Emcees also act as a timekeeper, holding up signs for the speaker to let them know they have a few minutes left. If there is a delay in the program, the emcee works with the Program Coordinator or Director to keep the event on schedule. We give our emcees headsets to use so that they can coordinate with the Director what changes should be announced. Of course, the emcee takes off the headset when she goes onstage!

> At some of the conferences we have used news reporters. One reporter wrote everything out word-for-word and followed a script. The other one ad-libbed the entire conference and we had no idea what she was going to say. But the Director trusted her based on the referrals and the emcee did a great job, adding significantly to an enjoyable conference experience.

Translation/Sign Language Interpreters

If your conference requires translators of any kind, don't forget to include their fees or honorariums in your budget, as well as any equipment that may be required.

Children's Program Coordinator

If you need childcare or a children's program, recruit a coordinator to handle it. He can enlist volunteers to help teach, pull together a children's curriculum, and make the arrangements to take care of the children. There are many resources available for children's programs so I won't go into detail here, but don't neglect this important aspect. Parents who know that their children are well taken care of can concentrate on the program in peace.

5   PROGRAM SCHEDULE

Now that you have all these wonderful program elements that will be used at the conference, how can you put them together in a way that will maximize the experience for those who are attending?

Keep this rule of thumb in mind: quality is more important than quantity. Make your goal to give the people the best experience, not the most experiences. If you have an option of packing your schedule as tightly as you can, or providing fewer well-done elements, go for the quality. Plan an interesting and relevant program and provide an experience that will challenge, encourage and inspire them.

SCHEDULING

Programming for optimal learning

Even if initially people come to a conference wanting to have fun or a good time, a goal for every conference should be to have people learn and grow in some aspect of their relationship with God. How can you put together a program that gives people the optimal learning opportunity?

TIPS FOR SUCCESS

Prepare the room

From the moment people step into the room, what they sense influences how they will learn. A room that is hot, stuffy, dark or dirty is not an optimal learning environment. But if they enter a room that is well-lit, visually appealing and with a pleasant scent, they anticipate an interesting session. Appeal to the senses by using color and light, adjusting environmental controls, and making sure that the smell is pleasant.

Use variety

Your audience will be a mix of people with different learning styles. That means that if you use only one teaching style, you'll be neglecting part of your audience.

Vary the program so that it will reach people with different needs. Use contrasting approaches: large groups mixed with small groups, quiet reflection and upbeat celebration. Combine entertainment with education. Offer general sessions that everyone attends but also sessions where people can choose where they would like to go. Scatter variety through the entire event because people learn in different ways and have different personalities.

> Usually the core staff are extroverts by nature so it's easy to plan programming around our personality styles. We need to ask what we are doing for the people who aren't like us, the introverts who find that being with people drains them. We try to offer something so that everyone feels like they are taken care of. For free time events, we had a spread of activities for the athlete and non-athlete. Some people are into playing volleyball, but we also had craft sessions and that took off. ✦ *Ron Sugimoto*

Worship before teaching

To prepare people, begin with worship. People come to sessions distracted or with other things on their minds. Worshiping helps them focus and be ready to hear what the speaker has to say.

SCHEDULING

> We always start with worship because we believe that worship is the basis for learning. What we learn comes out of our worship of God; it's encased in worship. We have a video and the speaker comes out, we close in worship, then we give people time to write down what they learn because unless you take the time to process and write it down you may lose what God might say to them. ✦ *Pam Chun*

Be wise in scheduling before the program. Whether you are using worship or drama or other elements, be careful not to make it too long.

> When a retreat starts on a Friday night, most of the people have been working. People are exhausted. Then they eat at seven and they have skits and singing for an hour. The program before any speaking needs to be short—twenty minutes at the most. If you add another forty-five minutes of speaking on top of that, you have over an hour where people are sitting. ✦ *Debbie Dittrich*

Use memorable experiences

Add unique experiences that people cannot have at home so that the event is memorable for them. At retreats, plan experiential events that are effective, as most people learn by doing. Use all senses to reinforce the message and help people learn.

Pacing

SCHEDULING

Varied pacing

Pacing also contributes to effective programming. The human body is not designed to sustain a constant level of activity for long periods of time. Remember this as you plan so that you don't expect your people to go from program to program without providing some down time.

Schedule a light session after an intense session. This allows people to have a chance to be refreshed. As the day goes on, people will grow more tired, so begin intense sessions earlier and end with lighter sessions.

Remember not to overschedule—don't pack in every moment of your conference. Allow times for reflection, recreation, and fellowship.

> A lot of retreats fall short in not giving women enough time to reflect and have quiet time. I've been in evening programs where they had way too much planned. They had skits, testimonies, singing, and by the time I talked, it was 10:30 at night. It was a small retreat for twenty women in a hotel. Some had been out to eat, some had wine, and they were very sleepy. Their dinner was Italian food with all the pasta. They came back to a big suite where they had 100 candles lit for a mood. They were on the floor and couch and chairs, and some were sound asleep! ✦ *Debbie Dittrich*

Watch the rhythm, the emotional high and low points of the program. Add appropriate light moments after intense heavy moments to release the tension so that you don't leave people hanging at the end of a session and leave with an unsatisfied feeling; plan for closure. Inspire and encourage them! Think of meal or break times as fellowship and ministry time and as an important part of the program. As you examine each part of the program, ask if the pacing is too fast or too slow and strike a varied but appropriate balance.

> We can't keep going on a level nine or ten the whole week—we'd have dead bodies! But if we kept it at a level three all week, they wouldn't break a sweat and that's not good either. We ask, "How do we build it up, then bring it down so they have a chance to recharge and reflect, and then to bring them up again?" ✦ *Ron Sugimoto*

Body rhythms

Remember another basic fact about human physiology: people have natural body rhythms throughout the day. Avoid scheduling sessions after meals where people will only be sitting. You are doing your speaker and your audience a disservice! Don't schedule anything before seven a.m. or after ten p.m. because night owls will not be awake in the morning and early birds will be tired at night. If you are at a conference center, plan for a way to signal the morning waking time. Some conference centers have bells that may be rung. Other groups assign a person to go around and knock on doors for wake-up calls. Ask a morning person to do this!

Be flexible

Plan every minute in your program (including down time) but be ready to make changes and adjust on-the-fly. Unexpected things always come up so expect to make changes! Plan flexibility into the program in case you need to swap program elements or eliminate something altogether.

Putting it on paper

EXAMPLES

Conference schedule

After you have determined how the program will look, draw up a conference schedule of what will be happening (page 108). This is the schedule that should go into the registration brochure. You may find that the schedule will change as you refine it and at this point it is more useful to have a general schedule to work with.

EXAMPLES

Cue sheet

An important tool for communication is putting together a *cue sheet*. The cue sheet lists a detailed schedule of the program, what will be happening, and who is responsible for each area. For complex programs, you may need to include a lot of detail in the cue sheet, including any transitions, audiovisual effects, sound cues, or any other information that your staff will need to make the program run smoothly. Scheduling minute by minute allows you to see whether you have enough time to do everything. Distribute this cue sheet to the staff, speakers, and key volunteer leaders (example on page 109).

Rehearsal schedule

Speakers, worship teams, and entertainers will need sound checks and rehearsals. The amount of time needed for rehearsal varies. Some speakers like to have a quick check of the microphone; others will rehearse part of their speech, walking up and down the length of the stage. Try to accommodate speakers as much as possible in the rehearsal schedule, and then give everyone involved a copy so they know when they need to arrive.

Program information

The last item to put together is information for the program booklet. Interact with the Speaker Coordinator to determine what content should go into the program booklet. Submit speaker biographies and schedule information to the Marketing Coordinator to put into the program booklet.

6   PROGRAM LOGISTICS

Assigning rooms

Assigning rooms should be a joint effort between the Program/Speaker Coordinator and the Site Coordinator. The Speaker Coordinator will be familiar with the speakers and their needs and the Site Coordinator will know which rooms are suitable for the workshop.

Work with the Volunteer Coordinator to recruit responsible volunteers to oversee the workshop rooms.

> We have a room host greeter in each room. They work directly with the speaker. If the speaker has problems with the audiovisual equipment, the host greeter makes a call. The greeters are responsible for the guest experience. If they see people fan themselves when it's hot, they adjust the temperature. They greet people when they walk in and give them a handout. Typically we have two for each room. Sometimes volunteers will

Time	Event	Details	Leader
Friday			
5:00	Registration	Welcome package, name badges, room	Registration Coor.
7:00	Dinner	Mixer activity	Fellowship Coor.
8:00	General session	Welcome	Conference Dir.
		Music worship	Worship Leader
8:30		Speaker intro	Conference Dir.
		Speaker session	Speaker
10:00		Announcements/rules	Registration Coor.
		Bring out snacks	Fellowship Coor.
	Snack time		
11:00	Lights out	Lights out at meeting room	Fellowship Coor.
Saturday			
7:30	Wake up	Morning wake up call	Fellowship Coor.
8:00	Breakfast/mixer	Mixer before breakfast	Fellowship Coor.
9:00	Quiet time		
9:30	General session	Music worship	Worship Leader
10:00		Speaker session	Speaker
11:30		End general session	
12:00	Lunch	Mixer	Fellowship Coor.
1:30	Talent show		Fellowship Coor.
2:30	Free time		
5:30	Dinner	Mixer	Fellowship Coor.
6:30	General session	Music worship	Worship Leader
7:00		Speaker session	Speaker
8:30	Small groups	Small group sharing	Fellowship Coor.
10:00	Snacks		Fellowship Coor.
11:00	Lights out		
Sunday			
7:30	Wake up	Wake up call	Fellowship Coor.
8:00	Breakfast	Mixer	Fellowship Coor.
9:00	Quiet time		
9:30	General session	Music worship	Worship Leader
10:00		Speaker session	Speaker
		Communion	Pastor
		Announcement about check-out procedure	Registration Coor.
		Announcement about group picture	Fellowship Coor.
11:30	Group picture		Fellowship Coor.
12:00	Lunch	Mixer	Fellowship Coor.
1:00	Check out		Registration Coor.

Note: The Fellowship Coordinator oversaw hospitality as well as small group/social times. Because food was served by the conference center, the team chose to not have a Food Coordinator.

Time	Cue	Person	Event	Audio	Lights/Video
8:30		Ushers	General session doors open		House at full
9:00	Director cues band	Worsh. Tm.	Begin prelude	Emcee mike up	
9:02	Song finishes Band sits down	Emcee	Welcome, doorprizes, prayer		
9:12	Emcee finish prayer	Video	Opening media piece		House and stage down/run video
9:15	Video over	Worsh. Tm.	Worship set 1	Worship up	House at half
9:35	Worship leader prays	Emcee	Walk to stage Intro speaker	Emcee up	
	Applause	Speaker 1	Speaker session 1	Speaker up	
10:10	End of talk	Emcee	Make announcements, dismiss		
10:15			Break		House at full
10:40		Worsh. Tm.	Worship set 2	Worship up	
10:55	End of set	Drama Tm.	Walk to stage Perform drama	Drama up	House down Spot on drama
11:00	End of drama	Emcee	Intro speaker	Emcee up	
		Speaker 2	Speaker session 2	Speaker up	House at half
11:35	End of talk	Emcee	Announcements	Emcee up	
11:40		Emcee	Dismiss to lunch		
11:45			Lunch 1/Workshop A		House at full
1:00			End workshop A		
1:10			Lunch 2/Workshop B		
2:25			End workshop B		
2:35			Workshop C		
3:45			End workshop		
3:55		Emcee	Doorprizes	Emcee up	
4:00		Emcee	Introduce guest musician		
		Emcee	Sit down		
		Musician	Walk to stage	Piano mike up	House at half
		Musician	Sharing and singing		
4:20	Applause last song	Musician	Sit down		
		Emcee	Walk up to stage, offering intro	Emcee up	
		Singers	Special music	Musicians' mike up	
		Ushers	Collect offering		
4:25	End of song	Singers	Sit down		
		Worsh. Tm.	Worship set 3	Worship up	
4:45	Last song	Emcee	Intro reading	Emcee up	
		Reader	Dramatic reading		
4:50	Last line	Reader	Sit down		Blackout
		Speaker 3	Speaker session 3	Speaker up	
5:25	Message ends	Speaker 3	Sit down		
		Emcee	Walk to stage	Emcee up	
		Emcee	Feedback cards		
		Worsh. Tm.	Closing song	Worship up	
5:30	End of song	Emcee	Close in prayer		
		Worsh. Tm.	Postlude		

come to us and want to hear a workshop and we will match them up that way. Sometimes volunteers are assigned to the workshop. ✦ *Terry Toro*

7   COMMUNICATE LOGISTICS

Distribute schedules and regular updates to everyone involved in the program. Let people know of any major changes.

PLANNING EFFECTIVE PROGRAMS

Ask for commitments

Here are Saddleback, when we program, we specifically ask for commitment. The reason is that most people will take a decision more seriously if they make a written commitment. We've learned and programmed it in. It's a successful way to help people. Most of the times there are things you look for. You want people to take an action. I'm not thrilled with just doing inspirational events. Oftentimes we leave things hanging and give them a great inspirational event and then never ask people to do something. Christian faith is about doing, not just about learning. Keep the end results in mind.
✦ *Andrew Accardy*

Be creative

Be creative with what you put in a program. Either add a new creative element into the program, or take what you have and adjust it so that people can see things from a new angle. How can you structure what you do in a way that will be effective and memorable?

We invited four speakers, each one representing a different significant community. We had a Korean pastor, African American speaker, Latino theologian, and a white woman speaker. The four of them were all asked to speak from the same text. The one instruction I gave to each of them was to speak out of the text from their community's perspective. We ended up with four very distinct and unique messages all from the same section of Scripture. It ended up being very powerful with the depth that we saw in the text.
✦ *Keith Hirata*

Partner with others to add creativity and interest to the program:

When the women's ministry did their first retreat at the conference center, the men took roses up for every woman at the retreat and personally delivered them at the first session. We did a videotape about how important they were, that we were praying for them, we loved them, and then we handed them a rose. They returned the favor and brought up Krispy Kremes and Starbucks. Last year we gave them a turndown service. Then they came out and gave us cookies. We've been trading back and forth. ✦ Chuck Caswell

The element of surprise also contributes greatly to an effective program. Do something unexpected to delight and surprise people:

Get away from the predictable so there is something to look forward to. When I go to one of our events, I know there is something that will amaze me. Last weekend we had a Friday night opener with an African-American choir from Boston. It wasn't listed in the program, but added as a surprise. On Saturday morning in the middle of the worship time there was a signing to a song. Use variety and diversity. Make sure that your teaching styles are diverse—use panels, discussions, roundtables, sitting in circles or at long tables. Salt and pepper the whole programming with creativity. ✦ *Stephen Macchia*

FINALIZING ARRANGEMENTS

The few weeks before the conference, your primary task will be confirming information with your team members to make sure everything is in place. Check that all details are ready and bring all your information to the site in case you need to refer to it.

CHAPTER

9 | SPEAKERS

A team from our church attended a conference where a musical artist was the speaker. I'm sure he was a wonderful musician, but his speaking skills needed significant improvement. A friend behind me squirmed in his seat, and after the speaker had droned on for almost an hour, my friend groaned and put his head in his hands. My husband was more proactive: he just got up and went home, right in the middle of the talk. I think he was the happiest one in our group that night.

Speakers are a central part of most conferences. Sitting through a conference with a poor speaker provokes in the listener an intense urge to bolt towards freedom. People perceive the quality of the conference to be a direct result of how good the speaker was. Therefore, the Speaker Coordinator's job is crucial to the success of a conference.

OVERVIEW

If you have a complex conference with multiple speakers (either main session or workshop), you may want to have one person whose sole purpose is to handle speaker arrangements. If you have a small event with only one speaker, then the Program Coordinator's responsibilities can be included.

TIPS FOR SUCCESS

Start finding speakers as early as possible. Well-known speakers are booked years in advance. Unless you are using someone who is not a frequent speaker (such as someone in your organization or a friend who does speaking), plan as early as possible for your speaker needs.

As with all areas of conference planning, you'll need to know the purpose and goals of the conference as you plan speakers. Who is your audience? Why are you holding the conference? What do you hope to accomplish with this conference? Knowing the answers to these questions will help you narrow down the speakers that are best for your event.

The Speaker Coordinator's main tasks are:

STEP-BY-STEP

1. Determining speaker requirements
2. Finding speakers
3. Contacting speakers
4. Evaluating speakers
5. Paying speakers
6. Confirming speakers
7. Making arrangements

At the conference, you, the Speaker Coordinator, handle the responsibilities related to the speakers, including communicating with them and directing the volunteers caring for them (see *Chapter 18: The Conference*).

The Speaker Coordinator handles arrangements for the speakers and entertainment.

Recommended skills/qualities

- Administrative/organizational skills
- Good communication skills
- Enjoys working with people
- Administrative ability to arrange for speakers' needs

Job Description

Before the conference

- Attend planning meetings
- Find speakers and entertainment
- Coordinate travel and accommodation arrangements for speakers
- Coordinate receiving speakers' information for the conference program booklet

Night before conference

- Oversee dinner with speakers

During the conference

- Handle arrangements for speakers and teachers
- Make sure speakers are comfortable (water, other needs)
- Make final payments

After the conference

- Send thank you notes to all speakers and speaker hosts
- Compile summary report
- Send notes of appreciation to speakers and speaker hosts
- Evaluate conference and suggest improvements for next time

Time Commitment

This position's time commitment is:

After the conference, your main tasks are evaluation, summarization of the event, and appreciation of speakers and volunteers who helped (see *Chapter 19: Wrapping Up*).

Because in some cases speakers, musicians and entertainers might overlap in their functions, all the information in this chapter pertaining to speakers can also apply to musicians and entertainers.

DETERMINING SPEAKER REQUIREMENTS

What kind of speaker would fit the purpose of the conference?

> Are you looking for someone to draw people to the event, or are you looking for someone to address a topic? Do you need someone with a certain experience? It's important to know what kind of speaker you want. ✦ *Brian Lord*

Discuss the budget with the Finance Coordinator to figure out what you can afford. Be prepared to compensate your speaker at a reasonable rate. Speaker rates vary from speakers who don't ask for anything (a love offering is taken or you can give them an honorarium) to ones who charge tens of thousands of dollars. Some travel alone; others bring a companion. Some are local; others will need airplane fare paid.

> Many well-known speakers like to travel with a second person. It's an accountability measure with speakers to uphold their integrity. A lot of speakers who are well-known won't travel by themselves, so you need to anticipate that. Sometimes speakers request using first class, which increases cost. If you are able, buy a full fare rate and then try to get miles from someone in your church to upgrade instead of buying first class fare.
> ✦ *Andrew Accardy*

Before you make a call, put together information for speakers in a summary fact sheet that can be e-mailed, mailed, or faxed, so that speakers can have everything in writing. It also allows you to give every speaker the same information.
- What is the sponsoring organization?
- What is the theme of the conference?
- What is the expected attendance and the demographics of the audience?
- How often will they be teaching?
- Will they be main session speakers or workshop speakers?
- If you are looking for workshop teachers, what kinds of topics are you looking for?

FINDING SPEAKERS

Now it's time to draw up a list of potential speakers.

The best way to find speakers is by personal referral from the staff, or people you know who have attended any churches or conferences where they've heard a noteworthy speaker. Here are some other sources where you can find referrals for speakers:
- **Church denomination.** Some denominations maintain lists of speakers. If your church is part of a denomination, check if there is such a list available for your use.
- **Church or organization.** Ask around your church network if anyone knows good speakers. Church leaders or teachers are also potential speakers you can contact.
- **Other local churches or groups.** Ask organizations in your area for referrals. If a nearby church has had a retreat or conference lately, find out who their speaker was.

- **Speakers bureaus/talent agencies.** Speaker bureaus maintain databases of speakers. Talent or booking agencies are sources for musicians and other performers. Many speaker bureaus tend to be more expensive (usually $5,000 +) and are more suited for larger events. Some agencies provide a variety of speakers as well as artists.

Speaker bureaus:
- Ambassador Agency, www.ambassadoragency.com, 877-425-4700. Provider of exclusive Christian speakers and other high-profile speakers through other agencies.
- America's Speaker Bureau, www.americasbestspeakers.com, 800-547-9263. Motivational speakers, paid public speakers, and keynote speakers.
- Christian Speakers and Artists Agency, www.christianspeakers.com, 800-220-8125. Source for both speakers and artists.
- CLASS Services Inc, www.classservices.com, 800-433-6633. Source for speakers and training for speakers.
- The Mitchell Group, www.mitchellgroup.org, 615-771-6644. Provides artists and speakers for many events.
- Nashville Speakers Bureau, www.nashspeakers.com, 866-333-8663. Source of secular and religious speakers.
- National Speakers Bureau, www.nationalspeakers.com, 800-323-9442. Source of secular and religious speakers.
- Premiere Speakers Bureau, www.premierespeakers.com, 615-261-4000. Source of secular and religious speakers.
- World Wide Talent, www.world-widetalent.com, 615-285-0729. Talent agency for musicians, dramatic and visual artists, and speakers.

Entertainers:
- Christian Comedian Index, http://christiancomedy.tripod.com. Contains links to many Christian comedian Web sites.
- Clean Comedians, www.cleancomedians.com, 800-354-GLAD. Wide variety of performers.
- Comedy Crusade, www.comedycrusade.com, 877-COMEDY-2. Resource for Christian Comedians and Entertainers.

Musical artist and talent agencies:
- Alabaster Arts, www.alabaster.com, 615-662-7400. Management and booking company for artists.
- Beckie Simmons Agency, www.bsaworld.com, 615-595-7500. Booking agent for Southern Gospel musicians.
- The Breen Agency, www.thebreenagency.com, 615-777-2227. Source for musicians, speakers, worship leaders, and comedians.
- Creative Artists, http://ccm.caa.com, 615-383-8787. Booking agency for music artists.
- Fishers Artists Agency, www.fishers.com, 909-684-FISH. Christian artist management/booking agency.
- GOA (Greg Oliver Agency), www.goa-inc.com, 615-790-5540. Promoter/booking agency.
- H20 Artist Agency, www.h20artistagency.com, 770-736-5363. Booking agency for contemporary Christian artists.
- Halo Productions, www.haloproductions.net, 800-225-9087. Booking agency for Christian recording artists and bands.
- The Harper Agency, www.harperagency.com, 615-851-4500. Booking agency for gospel music artists.
- Jeff Roberts & Associates, www.jeffroberts.com, 615-859-7040. Booking agency for Christian artists.

RESOURCE TOOLS

- Premier Productions, www.premiereproductions.com, 864-801-9266. Booking agent for Christian artists.
- Street Level Artists Agency, www.streetlevelagency.com, 574-269-3413. Booking agency.
- Third Coast Artists Agency, www.thirdcoastartists.com, 615-297-2021. Musical artists' booking agent.
- **Mailing lists.** Ask to be added to mailing lists for Christian organizations. Note the prominent people in the organization who may be potential speakers.
- **Magazines.** Read Christian magazines and look at flyers or advertisements to see who is speaking at conferences. If you see a new name, then it may be someone who is on his way up and it is good to catch him early before he is well-known.
- **Publishers.** Check out publishers and authors of books about the topic of your conference.

EXAMPLES

As you ask around, list the speakers and the person who recommended them. Update this list frequently. Use the *Speaker Referral* form on page 116 to track the potential speakers.

COMPUTER HELPS

Use a spreadsheet or database to track the data. You can easily do a search to find a speaker who you are looking for. Create a spreadsheet with these columns:
- Speaker Name
- Type of speaker (subjects, style)
- Address
- Phone
- E-mail
- Referred by
- Referral contact information
- Date referred
- Speaker references
- Notes

For a quality speaker, look for someone who has done extensive speaking. Sometimes an organization will be willing to try someone who is not as established, but don't open or close your sessions with this kind of speaker. Instead, try out these kind of speakers by putting them in workshop sessions. Use a well-established, proven speaker in your main sessions in order to have the most effective program.

> Don't just go after popular personalities because they tend to dominate your program with their own pet message. It's ok if they come in and do their thing if it matches your objectives. ◆ *Andrew Accardy*

CONTACTING SPEAKERS

EXAMPLES

After you have your list of potential speakers, begin contacting them to ask their availability. Use the *Speaker Status Information* form on page 117 to keep track of your contacts with speakers. Use one form for each speaker and keep all the pages together in a file or binder for easy access.

Initial phone call

Make an initial phone call and ask the speakers (or their agents/speaker bureaus):
- When are they available? If they aren't available on the dates you prefer, you can save yourself some time by automatically eliminating them from your list.

SPEAKER REFERRAL | Form

Speaker name	Address	Telephone	E-mail	Referred by	Date

S P E A K E R   S T A T U S   I N F O R M A T I O N | Form

Speaker name _____

Address _____

Telephone: (H) _____ (W) _____

Fax _____ E-mail _____

Referred by _____ Phone _____

Date referred _____

Date contacted _____

Type of speaker (subjects, style) _____

_____

Fees/honorariums _____

_____

Other information _____

_____

Date extended invitation _____ Date invitation accepted _____

Expenditures

Fee/honorarium	$ _____	❏ Honorarium check sent
Travel	$ _____	❏ Reimbursement form received
Housing	$ _____	❏ Reimbursement check sent
Other	$ _____	
Total	$ _____	

Forms

	Date sent	Date received	Notes
Session description	_____	_____	_____
Biography	_____	_____	_____
Travel information	_____	_____	_____
Housing information	_____	_____	_____
AV equipment	_____	_____	_____
Policy information	_____	_____	_____

Conference Information

Program speaking date _____ Start and end time _____

Host/hostess _____ Introducer _____

- What experience do they have? How long have they had speaking experience? What is their background? What qualifications do they have?
- What kind of speaking interests do they have? What is their passion?

Don't expect too many speakers out there to speak on things other than what they are passionate about. You can't ask someone big on prayer to talk about marketing even though that's what you may be interested in. Try to learn as much about a speaker as you can and try to fit them into a program in a way that gets it close to their passion. I speak with them to help them understand my objectives. We talk about what they are going to speak on: I say, "These are my objectives—how are we going to do it?" A lot of people are intimidated by speakers and most of the time I find that they are willing to talk with you and meet your goals. Be specific in your invitation about what you want them to do and what you want them to speak on. ◆ *Andrew Accardy*

- What kind of audiences have they spoken to? Have they spoken to audiences similar to yours?
- Can they interact with the audience before or after the program?
- How much are they capable of doing in one day while maintaining a good energy level? Some speakers may tire more easily and you would not want to schedule too much for them.
- What is the fee? Any additional expenses?
- What are their references?

Informational letter

After the phone call, if the speaker is interesting in continuing with the process, send them a letter with the main information about the conference:
- Your contact information
- Information about your organization
- Type of event you are holding
- Dates, times, and location of the event
- Purpose of the event
- Theme
- What the speaker would present (general or breakout session, what topic they would speak on)
- A follow-up date for a return phone call
- Reference request (if you haven't already requested them)

TIPS FOR SUCCESS

Never book a speaker unless you have heard them personally, listened to their tape, or really trust the person who recommended them. Even if you do trust your friend, it's still a good idea to check out the speaker because different people define a good speaker in different ways. Request the speakers' promotional materials and read them thoroughly. Sometimes a person may be a great speaker but just not a good fit for the type of event you are holding.

Ask the speakers for a copy of an audio or video tape to listen to or to watch. Better yet, if they are speaking locally anywhere, go hear them.

Check three to five of their references. Be sure they are recent references, as speakers change over time (hopefully for the better!).

Ask for their statement of belief. Different churches have different theology that is important to them. The speaker's theology might not fit with the church's. Ask about their statement of belief, and if they don't have a typed one, ask them what they believe.
◆ *Debbie Dittrich*

EVALUATING SPEAKERS

Selecting speakers should be based on more than how good their talks are or how much they charge.

- How reliable and timely are they in returning your phone calls or e-mails?
- How flexible are they in adjusting to your needs? Are they willing to customize their talk to fit your group?
- What kind of quality is their presentation?
- Will they appeal to your audience?
- Are their basic theological beliefs in line with with your organization's?

Look at the speaker's heart. When I'm talking to her, I would ask her, "What messages or message has God laid on your heart? What message are you doing right now?" There's a difference between a speaker who markets her material based on what she thinks the audience wants to hear, and a speaker who shares what God has laid on her heart. I would also want to hear what others who have heard her think about her. Call the last retreat committee person that she did a retreat for. Ask, "Was she easy to work with? Anything I need to know about?" ◆ *Debbie Dietrich*

PAYING SPEAKERS

There are three types of speakers:

1. Speakers who speak professionally or who do extensive speaking. They have a set fee.
2. Speakers who speak extensively and who don't have a set fee.
3. Speakers who do not speak professionally.

Paying a speaker ranges from speakers who don't ask for anything, to those who charge upwards of $10,000 per event. Every speaker is different, so clarify what their fees are. Be as generous with your honorarium as you can. Always try to honor your speakers in every way, including financially.

Speakers spend hours working on their talks. I spend forty hours for every hour I speak. It may be more than that if I'm doing a talk for the first time. It's a big time commitment. The Bible says the workman is worthy of his wages, so pay your speaker. ◆ *Vicki Hitzges*

We have a set fee schedule. If they are speaking in a plenary (general) session, we pay them "x" amount. Seminar (workshop) speakers are paid a lower amount. Some speakers make their living speaking. Sometimes they need to ask a little more. We try to negotiate with them. What we can't give in money we make up in amenities; most speakers love coming back. ◆ *Pam Chun*

You may not have the advantage of holding your event with Pam Chun in Hawaii, but ask your speakers if they would be willing to work with you to come up to a mutually satisfying agreement. If you can't afford their fees, be creative with your arrangements to see if you can work out something.

MONEY SAVERS

Ask the speaker if they will give discounts to non-profit groups, during certain times of the year, or to certain audiences. Or consider trying to book a speaker (or entertainment) that another local group may be using. Ask other groups what speakers they have and share the cost.

Some speakers are willing to negotiate. Consider exchanging something that's important to them:

- A mailing list of the registered attendees
- Publicity for the speaker at the conference
- Free spouse arrangements
- A contract for a future event

The most important thing is to talk with them frankly in advance, confirm in writing, and then look at ways to bless them. If you can do it, bring their spouses, and have the spouse as a guest in the same hotel room. Some of the places they go will let them sell their books and CDs but take 10%. We'll provide tables and volunteers and let them keep the entire amount. We tell them, "We'll put your books in the newsletter next week; we'll sell them after the conference." See what is important to them beyond the weekend. If there is some program your organization does, invite their kids to the camp; it doesn't cost you that much. Offer to cover their airfare or parking. ◆ *John Pearson*

Be up-front with speakers and let them know precisely what you will cover. This will avoid any future misunderstanding.

When you have selected your speakers, contact them immediately. Don't wait too long to book your speakers. Book them as early as possible because the longer you wait, the fewer speakers will be available. Some speakers raise their rates every year too, so book them early!

CONFIRMING SPEAKERS

As soon as the speakers confirm their availability, immediately send a confirmation packet with the following information:
- Thank them for accepting and confirm the topic information.
- Give the background of your organization.
- Tell them when they are scheduled to speak and how much time they have to speak.
- Ask for biographical information, photographs, exact title of presentation, and outline. Make sure that the topic of their presentation matches what the advertised title is. Give a deadline for when you need their information.
- Request information on room setup, equipment needs, and other facility-related issues.
- Give requirements for any submissions, handouts, or audiovisuals. If your speakers are producing their own audiovisuals, provide tips on how to make their visuals more effective—using text that is large enough, with only a few colors, and a few typefaces.
- Begin making travel arrangements. If they are making their own travel arrangements, give the information they will need. If they are flying in and you are meeting them at the airport, let them know what the arrangements for meeting them are.
- It's also helpful to let the speakers know why they were chosen. If they were chosen because of a particular style, communicate that to them so that they don't try a totally different style for your event.

The information can be combined into a single form (see *Speaker Needs Information* form, page 121), or, for complex events, create a packet including a form for each area.

EXAMPLES

Sometimes speakers will sign a contract, but smaller events usually do not use a contract. In these cases, it's still good to spell details out in a letter so there's no miscommunication. Just make sure that in all your interactions with the speakers you convey an attitude of professionalism. Cultivate a positive relationship with the speaker.

John Pearson found that he frequently communicated with the speakers' secretaries. Six months before the event, the secretary would send the speaker's photo. John would send a thank you note along with ten dollars to cover the cost of the picture. Sometimes he would send a Starbucks coupon to the secretary after the event. The secretaries were very grateful.

SPEAKER NEEDS INFORMATION | Form

Speaker name _____

Address _____

Telephone: (H) _____ (W) _____

Fax _____ E-mail _____

Session title _____

Session time _____

Room setup desired: ❑ Classroom ❑ Theater ❑ Round tables ❑ Other

Equipment Needed

❑ Lectern

❑ Microphone: ❑ Floor mike with stand ❑ Handheld mike ❑ Lavaliere mike (clip-on)

❑ Overhead projector

❑ Video projector

❑ Slide projector ❑ Carousel for projector

❑ TV monitor

❑ VHS Video player

❑ DVD player

❑ Computer

❑ Laser pointer

❑ Flip chart

If computer needed: What platform? ❑ PC ❑ Mac ❑ Other

What programs? _____ Version? _____

Transportation Information

How many people in your party? _____ Arriving via: ❑ Air ❑ Car ❑ Other: _____

If traveling by air:

Arrival date _____ Airline _____ Flight No. _____

Arrival time _____ Arrive from (city) _____

Departure date _____ Airline _____ Flight No. _____

Departure time _____ Depart to (city) _____

Reservations will be made for you at : (Hotel) _____ Address: _____ Phone: _____

Hotel check-in date _____ Check-out date _____

Comments/Needs: _____

_____

_____

Be in frequent contact with your speakers so they know what is happening. Ask their opinions for the parts of the program that they will be involved in. Asking your speaker if she has energy to do a question and answer time after her session shows her that you value her input.

> One church has done an incredible job keeping me in the loop. After they called back to confirm, I heard back via e-mail every few months. I wasn't too heavily involved, but they told me their ideas and asked me how it worked for me. About eight to twelve weeks before the retreat, the committee started sending me handwritten notes or e-mail every week. They said, "My name is… and I'm doing the social events. I just wanted you to know I'm praying for you. Just a little tip—the weather in Michigan might be cool so bring a jacket, but bring comfortable clothes because we're going to have fun. If you have any needs, here's my phone number." They've been very considerate. ✦ *Debbie Dittrich*

MAKING ARRANGEMENTS

EXAMPLES

When your speakers are confirmed, start making arrangements for when they arrive at the event. Use the *Speaker Status Information* form (page 117) to track the status of what has been completed and what is pending.

Contact information

TIPS FOR SUCCESS

One person should be responsible for being the final contact person once the speakers are confirmed (usually the Speaker Coordinator). This will avoid the confusion of speakers hearing conflicting information from multiple people. Ask your team to communicate everything to the speaker through you first.

Scheduling

SCHEDULING

Maximize your investment in your speaker. Are there ways you can include the speaker in other parts of the program? You're already spending a lot of time and effort to bring him in—why not ask him to help out in other areas?

Ask your speaker if he might be available to give a workshop after the general session. If he can, it's a win-win situation for both parties: you get another speaker without having to pay for additional transportation fees, and the speaker will have a workshop that is usually well-attended.

If your speaker is presenting both a general session and a workshop, schedule the general session first. This gives the audience an opportunity to hear the speaker and for the speaker to establish himself. Then when he teaches a workshop later, the audience will feel comfortable and connected with him.

When you contact your speaker to tell him about the schedule, give the start time two hours before it actually does. One reason is that if he is late, he will still be in time for the program. The other reason is that if the speaker does arrive two hours ahead of time, you can take him out to dinner and prepare him for the conference.

> Before our Saturday conferences, we ask the speakers to arrive the night before. The Director takes them out to dinner and they have an opportunity to eat together, meet each other, and discuss what they will be talking about. After the dinner, they are driven to the facility where they meet with the prayer team and pray over the event.

Presentation needs

Prepare for the time when the speaker will be presenting. Where will the speaker be before the presentation? Sitting in the front with the audience? Or backstage? Will there be a time of prayer beforehand and if so, where will that be?

What needs does she have? Will she need a clock? Water? A lectern? Any other special needs?

One of our speakers was a very small lady. When she went to the lectern, she seemed dwarfed by it. Plus the fact that she was on a five-foot stage contributed to the appearance that she could barely see over the top. One of our quick-thinking volunteers brought her a small step-stool and finally we could all see her better.

Housing

As you make housing arrangements, give the speaker the best room or cabin available. If you're using a hotel, always give a single room that is quiet and away from the busy crowds so he can get adequate rest. Pay for his housing in advance so that everything is taken care of and he has one less worry upon arrival. If you're using people's homes as accommodations for your attendees, avoid putting him in someone's home so that he can get rest and have time to prepare without distractions; if possible, pay for a nearby hotel room.

> Most speakers I talk to find it really hard to sleep, even though they are pouring so much energy into their speeches. Make sure you have a coffee pot or something else for the speakers so they can wake up and have coffee or bottled water. Some hotels provide it, but if you are in an area such as a cabin, be sure to provide something. ◆ *Debbie Dittrich*

> Have a little welcome gift in their room upon arrival. Write a little handwritten note following their event sessions. ◆ *John Pearson*

Meals

Arrange meals for the speakers if necessary. Find out if they have any special dietary requirements and discuss meal seating arrangements.

Transportation

If your speaker is local, you don't have to worry much about their transportation, other than making sure that they have a place to park. For those who are flying in, arrange for air and ground transportation if necessary. If speakers will be picked up at the airport, assign a responsible person to pick them up. If the speaker is making her own travel arrangements, leave a note at the front desk and let her know when you plan to contact him. Or, have a host at the hotel lobby waiting for her to arrive. Whether the greeters are at the airport or at the hotel, have all of them wear the same clothing so that they will be easily recognized.

Plan for after the conference too. Arrange for departure travel, checkout procedures, and other logistics to make the speaker's departure quick and and as painless as possible.

Break room

Ask the Site Coordinator to arrange for a speaker room or a quiet place where the speaker can prepare and rest before her presentation. Stock the room with water, drinks, and snacks. Speakers will appreciate having a quiet place where they can hide out and take a short break.

People

A host or hostess can make a big difference in adding to a positive experience for the speaker. He prepares water to be available during the presentation and oversees other small details that will help the speaker be comfortable. His responsibility is to take care of the speaker in every possible way.

> Provide VIP hosts/hostesses—people who like to hang out with the speakers. They have hospitality gifts and will meet the speakers at the airport, have conference materials and clue them in to what's happening. They can ask speakers in advance if they want to be rescued if the line is too long. They bring coffee or Coke to them during the break and say, "If there is anything day or night, here's my room number—call me." The hosts/hostesses go to the speakers' rooms, knock on the door, escort them, and protect them from

everybody. We provide someone who has lots of time for them and helps them get the book table set up. The speakers are so appreciative for these hosts. ◆ *John Pearson*

For the sessions, someone introduces the speaker. Who will she be? What will she say? Will the speaker provide the text for the introduction?

If your speaker is a workshop teacher, a workshop monitor is another invaluable helper. Monitors keep track of time, adjust temperature controls, and make sure water is available for the speaker.

Backup plans

Occasionally you may find that something unexpected comes up and the speaker is unavailable! Whether he's late, he must suddenly cancel, or his materials get lost, it's best to have a contingency plan. To avoid loss of materials, suggest to the speaker that they carry their materials as carry-on baggage. Be prepared for the unexpected to happen and have a plan if the speaker doesn't show up or is missing items.

One of our speakers came in from Singapore and wasn't feeling well. It turned out he had chicken pox. We had to quarantine him and an infectious disease physician visited him. He never got down to speak. ◆ *Pam Chun*

Follow-up

Make a decision whether or not the feedback results will be shared with the speakers, and ask the speakers if they're interested in hearing feedback results after the conference.

Appreciation is another important aspect of following up. Make plans to send a thank you note or a thank you gift to the speaker, an evaluation form for their conference experience (see *Chapter 17: Administration* for more information about evaluations), as well as any publicity or facts about the conference, such as an article that was written after the conference.

MAKING FINAL PREPARATIONS

Final confirmation

As the event draws nearer, send the speakers more detailed information to finalize the arrangements:

SCHEDULING

- **Purpose and theme:** objectives of the conference, theme, and a reminder to follow it.
- **Audience:** size, type, ages, gender, demographics, and any special needs they have.
- **Schedule:** confirm weekend schedule as well as the cue sheet (or give them the cue sheet when they arrive). Reiterate that they should arrive two hours before the program start time. Give the time to arrive and duration they should stay at the conference, and whether they have the option to attend the rest of the conference.
- **Rehearsals:** rehearsal times and location of rehearsal. Include sound check or audio-visual check times.
- **Presentation time:** remind speakers how long their presentation should be; whether they will have a timekeeper, or if there is a clock available in the room.
- **Program:** any elements of the program that will precede or follow them, particularly those items that are immediately before or after; format of their presentation (lecture, discussion, Q&A).
- **Travel:** what the arrangements are, driving directions if they are driving.
- **Location:** map to site and length of time it will take them to get there. Enclose a detailed site map and the location of the meeting room where

they are speaking and when it will be available, rehearsal room, and what other speakers will be talking about so they can see where they fit in. Other speakers that have spoken at your previous conferences might be helpful information also.
- **Map:** map of the facility. Location of meeting room, rehearsal room, as well as the staff break room.
- **Dress code:** any special requirements

Let your speaker know what kind of clothes you're going to wear. If you have a casual retreat in Dallas, it's very different than if you go to the hills of Kentucky. Casual in Dallas means you will be wearing earrings, and hair and makeup will be done. Most other places really mean casual. Tell the speakers how your people will be dressed. ◆ *Vicki Hitzges*

EXAMPLES

- **Finances:** what the expense policies are, what will be paid, travel, mileage, accommodations, meals, expense reimbursement procedure. (see *Expense Reimbursement* form on page 42)
- **Honorarium:** confirm what the honorarium will be and when they will receive it.
- **Audiovisual:** confirm what their needs are with the Technical Coordinator (page 130).
- **Spouse arrangements:** remind speakers what the arrangements are and what will be paid.
- **Feedback results:** tell speakers they can expect to hear feedback.
- **Accommodations:** where speakers will be housed and give information about their accommodations.
- **Permission form:** ask speakers to sign permission form allowing you to audio or video tape their presentation.
- **Registration form:** have speakers complete forms if they have not already done so.
- **Contact information:** provide your contact information, the site's information, and anyone else who will be helping them (such as their host, technical help, or workshop monitor). Also, give them contact information that they can leave with their spouse or family member.

If any information changes, let the speaker know as soon as possible. Keep them in the loop.

At this point it's also a good idea to discuss expectations with the speaker so that he knows what is expected.

We had a speaker who had forty minutes but took about fifty-five to sixty minutes. The last twenty minutes she added her own personal agenda. She was never asked to speak again, and it got us in trouble with the facility since she was the last speaker of the day. We were supposed to be out of there and it messed up our contract. Make sure that you have contracts on the front end. If your event isn't that formal, at least make sure that expectations are outlined completely. ◆ *Yvette Maher*

Prepare speaker packets

Prepare a packet to give to speakers when they arrive. Include the following information:

- Program handbook
- Reimbursement form
- Meal tickets (if applicable)
- Speaker evaluation form
- Name badge

Make sure their room is prepared, everything is in working order, and that they are given a quiet location so they can get enough rest. Then be ready to meet them at the conference.

10 | TECHNICAL

I have a friend who loves computers. He works for a computer company and eats, breathes, and lives computers. He has even come to our house after midnight to help a project full of technical difficulties. My friend has a special touch with computers—in fact the other day when I had a problem, as soon as I called him the computer started working even though he hadn't given me the solution yet! His presence strikes fear into the heart of computers because they know if they don't start behaving . . . they get upgraded!

My friend thinks it's fun to operate video and sound equipment too. People like him are perfect candidates for Technical Coordinators. Technical Coordinators oversee all the technological equipment involved in a conference. Most of this equipment is used for the main sessions and workshops. Having one person who is knowledgeable about technology is very useful because all too often, some kind of technology will go wrong!

OVERVIEW

Once the facility and the program has been set, the Technical Coordinator can begin determining what kind of equipment might be needed, drawing up a budget, and researching equipment sources. You'll be working closely with other team members to arrange for the equipment needs:

- Program Coordinator: finding out what kind of equipment will be needed in the meeting and workshop rooms.
- Speaker Coordinator: arranging for specific equipment and technicians that each speaker requires.
- Finance Coordinator: securing the finances needed to pay for the equipment and audiovisual technicians.
- Volunteer Coordinator: getting a list of names of volunteers who can assist you.
- Site Coordinator: arranging the site's equipment.

At the beginning, one of your first tasks is to provide the budget for the Finance Coordinator. Remember to add ten percent to the total for unexpected expenses, or have the Finance Coordinator add ten percent to the total budget.

The Technical Coordinator's tasks include:

STEP-BY-STEP

1. Determining equipment needs
2. Inspecting the site
3. Finding equipment sources
4. Making arrangements

At the conference, you oversee the setup, operation, and dismantling of the equipment (see *Chapter 18: The Conference*).

The Technical Coordinator oversees all technical and equipment arrangements for speakers and program events.

Recommended Skills/Qualities

- Technical knowledge and ability to operate equipment
- Able to coordinate speaker and planning team requests
- Servant heart to help others
- Attention to detail

Job Description

Before the conference

- Attend planning meetings
- Oversee selection and setup of equipment

Night before conference

- Coordinate volunteers to set up equipment
- Run through rehearsals and sound checks with speakers, worship team, and entertainers

During the conference

- Operate technical equipment, or oversee technical team

After the conference

- Return rented equipment
- Compile summary report
- Send notes of appreciation to technical operators and helpers
- Evaluate conference and suggest improvements for next time

Time Commitment

This position's time commitment is:

After the conference, you return equipment, summarize the event, evaluate, and express appreciation to everyone who helped (see *Chapter 19: Wrapping Up.*)

DETERMINING EQUIPMENT NEEDS

To figure out what equipment is needed for each session, go through each program event with the Program Coordinator. Communicate with the other conference staff so that they can tell you their equipment needs. Consider also the size of the room and how many people will be in the audience.

Send a form to each speaker (through either the Program or Speaker Coordinator, whoever is handling the speaker arrangements) asking what their equipment needs will be. This form may be included in the speaker confirmation packet (page 120).

- Podium
- Microphone (be sure to get the correct type)
- Overhead projector
- Video projector
- Slide projector
- TV Monitor
- Video player (VHS or other format)/DVD player
- Computer
- Laser pointer

Limit your choices. If you know that you can rent two different types of video projectors, don't put them both on the list. Make the decision as to which one to use and just offer one. And even though it might be impressive to list the brand, product number, or even the equipment specifications, avoid the temptation. Simple is better, especially if you have a speaker who is non-technically inclined.

MONEY SAVERS

To reduce expenses, consider whether the equipment is really necessary. A session with a small audience (such as less than fifty people) probably does not need a microphone.

Since many people are procrastinators by nature, set an early deadline that will give you plenty of time to make arrangements for the equipment. Then follow up with the speakers until you receive all the information that you need.

RESOURCE TOOLS

Another area to discuss is whether sessions will be recorded for distribution or sales. If there is a need for audio/video recording, it can be handled either by your team of volunteers or a professional recording studio. Check out the Web site of OT Studios (www.otstudios.com) for an example of a company that provides such services at conferences.

Communicate clearly to the site what equipment you need. It's good to let team members know that all equipment requests should be cleared with you and that they not personally request equipment from the site. Sometimes people who are not aware may request a podium not knowing that later a bill will arrive for $250!

INSPECTING THE SITE

Ask the Site Coordinator for a detailed floor plan. The floor plan should include dimensions, furniture, windows, and power sources. If there is no floor plan available (and even if there is), visit the site and draw a plan of the rooms that will need audiovisual equipment.

- **Equipment.** What kind of equipment is needed? Are you required to use the site's equipment or can you bring in your own?

- **Lights.** Where the lights located? Where are their controls? How are the controls operated?
- **Screens.** Where is the screen located? How large is it? Can you bring your own screen? Determine if you want front projection or rear projection screens. Rear projection screens need enough space behind the screen for the projector. Front projection screens need a place to put the projector in front of the screen without any obstructions (pillars, people's heads) getting in the way. What kind of screen is best suited to this room?
- **Windows.** How many windows does the room have? When the window coverings are drawn and the lights are off, how dark is the room? If you will be using video projection, a room with significant light from windows or doorways will need a projector with a bright bulb. If the rooms don't have window coverings, plan how you will cover or dim them.
- **Power.** Where are the power outlets? What is the maximum power capacity? Will power strips or extension cords be needed? Does the site provide them?
- **Cables.** Do you provide cables? Do you have a snake that will run to the back of the room? Is your equipment hard-wired into the wall?
- **Room.** How large is the room? What shape is it? What kind of sound system is needed for this room? What kind of layout will this room have and where can the equipment be set up? Rooms that holder fewer than fifty people may not need a microphone. Rooms that are deep may need larger screens; wide rooms may need multiple screens.
- **Acoustics.** What are the acoustics of the room? Is any dampening needed?
- **Labor.** What kind of labor do you require? Is your staff unionized? What is their fee? Some locations are unionized and require you to use their equipment and their people. Other places will allow you to bring in your equipment but you must use their unionized operator.

FINDING EQUIPMENT SOURCES

MONEY SAVERS

The most cost-effective way to provide equipment is to bring your own if it is adequate for your needs. Asking friends for equipment also works, especially if you have a technologically-oriented friend who may even volunteer to help run the equipment!

Check first with the site to see if they can provide equipment at no additional cost (such as microphones). If they charge fees, compare their prices to an outside AV source. Sometimes hotels will mark up equipment usage significantly and it is more cost-effective to rent from an outside source.

Call vendors nearby the conference site and ask them about:
- **Fees.** What are their rental fees? Do they give discounts for multi-day rentals? How are rates charged—hourly or daily?
- **Redundant systems.** Do they provide redundant systems in case of equipment failure?
- **Policies.** What are the deposit, cancellation, and insurance policies?
- **Times.** When are the pickup and drop-off times?
- **Maintenance problems.** What if there are maintenance problems with the equipment at the event?

- **Technicians.** Do they provide technicians? What is the rate? What kind of experience have the technicians had?
- **References.** Ask for a list of some recent references.

When contacting AV companies, look for companies that are reputable and experienced. If they are providing technicians, ask about their experience and only use qualified technicians. A poorly run sound system with distracting noise, or missed cues with audiovisuals can ruin the message.

Read any fine print carefully when you rent equipment and arrange for backup equipment. Schedule enough time to pick up, deliver, and set up the equipment. Arrange for return of the equipment as well.

One option is to hire an audiovisual company that specializes in handling conferences and meetings. Although it can be an expensive option, you'll know you are getting professional service. It's also worth considering if you prefer not to handle all the areas yourself; for example, if you want someone to handle the video recording only, you can hire the audiovisual company to do just the video.

For a Web site that shows what kind of services an audiovisual company can provide, check out Swank Audio Visuals, www.swankav.com, 800-876-5141. They also have nice examples of lighting and set design.

RESOURCE TOOLS

MAKING ARRANGEMENTS

Equipment

EXAMPLES

Once you have drawn up a list of equipment needs, record them as a chart (page 131). A schedule of what equipment needs to be in each room as well as the operators needed helps you see who you will need to recruit at what time. Include spaces for sessions that do not require technical support in case of last-minute requests.

Communicate clearly with the Program/Speaker Coordinator so that the speakers' needs are taken care of. Some speakers like to bring their own equipment such as laptop computers or projectors. If they plan to do so, check that their equipment is compatible with what will be used.

Get permission from the speakers if you are recording their sessions. A permission form should be included with the confirmation packet that is sent to speakers (page 120).

If the site allows you to bring your own volunteers to operate equipment, ask the Volunteer Coordinator to help you find volunteers. Or, recruit any reliable friends to assist you. Plan how you will orient and train the volunteers, either before the event or on-site.

Rehearsals/Sound Checks

Speak to the Program Coordinator about rehearsals. The speakers or entertainers will ask for rehearsals if they are needed. How will rehearsals be handled? How long will they take and where will they be? Speakers may use a separate room to rehearse, but a worship team or band will need the actual stage. All people involved in the program will need to do sound checks, so work to schedule the sound checks with the Program and Site Coordinator.

Security

Equipment is expensive and security may be an issue at your site. Arrange for equipment security and a storage location with the Site Coordinator:
- How secure is the location?
- Can the equipment be kept overnight in a locked storage area?
- If the equipment cannot be moved, can the meeting room be locked?

EQUIPMENT NEEDS | Example

Date: Monday March 1

Room	Green *General session*	Red *Workshop*	Yellow *Workshop*	Purple *Workshop*	Blue *Workshop*
All day:					
Stage	50'x100'	30'x50'	10'x20'		
Screen	Motorized 100'x75'	Wall 80'x60'	Portable	Portable	Portable
Projector	Built in video	Built in video	Bring video	Overhead	Overhead
Lectern	Requested	Requested	Requested	Requested	Requested
Mikes	1 lav, 4 wireless 2 drums	1 lavaliere	1 lavaliere	1 lavaliere	1 lavaliere
Other	4 DI boxes 3 mike stands 1 boom mike stand 5 music stands 1 remote controller		1 TV Monitor 1 VHS player		
9:00–10:30	GENERAL SESSION 1 lavaliere 4 wireless mikes 3 mike stands 1 boom mike stand 4 DI boxes 2 drum mikes 5 music stands 1 remote controller	no tech	no tech	no tech	no tech
10:30–11:00			BREAK		
11:00–12:30	PANEL 1 wireless 4 tabletop mikes	WORKSHOP 2 1 lavaliere	WORKSHOP 3 1 lavaliere 1 TV monitor 1 VHS player	WORKSHOP 4 1 lavaliere	WORKSHOP 5 1 lavaliere
12:30–1:30			LUNCH SESSION		
1:30–3:00	WORKSHOP 6 1 lavaliere	WORKSHOP 7 1 lavaliere	WORKSHOP 8 1 lavaliere	WORKSHOP 9 1 lavaliere	SMALL GROUP no tech
3:00–3:30			BREAK		
3:30–5:00	WORKSHOP 11 1 lavaliere	WORKSHOP 12 1 lavaliere	WORKSHOP 13 1 lavaliere	WORKSHOP 14 1 lavaliere	SMALL GROUP no tech

- Where can small items be locked up?
- Does your insurance cover the equipment? If not, add a rider to your insurance policy for this event.
- Engrave or label all equipment, cables, extension cords, and power strips.

Supplies

Begin collecting items that need to be brought to the site. Don't forget to bring backup items: extra cables (in case a cable fails), spare bulbs, extension cords, and power strips. Bring tape to tape down the cords. Gaffer's tape works best because it doesn't leave a residue; it is available at audiovisual companies. A well-stocked tool kit is also a must. Sometimes you will wonder if you will really need something. If in doubt, bring it! It's not that extra trouble to pack a few more pieces and it may end up saving the day!

Bring extra cables and power strips. They come in handy and will save you the cost of renting them from the facility if you discover you are short.

FINALIZING ARRANGEMENTS

The week before the conference, confirm with the speakers their equipment needs in case they have changed. Briefly give them guidelines and instructions for the equipment. You may wish send the information in advance or give them a brief orientation when they arrive (or both!).

Pack up all the supplies and equipment needed in preparation for leaving for the site.

Finalize with the equipment rental company what equipment is rented and when it will be delivered or picked up.

Check final details with the audio/video recording company.

Confirm with volunteers arrival time and location.

11 | HOSPITALITY: FOOD AND DECOR

On first attempt at cooking, I poured oil into a pan and turned on the heat. As the stove got hotter, I suddenly noticed some movement at the edge of the pan. A tiny ant was running back and forth frantically, trying to escape the growing heat. It dashed back and forth until finally it toppled over into the oil and started sizzling. I was so traumatized that to this day I can't enjoy cooking. (I told you that bugs and I just don't get along!)

So it is with great admiration that I work with people with hospitality gifts. These people seem to have a special way with food and appearance and know how to add a special touch to every event. They are able to oversee the comfort of guests and have a special gift for knowing how to help people feel welcome. They enjoy serving and feeding people. They actually think that food and cooking are fun! Imagine that!

The Hospitality Coordinator oversees the physical needs and helping attendees feel welcome. She recruits a team to oversee the food, decorations, and overall comfort of the attendees.

OVERVIEW

The hospitality area oversees more than just food. Think about the entire experience for the participants. How can their experience be enhanced?

> At a women's event, I would rather spend money on a little gift at each woman's table place setting every time she comes to the table, rather than have an exquisite catering company do the food. The food will be good, but they won't care much if Aunt Betty donated it or whether it came from the Pampered Chef. So I would rather have a little something, like an ink pen with a bow around it and a note that says to use the pen to journal your prayers this weekend. Little gifts are great for the take-away value. They will remember it. ◆ *Yvette Maher*

Planning all the aspects of hospitality involves:

STEP-BY-STEP

1. Determining food needed
2. Planning the menu
3. Considering food sources
4. Making arrangements
5. Working with the site
6. Setting up logistics plans
7. Planning décor

At the event, the Hospitality Coordinator oversees setup of food areas and decor, and directs volunteers in these areas (see *Chapter 18: The Conference*).

After the conference, you return any borrowed or rented items, summarize the event, evaluate, and express appreciation to those who helped (see *Chapter 19: Wrapping Up*).

The Hospitality Coordinator oversees physical comfort and care of the attendees by taking care of food, decorations, and overall comfort.

Recommended Skills/Qualities

- Administrative skills
- Able to manage volunteers for food logistics
- Good people skills
- Attention to detail
- Creative eye for decorations and food presentation

Job Description

Before the conference

- Attend planning meetings
- Find and make arrangements with caterer or food outlet
- Coordinate details with Site Coordinator
- Find and rent equipment, linens
- Develop logistical plan for serving meals and snacks
- Work with Volunteer Coordinator to recruit helpers needed for preparation, service, and cleanup
- Develop decorating scheme for eating area
- Work with Marketing Coordinator to create signage for food areas

Night before conference

- Set up food tables and kitchen area
- Oversee dinner arrangements for staff and volunteers helping to set up
- Pick up any equipment, linen rentals

During the conference

- Set up meals and snacks
- Prepare food and refreshments for conference staff and volunteers

After the conference

- Compile summary report
- Send notes of appreciation to site staff and volunteers
- Evaluate conference and suggest improvements for next time

Time Commitment

This position's time commitment is:

DETERMINING FOOD NEEDED

Food is one area that attendees remember—they won't recall if the program started late, but they will remember if the food was awful. Take time and care to investigate food options, check the experience and background of those providing the food, and taste samples beforehand.

In order to begin planning, review the information that impacts the Hospitality area.

- Approximate date of the conference
- Purpose, goals, and any themes
- Location, facility where conference will be held
- General program schedule (to know what meals or snacks will be needed)
- Type of audience (and their food preferences).
- Estimated attendance
- Budget allocated for food and decorations

As with the other areas of the conference, keep in mind the purpose and audience. What may be appropriate for one group may be inappropriate for another group. You don't want to serve meat to a group that is primarily vegetarians! The purpose of the program should be considered too; if people are going to be working after lunch, don't feed them a meal heavy in carbohydrates that will put them to sleep.

As you review the conference schedule, list the meals that will be required. Are snacks needed? Will speakers or volunteers need food too? Do you need to plan for food for the staff or volunteers? Will people be eating at once or is eating staggered?

Keep your budget in mind as you plan. You don't want to have a menu that will blow your entire budget in the first meal! What is reasonable given the amount you have to work with?

Breakfast/Brunch

What kind of breakfast is needed? Sit down? Buffet? Continental? Or just a simple coffee service? A typical continental breakfast includes: bagels, pastries, cereal, oatmeal, toast, muffins, fruit, juice and coffee. Sit down meals are more labor-intensive and have warm entrees.

One area you can save money in is the serving size of the items. Many muffins or pastries are large and can be divided too reduce waste. If you can bring in your own food, consider buying in bulk and dividing the muffins. Or serve food with smaller serving portions, such as mini muffins.

Consider your audience when planning. Some groups may not be breakfast eaters, so provide a light continental breakfast.

Refreshments/snacks

Is the break time a coffee break, or are refreshments needed? How many drinks and snacks are required and when will they be served? How many should be provided? Salty and sweet snack options are appreciated. Bottled water, juice, or soda are popular as beverages. Remember to allot transition time for people to get in and out of the meeting room, go to restrooms, get their food, and eat it.

Lunch/dinner

What kind of meals are scheduled? A sit down meal? Buffet? Box lunch? Picnic? Potluck?

One way to save on cost is to schedule an evening for the attendees to go out on their own. You'll save on the cost of a meal and the attendees will have an opportunity to relax, sightsee, and spend time with others.

Receptions

Receptions range from serving hors d'oeuvres to having what amounts to a light dinner. The time of the reception may be in the afternoon or late evening.

PLANNING THE MENU

When selecting the food, choose a menu that offers variety, and is nutritious, balanced, healthy, and visually pleasing.

Is there a theme that your menu could follow? Maybe a regional or thematic menu would add interest to the meal.

> We were doing an Asian-American Men's Conference and one of the leaders said, "I know this great guy who does great Mexican or Italian food." I had to stop and say, "Guys, think about it. It's an Asian-American conference. Tacos are just not going to do it!"
> ✦ *Ron Sugimoto*

Plan for how leftovers will be handled. Rewrap any pastries, cookies, or whole fruit (for example, from breakfast) and reuse it for a break or dessert. Donate leftover food to volunteers, your church, or a nearby shelter.

Special diets

Some delegates will need special meals such as vegetarian, diabetic, or special diets. Ask the Registration Coordinator to provide a line on the registration form so people can inform you of their needs. Discuss with the site or food outlet what to do about special dietary requests. Some food outlets may prepare a certain number of meals in advance without knowing the exact number of meals. Others require you to give the number of special meals to them. Communicate clearly with the food service staff so they can adjust for your needs. If available, the site may also have accommodations with kitchenettes for people with special dietary needs so they can make their own meals.

Beverages

MONEY SAVERS

Offer a variety of drinks—cold drinks, iced tea, hot water, juices, coffee, water, bottled water. To save on cost, ask the site if you can buy your own beverages to serve. Serving drinks mixed from a concentrate or powder is more cost-effective than using soft drinks.

> You can never have too much bottled water. ✦ *Terry Toro*

Food for children

If your conference will have children, plan for food that will be suitable for them too.

> We have a banquet [for the kids]. We have to make it affordable if they are going to buy tickets. Hotdogs and chicken strips are fine; cost is more important to parents than what is served. We use white butcher paper and crayons; it occupies their time while they are waiting for food to show up. We don't preset the dessert and don't serve a buffet. We go with something they prefer—mac and cheese and hamburgers are fine. ✦ *Dean Jones*

CONSIDERING FOOD SOURCES

COMPUTER HELPS

A wide variety of options exist for providing food for your attendees. If you have a small event, you can bring your own food. Large events benefit from using hotel's food outlets (such as a restaurant), or bringing in a caterer.

As you research your options, keep the information on a spreadsheet so you can compare the costs, whether you are ordering a la carte, buying bulk items, or looking at package deals.

Bringing own food

Can attendees bring their own meals? If you're having a one-day retreat or conference, consider asking people to bring their own lunches.

Even if a caterer is providing the meals, you might want to consider bringing your own food for the breaks if cost is a big issue. Sometimes grocery stores or discount warehouses donate food items from their community donation budget; they require the request to be written on your organization's letterhead.

If you are buying snacks, buy individually packaged items so that unopened items may be returned. Drinks such as bottled water or snacks such as individual cookies or cracker packages, are such items. Or plan ahead to donate the additional snacks to another ministry in your church, such as the children's ministry, which is always in need of snacks!

MONEY SAVERS

Making own food

Making your own meals might be a good option if you're having a small retreat in a rented house or in a church with a kitchen. Schedule the shopping, cooking, and cleaning to rotate among the participants. Think of kitchen duty as a bonding time, especially if people are put in teams with the same people for more than one rotation.

If the conference is a one-day event held locally, consider having a potluck for lunch. You'll get a great variety of food!

If your church is holding a conference, maybe there are members of your congregation who would enjoy cooking and serving meals to the attendees.

> Catering is expensive. If you can offset your expenses by having your event at a church, that helps. Having the food prepared by your church or by volunteers in the church is a lot less expensive than catering costs. ◆ *Yvette Maher*

Going to restaurants

Can attendees go to local restaurants instead of eating on site? If your group is small, this option may be less costly than hiring a caterer.

What kind of restaurants are available in the area? What are the price ranges in the area? Are they operating during conference hours? Some restaurants are not open during lunchtime on weekends, so check the restaurants' hours if your conference attendees need to find lunch.

Will you be booking a restaurant for the entire group, or letting the participants choose their own restaurants?

Compare restaurant prices for your group to caterer costs before you make a decision. If you find that using a restaurant is a price-wise option, make a list of restaurants to visit, then visit the restaurant personally to ensure it is up to standards in quality, service, size, and cleanliness. Ask to meet with the manager so you can ask questions and check out the facility.

- **Outside.** Is the area clean? Is the restaurant well-marked and easy to find?
- **Parking.** Is there adequate room for parking? What kind of parking is available?
- **Inside.** Is there enough space for the group? Is there a banquet room that can be used? What is the capacity? How long can the room be rented? Will other groups be using the facility as well?
- **Menu.** What kind of food and beverage items are served? What are the prices? Do they give group rates? Be sure to ask for estimates and get everything in writing.
- **Service.** What is the quality of the service? Watch how the customers are being served. Are their needs being attended? Some restaurants are

also rated online on restaurant feedback sites, such as www.epinion.com. Only use a restaurant with reputable service.

- **Payment.** What is the payment policy? When is payment made? How and to whom is the payment made?

If the food, facility, and service are satisfactory, make advance reservations for your group. Read the contract carefully and sign it, checking all the information carefully to make sure that all agreements are in writing. Then make arrangements for the payment.

If the conference attendees prefer to choose their own restaurants, provide them with a map of local restaurants. Be sure to provide a wide variety in menu selection as well as price ranges.

MONEY SAVERS

If you are looking for a way to cut costs, consider providing delegates with hotel restaurant vouchers for the last meal. Some people will not use the vouchers, saving you money.

Using the site's food outlets

Large hotels have on-site restaurants and food services. Discuss with their food managers what the menu items are and what services they provide. Retreat or conference centers have dining halls that have set menus. Their food prices are included in the package price. Daily participants who attend the program without staying overnight are charged an additional fee for the meals only.

Ask your facility what kind of food outlets are available:
- Are any meals included in the package price to the site?
- Does the site provide meals and snacks?
- What times are the meals served?
- What items are on the menu? Are these choices appropriate for our audience?
- Can you customize menus for our event?

Alternative options

What are other creative ways to provide food? Can you request a lunch wagon to come on site to provide food?

> We had lunch wagons pull up and provide cheap lunches. We just looked in the phone book, called them up and asked, "We are having an event; would you be willing to sell meals here?" ◆ *Pam Chun*

Hiring a caterer

If the site doesn't provide food services, find a reputable caterer. Professional caterers provide a variety of services depending on your need.

MONEY SAVERS

Where do you find a caterer? Delis, sandwich places, or local restaurants that cater are some options. Some restaurants have a Web site where you can check their menus, prices, and services. Sometimes small restaurant businesses will donate to nonprofit organizations in exchange for publicity or acknowledgement. If the restaurants are unable to donate an entire meal, they may be willing to make a small donation or offer a discount.

If your friends can't recommend any caterers, check with other churches or organizations in the area if they can recommend anyone. Or look in the phone book under "Caterers."

MAKING ARRANGEMENTS

STEP-BY-STEP

Here's a general outline of the process of working with a caterer:

1. Call a caterer and give them a summary of your event and food needs. Hotels and other facilities initially just want to know approximately how many people will be eating and what type of food needs that you have, and approximately how much you want to spend on food.

2. The caterer quotes a rate based on the food amount as well as the number of rooms you plan to book.

3. About three months before the event, the caterer will send menus at different price ranges. Select the menu that fits your price range and swap more appealing items from other menus. Ask for recent menus because food prices change, sometimes at a rate of six percent per year.

4. A week before the event, the caterer will request a final number and order the food.

5. Three days before the event, sign off on everything and verify that this is your guaranteed minimum number (see page 141).

6. The caterer arrives early to prepare the food. Sometimes a caterer will request to arrive at the facility the day before in order to drop off any food or equipment

7. At the event or immediately after, pay the remainder of the deposit.

Menu

If you are at a conference center that serves all the people there at once (different groups at the same time), you won't have much of a choice for menu selection. But if you are at a location which provides a variety of menus, or if you are using a caterer, you'll have more freedom with your choices.

TIPS FOR SUCCESS

Allowing caterers to be creative is one way to develop your partnership with them to create a successful event. Caterers are aware of ingredients that are seasonal and available locally, geographic preferences, and can craft a menu appropriate for your audience. They are able to create quality menus to fit your budget.

Questions to ask a caterer, restaurant, or the food outlet you are selecting to provide the food include:

- **Menu.** Does the food outlet have a set menu? Can guests select from different choices of entrees? Can guests order multiple choices? Can the caterer develop a menu to fit the budget? Does the food outlet have any specialties?

- **Food tasting.** Can a food tasting be arranged in advance?

- **Special diets.** Can the food outlet provide for special needs diets? How far in advance do they need to know how many of these meals to prepare? What can they do about last minute requests?

- **Portion size.** How large are the portions? For appetizers, plan eight to twelve items per person. For meals that are finger food/appetizers, plan fifteen to twenty items.

- **Appetizers.** Can appetizers be prepared quickly in case they run out?

- **Beverages.** What size are the servings? Is "one cup" a juice-size cup, coffee-size cup, or a mug? How are the drinks served—by the staff, or left in pitchers on the tables?

- **Deadlines.** What kinds of deadlines does the food outlet have for types of meals and number of meals?

Budget/Finances

When talking to the food service provider, be up-front about what your budget is. This will make their job easier and they will know what they have to work with. Prices may vary in different regional areas and according to season.

MONEY SAVERS

- **Saving money.** What package deals do the food outlet have, or do they provide price breaks? Are there certain foods that are less labor intensive? (Labor-intensive foods will cost more.) Will they provide a discount if there is another group at the site using your services? Can volunteers, crew, and entertainers be served sandwiches to save on cost? Compare a la carte vs. package prices to see what is less.
- **Additional charges.** What is the charge for labor, gratuity, and taxes? Is gratuity taxable?
- **Payment policies.** What is the payment schedule? When do they require deposit? Final payment? What is the policy in case of cancellation?

Service

- **Service time.** How long does it take to serve a meal? To save time, can the salads or the first course be on the tables when people enter? If lunch is being served, can the lunch be put in a box for quicker service?
- **Labor.** Does the food outlet provide their own people? If so, how many do they provide? Are their services included in the cost or are they additional? Is there an hourly charge, overtime charge, or gratuity?
- **Ratio.** What is the ratio of staff to guests? A rule of thumb is one staff for every twenty people. If your event is formal, use a lower ratio for more personalized service.
- **Costumes.** Can the staff wear costumes related to the theme?
- **Additional services.** Can the staff collect tickets, distribute menus, or giveaways?
- **Stand-by staff.** If there are more attendees than expected, will there be additional staff? Is there an hourly charge to have them standing by? If not, what arrangements can be made in case of increased attendance? Can the food outlet provide extra food? Can there be extra "stand-by tables?" Will there be a charge for these tables?

Experience

- **Size.** Has the food outlet handled events similar in size to this event in the past?
- **References.** Ask for a list of references, and check that their references are fairly recent. When you call the references, ask how big the group was and what their experience was working with the caterer.

Contract

Before signing the contract, review it to see that all verbal agreements have been written. Check the menu—is it on budget? The menu should list what food and beverages are provided for each break and meal, minimum number of guests required, services provided, table service items, and extra fees such as gratuities or delivery.

Make sure that you include tax and gratuity on top of the food and beverage. Some non-profits don't have to pay taxes. If you have a tax payer ID, check with the hotel to see if it is covered. Know in advance if you have paid the tax. Gratuity is usually eighteen to twenty percent of the food and beverage bill. Negotiate a food and beverage price in the original contract with the property so there are no questions asked. ◆ *Steve Jacobs*

EXAMPLES

Visiting the site with the caterer will help familiarize you with what kind of food preparation and serving facilities they have. What kinds of equipment, services, and items are available? Use the *Site Equipment* form on page 142 to record what they have. Note what they provide and what costs are additional. Can they also provide complimentary items or services, such as beverages or snacks? See if they are willing to negotiate

Facility

- **Location:** How far is the kitchen from the dining area? Where will the food be served?
- **Breaks:** Where will the breaks be? Is the break area centralized in relation to the meeting rooms? Centralizing the break area may help reduce the cost because it involves less labor serving than break areas distributed throughout the facility.
- **Setup:** What kind of tables are available? How many? Sixty-inch round tables seat eight to ten; seventy-two-inch tables seat up to twelve. Allow two feet for aisle space. Round tables take up more space than rectangular tables, but they allow easier conversation.
- **Permits:** Are permits required? How much do they cost?
- **Insurance:** Is liability insurance or worker's compensation provided?

Equipment

MONEY SAVERS

If the site doesn't have certain items, you may have to rent or bring your own. If you need to rent equipment, ask the rental company if it has special rates for non-profit organizations. Some companies request that you submit the request on your organization's letterhead. Some also require deposits. Find out the policies and make arrangements. Confirm when the pickup and return time is.

Guarantees

Some facilities require guarantees for the number of people to be served. Guarantees are usually required forty-eight to seventy-two hours prior to the event. Find out when the deadline is and if you need to change the guarantee, allow yourself enough time. It's easier to increase the guarantee rather than decrease it, so start with a conservative number. Some facilities have an *overset policy*. This means that they will take your guaranteed number and prepare a number of meals three to five percent over what you tell them, so keep this in mind as you do your calculations.

Check the documents they give you and read the fine print carefully; some sites will also add a minimum service labor charge. Hotels use a *banquet event order* (BEO) which is the document that details the guarantees.

SETTING UP LOGISTICS PLANS

Now it's time to begin figuring out how all the food will be served.

Location

First, the location: where will the food be served? How far is the dining area from the meeting room? Develop the schedule with the Program Coordinator so that there's enough transition time for people to get from the meeting area to the dining area and then to eat their meal.

To save on costs, you may also consider serving the buffet right in the meeting room, if it's appropriate for the event. Some meeting planners prefer

Contact person

Phone number   E-mail

Food preparation
- ❏ Stoves
- ❏ Ovens
    - How are they operated?
    - How much capacity?
    - Are oven trays available?
- ❏ Heating lamps
- ❏ Refrigerator
    - How much space?
    - Does food need to be labeled?
- ❏ Freezer
    - How early can we put food in?
    - Does it lock? Who can unlock it?
- ❏ Cooking utensils
- ❏ Coffee makers
- ❏ Storage area
- ❏ Ice machine

Serving
- ❏ Plating tables
- ❏ Serviceware
- ❏ Serving dishes
- ❏ Dishes, cups
- ❏ Silverware or plasticware
- ❏ Paper cups, plates, napkins
- ❏ Punch bowls
- ❏ Carafes, pitchers, coffee pots, teapots
- ❏ Coffee stirrers

Tables
- ❏ Number of tables:
    - Rectangular:
    - Square:
    - Round:
    - Oval:
- ❏ Number of chairs available
- ❏ How many people can be seated around each table
- ❏ How many tables the facility holds
- ❏ Number of serving tables

Linens
- ❏ Number of tablecloths
- ❏ Shape and size of tablecloths – how far do they hang?
- ❏ Linens color, texture, patterns
- ❏ Additional charge or included?
- ❏ Overlays?
- ❏ Chair covers?
- ❏ Table skirts?

Decor
- ❏ Decorations
- ❏ Candles, candle holders, hurricane lamps
- ❏ Greenery/flowers
- ❏ Centerpieces for serving tables

not to do this, since the smell of food is distracting, but it may save you the cost of reserving an additional room just to serve meals.

For break areas, centralize them in one location for more efficiency and to save financially. If you are using outdoor facilities to serve meals or breaks, be sure to have a backup plan for inclement weather.

Traffic flow

Put yourself in the shoes of an attendee heading off to lunch. As he walks to the eating area, is it obvious where he needs to go? Or is signage needed?

> We didn't expect that people wouldn't check their maps beforehand to find out where to go. People got lost trying to find the dining area. To try to direct the crowd, the conference coordinators stood holding up their arms to direct people toward the hallway where the food was being served.

When they arrive at the dining area, how will they enter? Will you be using a ticket system for meals? The advantage of using tickets is that you will get a more accurate number for the guaranteed minimum. If you're using tickets, station the ticket collectors near the entrance.

Place the buffet serving tables away from the wall so that people can line up on both sides. A rule of thumb is to allow one serving line for every fifty people. One buffet table using both sides will serve 100 people.

Where will people get their drinks? Having a separate beverage table allows people to put down their food first and then get a drink. Or, you can serve bottled drinks at the end of the buffet table so people can just pick up a bottle on their way to their tables.

A separate station for cream, sugar, and other condiments can be available for people who want these items, avoiding long lines.

Having a separate dessert table is also another option. Put coffee here too, for those who want coffee with their dessert.

Floor plan

Draw a floor plan of serving tables, dining tables, and a line to show the traffic path people will take from the moment they enter the room. Try to arrange the traffic flow so that people can be efficient in getting to where they need to go. It's human nature to take the shortest route between two points: the more buffet tables you have, the more opportunity that people will take to fill up, and the farther away you put the buffet table, the less chance they will take to fill up their plates.

> At one of our church events, we had four serving stations set up, one in each corner of the room. But even though announcements were made asking people to go to all the serving stations, the two stations farthest from the door were practically untouched. People just wanted to come in the door and go directly to the first table they saw.

EXAMPLES

If you have complicated decorative or serving items, you can also add these to the diagram so the volunteers will know how to set up everything.

See page 143 for sample traffic flow diagrams.

Scheduling

SCHEDULING

When scheduling the day, include the input of both the caterer and the site, as well as times for when to close an area.

> When we served breakfast at the registration area, the coordinator had to close down the breakfast line ten minutes before the program started so that people could get to the program in time.

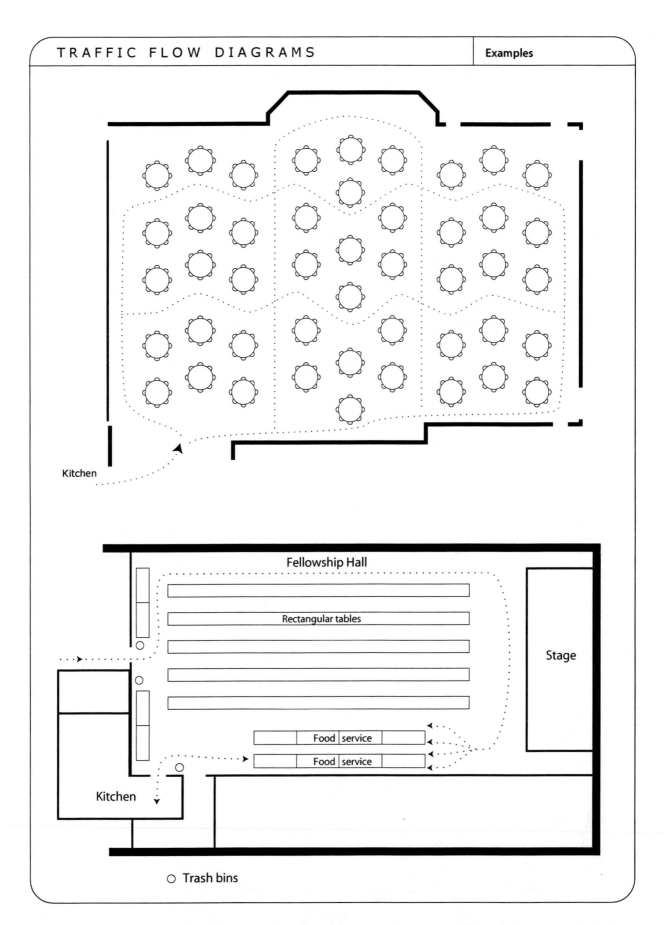

Kitchen

Fellowship Hall

Rectangular tables

Stage

Food | service

Food | service

Kitchen

○ Trash bins

Include in the schedule:
- The time entrances, kitchen, and loading areas are open and available
- The time caterer arrives
- How much time is available to decorate and prepare the eating area, or what time the site begins and ends setup
- The time serving staff arrives
- The time guests begin arriving or enter as a group
- The time to begin serving the food
- How long it takes to serve guests
- Time room must be vacated

EXAMPLES

Here is an actual timetable used at a one-day conference:

FOOD TIMETABLE	Example

5:30 Doors unlocked	9:00 Clear out dining hall and finish cleaning up
6:00 Caterers, Hospitality Coordinator and breakfast setup team arrive	breakfast
Greet and get instructions	Prepare pasta
6:30 Make coffee	Toss salad
Make tea	Prepare lunch boxes
Make juice	Stack serving tables with lunches and drinks in
Fill breakfast baskets with bagels, muffins and	each hall
danishes	Fill water jugs for tables and set out cups
Cut fruit and fill fruit cups	12:00 Continue preparing lunches
Put out coffee/tea urns, cups and plates	Refill supplies as needed
Stock staff break room	Serve requests as needed
7:30 Finishing touches	1:00 Lunch
Start cleaning up kitchen and begin preparing	2:00 Clean up and prepare snacks
for lunch	3:00 Snack time
8:00 Lunch volunteers arrive	3:30 Final clean up
Clean up or refill supplies as needed	

Used by permission of Karen Miya

Serving staff/volunteers

Discuss your needs for help with setup, preparation, and serving food with the Volunteer Coordinator. Here are some ways volunteers can help out:
- Food shopping (if you're buying your own)
- Delivering the food to the facility
- Setup helpers
- Food preparation
- Beverage preparation
- Ticket collectors
- Food servers
- Clean up helpers

Another volunteer you may need is someone to pray before the meal or make announcements during the meal. This may be done by you, the emcee, or another person you designate. This person can also make a reminder at the end of the meal for people to proceed to the next program.

Make plans to have someone direct the volunteers and oversee the food serving. Let the Volunteer Coordinator know:

- Where the volunteers go when they arrive
- Who they report to for orientation or training
- Who oversees them during the event
- What the specific volunteer assignments are

Plan ahead for any appreciation gifts for volunteers as well.

PLANNING DÉCOR

The visual aspect of the conference can make a significant difference in the overall perceived experience. Think of a time you went to a bright restaurant with glaring lights and tacky tablecloths, then compare it to an experience in a restaurant with low lighting, candles, and flowers and fine linens on the table. Which ambience helped contribute to a more positive experience? Even if people aren't aware of it, the décor can make a significant difference in their perception of the event.

Theme

Be creative when considering the theme for the conference. Can decorations be centered around the theme? What decorations can be used?

> The theme of the conference was "Discovering the Anchor for Your Soul." The Hospitality Coordinator found inflatable anchors that were used as swimming toys. She put a pile of sand in the center of each table, scattered seashells, and propped up the anchor in the middle of the sand. It was a great visual reminder of the theme.

RESOURCE TOOLS

Other decorative elements:
- **Balloons.** Companies that specialize in balloon design can come up with decorations that fit your event. For an example, see Balloonatics' Web site: www.balloonatics.com.
- **Ribbons/streamers.** Hang ribbons or streamers from the ceiling. Scatter them on the table. Hang them from the table. Hang them on the walls.
- **Table confetti.** Confetti is available in various shapes and colors. It adds a festive atmosphere when sprinkled on tables.
- **Napkins.** Hotel professionals begin setting banquet tables by placing napkins because they know that a beautifully folded napkin is one of the first thing a person sees upon entering a room. Use color and creative folding techniques to add an elegant look to the event.

The site's custodial staff may have limitations, such as if tape can be put on walls or if confetti can be used (it may be hard to clean). They will appreciate your willingness to cooperate with them.

Color scheme

A color scheme can bring effective visual reinforcement of the theme to people's minds. Partner with the Marketing Coordinator to coordinate the color theme with the marketing materials.

Centerpieces/flowers/greenery

Flowers and greenery add a pleasant and natural touch to the site and can be provided in centerpieces, floral arrangements, or silk plants. (Nonfloral centerpieces can be used too.)
- Corsages
- Boutonnieres
- Flowers presented to speaker
- Flowers or greenery for stage, registration, or lobby area
- Flowers for head table
- Centerpieces for serving tables

- Centerpieces for dining tables. Check the height of the centerpieces so that they are under fifteen inches, not high enough to block people's view of each other.

Stretching your decorations budget

MONEY SAVERS

- Are centerpieces necessary? Don't assume they are; only use them if they will contribute positively. Some groups of people won't even notice centerpieces!
- Decide whether you will borrow, rent, or buy silk plants. Save on cost by borrowing silk plants from other areas of the venue. If you need to buy, see if you can find someone with a connection to a floral supply or craft supplies wholesaler.
- Use items that can be stored and reused, or that can be donated to other organizations (such as stuffed toys).
- Place visually appealing food, such as bread or fruit, in interesting arrangements.
- Move centerpieces around so they can be used at different events in the program.
- Use flowers in rented vases so you don't have to pay for storage. Or, use vases that are bought in bulk as a discount and give the flower arrangements as thank you gifts to volunteers. Live potted plants are also another alternative.
- Avoid ordering flowers through the hotel; instead, go directly to a florist.

Stage design

The stage is another area that you can use décor to unify the them. Consider:

- Backgrounds
- Lighting
- Props
- Banners

Try to think of creative ways that elements (such as props) can be arranged in different ways throughout the event to give a new look.

FINALIZING ARRANGEMENTS

Buy supplies needed to create your own decorations. If you are using vendors (such as reserving balloons), book their services in advance and pay any deposits.

The week before the event:

- Submit the final registration numbers to the caterer by the deadline that the caterer has set.
- Confirm arrival time and arrangements with the site and the caterer.
- Purchase any necessary food and deliver to site.
- Pick up rental equipment, linens, and decorations. Pack utensils, kitchen supplies, and bags or containers for distributing leftovers.

TIPS

TIPS FOR SUCCESS

Communication is key to a smoothly functioning event. Keep your caterer informed and updated throughout the process. Let them know early about changes so that they can prepare adequately. It's better to give them too much information than not enough! It doesn't hurt to repeat yourself either, just to make sure that they have received all information. Give your caterer the program schedule, seating plans, and VIP seating information, tell them the arrival and departure time of the guests so they can time their serving schedule and, when possible, fax them all the information so they have it in writing.

If you are using more than one caterer, distribute menus from the other meals so they know what is being served.

12 | TRANSPORTATION

In order to attend the conference, people need to get from their homes to the event. Those who live locally will drive or take public transportation over. Other people come from farther away—they will use car, train, bus, or air transportation. If you are holding your retreat on a remote island or in an area with a lot of water, you'll even have to worry about water transportation!

OVERVIEW

Does your event need transportation? If you are holding a local conference with local speakers, transportation will not be much of an issue, other than planning for adequate parking. But a conference that has people flying in from all ends of the country and uses multiple facilities throughout the city is a different story.

TIPS FOR SUCCESS

Depending on what your transportation needs are, the Transportation Coordinator oversees the transportation arrangements for the conference staff, the speakers, and the attendees. Your job is to care for the well-being of people before they arrive at the conference. If a participant needs to switch multiple planes, finds the travel schedules to be inconvenient, or experiences unreliable service, he'll arrive at the event tired and unhappy. Check the transportation vendors carefully and follow up the details to prevent future problems.

STEP-BY-STEP

Your responsibilities are:
1. Determining transportation needs
2. Investigating options
3. Arranging parking
4. Arranging transportation for speakers or staff

At the event, your main job is to make sure all transportation arrangements go smoothly, and if they don't, to find a solution! (See *Chapter 18: The Conference.*)

After the conference, your tasks are to evaluate, summarize the event, and appreciate those who helped (see *Chapter 19: Wrapping Up*).

DETERMINING TRANSPORTATION NEEDS

When will transportation be needed? How many people will need which mode of transportation? Estimate rough numbers.

INVESTIGATING OPTIONS

Handling transportation can be done in one of two ways (or a combination of the two):

TRANSPORTATION COORDINATOR	Job Description

The Transportation Coordinator oversees transportation arrangements for the conference staff, speakers and attendees.

Recommended skills/qualities

- Knowledge of transportation industry
- Negotiating ability
- Able to think and function under pressure and make decisions
- Attention to detail
- Ability to organize team needs

Job Description

Before the conference

- Attend planning meetings
- Oversee selection and setup of equipment

Night before conference

- Coordinate volunteers to set up equipment
- Run through rehearsals and sound check with speakers, worship team, and entertainers

During the conference

- Operate technical equipment, or oversee technical team

After the conference

- Compile summary report
- Send notes of appreciation to site staff
- Evaluate conference and suggest improvements for next time

Time Commitment

This position's time commitment is:

1. Handling all transportation yourself: researching, booking, and confirming all travel arrangements.
2. Finding an agency to oversee transportation arrangements. This is particularly helpful if you are holding a national or international conference requiring multiple modes of transportation. Travel agents take care of arrangements for air transportation and car rentals. Transportation management companies may also offer lower rates as well as other services (such as maps).

As you begin contacting transportation companies, keep these tips in mind:

- Determine which sources are cost-effective and available. For example, some hotels offer a free shuttle service from the airport. This saves you the cost of having to hire a cab, take a train, or take a bus. Compare the different options. Is it more cost-effective to rent a van or take the train?
- Ask about policies for deposit, cancellation, insurance required, and age limitations.
- Before signing the contract, check the vehicles to make sure they are in good condition so you won't be inadvertently charged for any damage that already exists.
- Don't prepay in full, in case problems arise and you need to negotiate.

Air transportation

MONEY SAVERS

Contact airlines early to make arrangements. Call them first and give pertinent information—how many people are expected, arrival and departure dates, etc. Ask them what incentives they can give to you if they are designated as the "official" airline. Most have conventions and meetings arrangements and will negotiate rates for your group. They may offer discount fares or special rates for your conference, sometimes up to five percent off the lowest published price. Some offer a free ticket for every twenty-five to forty tickets issued. There are also discounts or free tickets for site inspections. Ask them if they provide any special amenities: pre-boarding, free headsets, or help with promotion.

See if they will give discounts to people who book very early, such as sixty or more days in advance. Some airlines may offer "zone fares," which are discounts given to people from the same area; requirements vary from airline to airline. "Group fares" are negotiated for a number of seats on the plane, usually through a travel agency. The airlines may also allow you to arrange for a block of seats on a flight. Publicize the official or preferred airlines so people are aware of the discounts.

Airlines can provide information to help you with your decision process. If you're trying to decide between two sites, they can tell you which one is easier to access via air travel. They also have information about traveling patterns and which days are lighter for your attendees to travel.

Don't forget to plan for how people will get from the airport to the facility. Major hotels may provide free shuttles from the airport to the hotel, or from the hotel to the conference venue if it is in a separate place. Clarify the times the shuttle is available, so that people leaving early know to make their own arrangements. Other options available are buses, cabs, and personal drivers (such as for speakers).

For people making their own air arrangements, give them clear directions on how to proceed from the airport to the conference.

Ground transportation

Ground transportation options include: train, bus, shuttle, car, and van. If you are contracting a company to provide services, check the company's history and references. When contacting and visiting these companies, find out:

- How long have they been in business?
- Are they insured and bonded?
- What is the size of their fleet? How old are their vehicles and what is the condition?
- How long have the drivers been driving?

MONEY SAVERS

EXAMPLES

MONEY SAVERS

Buses

If you are transporting larger groups of people, such as a church retreat, renting buses may save money. One church found that renting a Greyhound bus was cheaper than using a school bus for youth retreat

Whether you are using buses to transport people to the hotel, or to be transported from facility to facility, you'll need to calculate how many buses are needed. Use the *Bus Calculation* worksheet below which gives a rough estimate of how many buses are needed. The duration of each trip is impacted by such factors as how long it takes people to get to the bus, loading and unloading times, local traffic patterns, and how many buses can be parked at the facility.

Reduce expenses by scheduling more buses during the busy times and less during the rest of the day, or negotiating lower costs if you are booking a large number of buses.

Check the rental policies for buses, and if you are driving the bus yourself, check the insurance policies. When you discuss arrangements with the transportation company, ask about deadlines for reservations. Is there a minimum hour usage? If so, arrange the hours so that they match with your schedule.

Visit the rental site so you can check the condition of the vehicles before you sign the contract.

A month before the conference, prepare liability waivers for people to sign, and run them by your insurance agent to see if they are adequate.

BUS CALCULATION   Worksheet

A.	Number of hotels	_____
B.	Number of people at each hotel	x _____
C.	Total number of people needing transportation (A x B)	= _____
D.	Number of seats on bus (average is 47)	÷ _____
E.	Number of bus trips (C ÷ D)	= _____
F.	Length of time for each roundtrip (minutes)	x _____
G.	Total transportation time (E x F)	= _____
H.	Time allotted for transportation (minutes)	÷ _____
I.	Number of buses needed (G ÷ H)	= _____

Example:

A.	Number of hotels	2 hotels
B.	Number of people at each hotel	x 100 people
C.	Total number of people needing transportation (A x B)	= 200 people
D.	Number of seats on bus (average is 47)	÷ 50 seats
E.	Number of bus trips (C ÷ D)	= 4 trips
F.	Length of time for each roundtrip (minutes)	x 10 min
G.	Total transportation time (E x F)	= 40 min
H.	Time allotted for transportation (minutes)	÷ 20 min
I.	Number of buses needed (G ÷ H)	= 2 buses

Prepare the location for drop-off and pick-up too. The location should be set away from the main entrance, away from traffic, so there's not a big crowd of people blocking the entrance. If there is a chance of inclement weather, check if the site has a location with an overhang that can serve as the waiting area.

Will there need to be signage for the bus area? Possible signage might include a sign to post where people are to wait and signs to place inside buses to show the destination. See page 189 for more information about signage.

If you are asking buses to arrive at the conference, and if they do not arrive on time, call the rental company immediately.

> Many times you have the contact number of the the person who [made the arrangements at the company], but you arrive at the event and there's a new on-site contact person. Make sure you have [the original person's] cell phone and how to reach them at the office. They should also provide phone numbers of everyone they have outsourced (hired). If they are outsourcing, how are they contacting the bus drivers? How are they going to handle changes? Know how to get to that bus driver; make arrangements to contact them an hour prior [so you know where the driver is]. Thirty-five to forty minutes before, you have spoken [face-to-face with] the driver. Remind them that it's round trip—sometimes that one little detail gets left off! ◆ *Brad Weaber*

Don't forget to tip hired drivers. Allow a tip of about $10 to $20 per day, although amounts may vary according to region.

Car rental

If your attendees will be doing sightseeing during their visit, they may want to rent cars. Most car rental companies usually have desks at the airport. Since people really appreciate it if you tell them where those desks are located, call the companies ahead of time to find out.

Carpooling

Arranging carpooling conserves gas and reduces parking and traffic congestion. Only use vehicles that are licensed and insured. Give all drivers clear directions for getting there as well as for parking.

For those who are driving, clear directions are critical! A lost attendee will arrive stressed—and you don't want people to feel stressed while they are sitting through your conference!

ARRANGING PARKING

If people drive but have no place to park, they'll arrive with a negative attitude about the event before it has even begun!

Conference or retreat centers usually have adequate parking for your group. Some places provide a parking permit that is placed in each driver's car.

If you're using a location in a city with limited parking, check with the city about possible special event parking permits.

Churches with parking lots may benefit from a parking crew that assists with directing people. Ask the church if they can provide a parking crew. If they do not, work with the Volunteer Coordinator to recruit parking attendants.

ARRANGING TRANSPORTATION FOR SPEAKERS

EXAMPLES

When the speaker is confirmed, send them a form asking for information about their transportation needs. Or, if you have a Speaker Coordinator, as her to include the form in the materials that are being sent to the speaker. Page 121 shows an example of a form where transportation requests are included with other information desired from the speaker.

If speakers are flying in, make arrangements to meet them at the airport.

If they are driving in, give clear directions and have a host available to greet them at the facility.

For speakers who arrive at a late time (or if you don't know when they will arrive), leave a note and a welcome package for them at the front desk.

FINALIZING ARRANGEMENTS

Contact the Volunteer Coordinator if you need any drivers or helpers to direct people to buses.

Check with the organization's insurance company to make sure all transportation arrangements are covered.

If you will be using ground transportation, set up one person to be the dispatcher. This person will be the central communications hub for any questions, problems, or updates. This person should be supplied with a list of arrival/departure times of attendees, transportation vendor schedules, and contact information.

The week before the conference, double check all arrangements.

- Call rental companies to confirm rentals.
- Contact volunteer hosts or drivers to check that they know where to go and what their jobs will be.
- Prepare checks to pay off the remainder of the invoices.
- Put together lists and records to bring to the conference. Include contact information, what is being rented, and schedules.

13 | REGISTRATION

People with the spiritual gift of administration make excellent Registration Coordinators. That's because this job is full of handling little details that, if they were lost, would cause headaches for the attendees as well as the conference staff. The Registration Coordinator keeps records of all the people attending and distributes, to the conference staff, the data pertaining to their areas.

OVERVIEW

The Registration Coordinator oversees the process of registering attendees for the event. This may be as simple as processing forms that come in, to handling multiple options of phone, mail, fax, and online registration. Registration Coordinators also prepare materials to give to the participants when they arrive—nametags, a welcome packet with information, and other items that participants will use.

Your responsibilities include:
1. Setting up a registration process
2. Producing a registration form
3. Encouraging registration
4. Confirming registration
5. Producing name badges
6. Planning on-site registration

STEP-BY-STEP

At the conference, the Registration Director checks everyone in to the event and registers last-minute participants (see *Chapter 18: The Conference*).

Afterwards, your tasks are evaluation, summarization of the event, and appreciation of those who helped you (see *Chapter 19: Wrapping Up*).

SETTING UP A REGISTRATION PROCESS

Begin by determining the scope of the registration procedure. How many do you expect to attend and what kind of procedures will you need to handle those numbers? Try to keep the process streamlined and simple to make it easier for the attendees as well as for yourself!

Set registration limits

Will you need to set a cap on how many people will register? Registration numbers need to be limited if your facility has limited space, but if your facility has adequate space, then you'll need to consider the advantages and disadvantages regarding registration limits. The advantage of having a cap is that it encourages people to register early.

REGISTRATION COORDINATOR	Job Description

The Registration Coordinator oversees registering people for the conference and checking them in upon arrival. The Registration Coordinator is the main contact for attendees until they are registered on-site.

Recommended skills/qualities

- Administrative/organizational skills
- Attention to detail
- Able to function under pressure and make decisions
- Good at tracking numbers
- Good people skills

Job description

Before the conference

- Attend planning meetings
- Establish registration procedures
- Oversee registration form production
- Oversee volunteers helping with registration data entry
- Process registration forms
- Create name badges
- Assemble welcome packets
- Make arrangements for people with special accommodation needs

Night before conference

- Set up registration area

During the conference

- Sign in attendees at conference
- Register walk-on registrants

After the conference

- Return rented equipment
- Compile summary report
- Send notes of appreciation to technical operators and helpers
- Evaluate conference and suggest improvements for next time

Time Commitment

This position's time commitment is:

If you decide to have unlimited registration, everyone is able to attend. However, you might miss the guaranteed minimum required by the facility and may have to pay extra charges if attendance is not as high as you had estimated.

Set a schedule

SCHEDULING

When is the absolute last date that the majority of the registrations need to be in? Often this date is decided by cancellation deadlines given by the facility, caterer, or other suppliers. Plan a date to cancel the event also, in case of very inadequate attendance.

Once you have set this date, work backwards. When are discounted fares offered? When do registration forms need to go out? When does the registration form information need to be given to the Marketing Coordinator?

Establish registration policies

Since people will ask questions, it's helpful to have your registration policies written out, because it will provide consistency in the way you deal with the registrations. Detail any policies, such as:

- What space limitations are there? How will you handle waiting lists?
- What if people cancel? How will you handle people who request refunds? It's easiest if registrations are nonrefundable. Costs have already been paid and giving refunds may be a financial strain to the organization.
- How will you handle lost registrations?
- If people want to attend only a part of the conference, will you prorate their registration fee or do they still have to pay the full amount? What special arrangements will be needed for these people?
- If people are only attending the conference and staying off-site, how much will their registration fee be? Set a clear pricing structure.
- How will people who want to transfer their registration to another person be handled?
- What payment methods will you accept? Will you accept credit cards? Check with the Finance Coordinator to see what limitations there may be in this area.
- What is required for admittance? (name badges, tickets, or confirmation letter)
- How will you register children?

Set registration rates

Work with the Finance Coordinator to set the rate structure (see page 35).

Organize advance registration procedure

STEP-BY-STEP

Write a step-by-step list for processing advance registrations.

1. Receive registration form and payment.
2. Write down check number on registration form.
3. Log registration form information into database or spreadsheet.
4. Deposit money into bank account.
5. At regular intervals, submit an income status report to the team, particularly the Finance Coordinator.
6. Submit numbers to coordinators who need the information (Hospitality, Site, etc.)

Family conferences must also develop a registration procedure for children. Because security is a concern, if your group is large enough that people don't all know each other, you'll also need to develop some kind of identification system for children's program workers, parents, and children.

We offer a service where children can preregister. We limit our preschool registration to the first 100 people, and we charge $100, first come, first served. We mail forms in advance to people so they can fill them out before they get there. We use wristbands that have a tear-off number on the end. One end goes on the child and the end piece tears off [for the parent]. They are color coded by age; we band everyone from two years to sixth grade, assuming junior highers and high schoolers are more responsible and probably don't want to be picked up by Mom and Dad. If a child escapes out of the room, we know how old he is and put him back in the right place. The wristbands are less than ten cents a piece; you're investing twenty cents a week for a child's safety.
◆ *Dean Jones*

RESOURCE TOOLS

For an example of a company that Dean uses to buy these type of wristbands, check out www.medtechgroup.com, 800-361-1259. (Click on "Supertek" wristbands.) Some companies will sequentially number the bands for you. If the box has too many for your group, save the rest for the next year.

One option for processing registrations is to the use a registration service. Some local Convention and Visitor's Bureaus also provide registration services.

We contracted a secular registration company that sells sporting event tickets. They charge us a fee for each person registered and they get a confirmation via e-mail. People can register any way they feel most comfortable. They send in a check or pay by credit card. They can fax it too. ◆ *Pam Chun*

RESOURCE TOOLS

Some companies that provide registration services include:
- Afficent, www.afficient.com, 312-932-4400. Online registration company for registration and payment transaction.
- Cvent, www.cvent.com, 866-318-4358. Online registration, eMarketing and data analysis.
- eRSVP.com, www.ersvp.com, 212-201-7799, Web-based registration and response management.
- 123Signup, www.123signup.com, 877-691-9950. Online registration, association management, and credit card processing. Offers discounts to non-profits.

PRODUCING A REGISTRATION FORM

A registration form should be clear and easy to fill out. In many cases, a designer or Marketing Coordinator will design the form, so give the registration information to the designer to format. (See page 182 for more information about the conference brochure.)

Your registration form may request some or all of the following:
- Name
- Address
- Contact information (telephone, e-mail, fax)
- Gender
- Birthdate
- Marital Status
- For family conferences: children's names, ages, allergies
- Church information
- Medical/special diet needs
- Type of housing selected (and roommate requests, if pertinent)
- Fees
- What the fee covers (meals, accommodations, materials, etc.)
- Cancellation/refund/transfer policies
- Information about who to make check payable to, and where to send the registrations

- Liability release form for adults (and also children, if your program includes children)
- Emergency contact information

At one of our large conferences, a man was crossing the street and was hit by a bus and killed. He had nothing on him, and a lot of people didn't know him or where he lived. It took us a long time to find out where he lived and we had to send someone to his home. We had to ransack his apartment look for numbers of family or anyone who know him. It took us hours. Ask for addresses, emergency contact information, and any medical information. ◆ *Jeanne Gregory*

ENCOURAGING REGISTRATION

Because there are people who hate filling out forms, make the process as easy as possible. In order to encourage as many people as possible to register, make the process as easy as possible. First, ask what discourages people from registering? Then try to eliminate the barriers so that people can register quickly and easily.

A form that is simple to fill out encourages registration. A complicated form is intimidating to fill out and people will procrastinate registering (or not register at all) if they feel it is too complicated and difficult. Use a clear form that is easy to follow.

With the popularity of the Internet rising, online registration is a convenient option. Online registration forms can be accessed at any time of day and from anywhere there is an online connection (great for early birds and night owls!). People can access the information instantly and have their questions answered instead of waiting for a brochure to arrive in the mail. It also saves you time because since it's automated, you don't need people to enter the data.

We've gotten to a point where 70% of the people register online. That means you don't have to process checks. You don't have to run credit card numbers. All data has been entered by an individual so you don't have to rekey in information. Online is really great but we always offer other alternatives. ◆ *Andrew Accardy*

If you are using the Web to register people, keep these tips in mind:
- Make your Web site secure so people feel comfortable registering online.
- List contact information. After looking on your site, some people may decide to register another way. Make it easy for them by listing your phone, address, or other contact information on your Web site. Or if they do want to register online, they will be assured that their questions can be answered with a phone call if necessary.
- If the registration process requires more than one page at a time, let the registrant know how many more pages to go so he doesn't get frustrated.
- At the end, let the registrant know what will happen, such as receiving a confirmation e-mail or fax.

The best publicity is word of mouth. Use this effective means of attendee recruitment by encouraging friends to tell others about the conference. Offer group registration rates so people enlist their friends or coworkers to attend. Or give a discount to a group leader who signs up a certain number of people.

Because many people are procrastinators by nature or like to leave their options open, early registration incentives, such as offering an early bird discount, are effective. The majority of your registrations usually arrive at the early bird discount deadline. Another option is to let people know ahead of time that the earlier they register, the greater their chance of winning a

EXAMPLES

doorprize. Then set aside one prize for a special drawing for say, the first ten people who register. Or offer each of them a small gift for being the first to register.

A good time for many registrations is offering an opportunity at the end of the conference to register for the following year. Those who enjoyed the conference will be more apt to re-register for the next year, especially if you offer a discount. Give them a month or two to take the form home and register for the next year's event.

CONFIRMING REGISTRATION

Registrations begin trickling in once the brochures are distributed, but don't expect the majority to come in until the deadline. As the registrations arrive, process them immediately.

As soon as you receive the registration, send out a confirmation letter (example on page 160) with the following information:
- Sessions or workshops they will be attending
- Program schedule
- Policies (refunds, cancellations, transfers, etc.)
- What to bring
- Map to site
- Weather information for people traveling from out of town
- Check-in information
- Travel or transportation information
- Tickets for admittance or for meals

See the sample confirmation letter on the next page for an example.

PRODUCING NAME BADGES

Although name badges can be included with the confirmation letter, it's usually better to keep the name badges and hand them to the participants when they check in. If you send them ahead of time, people forget to bring them and you'll end up making new badges.

First make some decisions about the actual appearance of the badges:
- What kind of badge will you use? Paper in a plastic holder? Or self-adhesive? If you are using self-adhesive badges, plan for one badge per day.
- If you're using plastic holders, will you use clip-on, pin-on, or hanging? If you're using clip-on badges, add a small safety pin (they usually have a little hole by the clip) for people who wear shirts without collars.
- What size is the badge?
- How will you generate the badge?
- What information will be on the badge? How will the information be shown? Use a large font for the name!
- How will you replace lost badges?

COMPUTER HELPS

Some word processing programs let you make mail merge files for printing. You can set up a nametag template in the word processing program, import the spreadsheet information of the registrants, and print out the nametags onto pre-perforated nametag paper. Check your word processing and spreadsheet software manual for instruction on how to do this.

One helpful tip is to print on the back of the nametag, "In case of emergency, contact:" with a line for the attendee to fill in a name and phone number. In the event an emergency occurs, the contact person can immediately be reached, without having to dig through paperwork.

Dear Lisa:

Thank you for registering for the Annual Retreat. This year our theme is "Bringing Out the Best." We've brought together our best efforts to plan a retreat that will provide practical encouragement for you in your walk with the Lord.

As a reminder, the retreat will be held March 1-3 at the Oak Springs Conference Center in Oak Springs City, located about two hours from our church. Enclosed is a map and driving directions for your convenience, as well as a program schedule. The program starts at 7 pm Friday night so please try to allow adequate time to register. Parking is near the entrance and registration begins at 5 pm in the Oak Forest building. Although dinner is not included, see the enclosed map for nearby restaurants.

You have registered for the following workshops:

"Bringing Out the Best in My Children"	Sat 1 pm
"Bringing Out the Best in My Marriage"	Sat 3 pm

The program handbook you will receive at the retreat will list the locations of these workshops.

Don't forget to bring the following items: Bible, pen, notebook, and anything you want to do during recreational time. Oak Springs is cool during March so bring warm clothes for the evenings.

Please be aware that there are no refunds or cancellations for this event. However, you may transfer your registration to another person up to two weeks before the retreat. If you have any questions, please contact me. I look forward to seeing you at the retreat!

Joan Brown

Registration Coordinator
444-5555

You might find it helpful to print badges in different colors for the different groups of people at the event. Having volunteers with one color badge helps registrants identify people they can go to with questions. There's also the added security of knowing that a stranger can't pose as a volunteer without being registered.

MONEY SAVERS

If you want to recycle badge holders to save on costs, have a plan for how you will collect the holders at the end of the conference. One way is to have a large basket by the door nearby the feedback form collection basket. Remember to plan for where you will be storing the holders until the next conference.

RESOURCE TOOLS

An example of a company that provides a wide variety of badge products and other registration materials is pc/nametag, www.pcnametag.com, 800-233-9767.

PLANNING ON-SITE REGISTRATION

Besides processing registrations, another major task is handling the registrations of people when they arrive on site.

Establish on-site registration process

The goal for on-site registration is to make the procedure as simple as possible. Registration is often the attendee's first impression of the conference. A participant who goes quickly and smoothly through registration begins with a positive view of the conference, but if the wait is long or complicated, they start with a negative impression.

At the conference, the people who arrive can be separated into two groups: a group of people who have already registered (pre-registered) and those who will be registering at the event (walk-ons or on-site registrants). The process for each group is different so plan each process separately.

Drawing up a plan for registration is easily done by considering these questions:

- What will the on-site registration procedure be? Will you use computers or process information manually?
- Where can you store your equipment before and after the registration time? When will equipment be set up?
- What volunteers will be needed? How many people? What jobs will the volunteers need to carry out?
- How will you divide the registration lines (alphabetical pre-registered or walk-ons)?
- What will you do with the on-site registration money? If you will need a lock-box, find one and figure out where to put it after the registration period is over.

Inspect registration area

Ask the Site Coordinator to arrange a time when you can visit the registration area. Inspect the area to see how the registration area can be used effectively:

- How near is the area to the general session room?
- Is there enough lighting?
- How many doors and hallways are there?
- If you are using computers, where are the power outlets?
- How many tables can the facility provide? Will tables be draped? Chairs will also be needed for volunteers processing registrations.
- Is there storage for equipment and registration materials?

- Does the site have any signage that you can use for registration, or will you need to make your own?
- What time will the area be available?

Make any arrangements needed with other Coordinators, such as reserving tables, equipment, or signage.

Traffic flow/distribution

Consider the traffic flow from the time the attendee enters the door to when they leave the registration area and how they will travel around the registration site. When will the traffic peak? Plan the traffic flow for peak periods because that is when smooth traffic flow will be crucial.

The most efficient way to register people is to establish a smooth traffic flow. One-way traffic is most efficient. To make the process simple, break it down into separate areas:

- For pre-registered, break down the registrations by letter (A-L, M-Z). Quickly check people off the registration list, hand them their nametag and a packet, and direct them to the next location (housing, dining, or meeting room).
- For on-site/walk-on or non-paid registrations, have a separate table where people can go. Streamline the process by having pens and registration forms ready on clipboards so people can fill them out while they are standing in line.
- Have another table for speaker/staff/volunteer check-in. The Speaker and Volunteer Coordinators stay here throughout the registration process so that they can greet people.
- Establish an information or question area for people who don't know where to go. Place this table near the door.

Draw a map of the registration area:

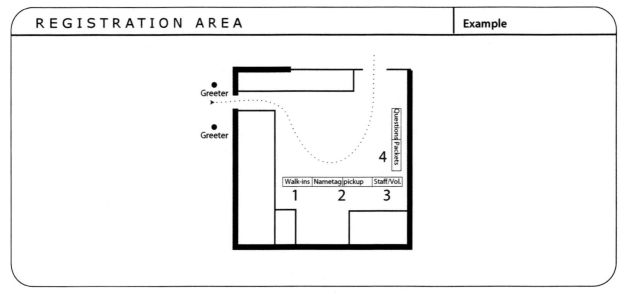

Determine what signage is needed to clearly direct people to the proper locations and work with the Marketing Coordinator to produce it (page 189)

SCHEDULING

Discuss the schedule with the other members of the team. When does the line need to be closed? If people are getting breakfast before the session begins, maybe you need to close the line ten minutes before the program starts so people can start getting seated.

Establish some contingency plans for unexpected crises. What will you do if the computers go down or a crowd of people appears right before the session is going to start? See page 207 for more information about crisis management.

When registration closes, store all the supplies until the end of the day or until they can be moved to a more permanent place.

Volunteer staffing

Work with the Volunteer Coordinator to develop a list of volunteers needed and to communicate advance information to the volunteers.

Determine volunteers needed

The number of volunteers needed for registration depends on the expected attendance for the event as well as what kind of tasks need to be covered. Calculate the total number of people registered. An additional ten to twenty percent walk-in registrations is normal, but no-shows usually balance out the final number. Plan one registration volunteer for every fifty to 100 attendees during peak periods. Designate an additional volunteer to be the troubleshooter (someone with good diplomatic skills that will be able to handle upset registrants) and another volunteer to help with any errands that may be needed.

Excellent volunteers are those who are patient, calm, and have good people skills. These volunteers might be one of the first people the attendees interact with, so you want them to be positive! Be sure that the volunteers are responsible too, so that they show up when they are needed.

EXAMPLES

Communicate advance information

To help your volunteers be adequately prepared for their arrival, send them helpful information such as travel directions, check-in procedures, dress code, and other instructions (see page 203 for sample instructions for a volunteer).

Prepare training

When your volunteers arrive on site, they'll need to be trained. Take some time to list out responsibilities and what the volunteers will be told.

- **Knowledge.** What do they need to know? At the very least, volunteers should be aware of general information such as schedules, locations of meeting rooms, restrooms, telephones, and other important areas.
- **Responsibilities.** What kind of duties will the volunteers have? Explain job descriptions and boundaries of who does what.
- **Behavior guidelines.** Encourage volunteers to smile and be friendly, and remind them their first priority is to serve the people attending. Discourage personal conversations with other volunteers at the registration tables and unprofessional behavior.
- **Emergency contact.** Let them know what to do in an urgent situation. As the coordinator, you should be in the registration area, but in case you are not there it's always wise to have a backup plan.

FINALIZING ARRANGEMENTS

Assembling welcome packets

EXAMPLES

After check-in or registering on-site, the attendee may be given a packet with all the materials and information that they will use. Because this information will be referred to over and over, it's helpful to make it accessible and convenient by using a 9x12 envelope or a large folder. Some conferences even bind all the materials into a book. See page 188 for an example.

Information to include:
- Facility map and information
- Program schedule
- Check-out procedure and time
- Local information: restaurants, attractions
- Writing materials: pen, paper
- Name badges and badge holder
- Speaker biographies, outlines/notes
- Small group locations
- Announcements
- Safety/emergency brochure or procedures
- Feedback/evaluation form (ask hotel or Convention and Visitor's Bureau if they have any)
- Blank envelope for offering

Produce enough packets for the number of people who registered, plus an additional ten to twenty percent for walk-in registration. Remember to include packets for the speakers, staff and volunteers as well. For volunteers, include their instruction sheets with the packet.

Collect supplies

Assemble the following supplies to bring to the registration area to have on hand in case you need them.

- Clipboards
- Pens
- Registration form
- Stapler/paper clips
- Staple removers
- Receipt forms
- Lock box
- Computer
- Printer
- Calculator
- Wastepaper basket
- Tape
- Spare cash
- Credit card terminal

Also, pack up the registration materials:
- Registration records
- Registration signage
- Extra brochures, maps, schedules
- Welcome packets
- Name badges and badge holders

CHAPTER

14 | EXHIBITS

Attendees find exhibits to be helpful sources of information, products, and resources. The extent of your exhibit area depends on what kind of conference you are having and how many people are expected to attend. A small exhibit area might be a few tables, whereas a large exhibit area can have many booths. Exhibits are also called *tradeshows* and *exhibitions.*

OVERVIEW

At the initial meeting, you will get an idea of the scope of the exhibits area. If there will only be a few tables or booths, the exhibits area can be included as the responsibility of another team member—the Program Coordinator, for example. Conferences with extensive exhibits should assign one person who is dedicated to overseeing this area.

STEP-BY-STEP

The responsibilities of the Exhibits Coordinator include:
1. Determining exhibit requirements
2. Visiting the site
3. Arranging booths
4. Setting exhibitor fees
5. Drawing up the contract
6. Making arrangements
7. Compiling the exhibitor prospectus
8. Contacting exhibitors
9. Confirming exhibitors

At the conference, the Exhibit Coordinator oversees the setup of the exhibit area and helps exhibitors setup (*Chapter 18: The Conference*).

After the conference, your main tasks are returning items, summarizing the event, evaluating, and sending notes of appreciation (*Chapter 19: Wrapping Up*).

DETERMINING EXHIBIT REQUIREMENTS

Your first task is to discuss with other team members the scope of the exhibits at the conference. Will there just be tables for a few organizations? Or will there be an entirely different section that will be quite extensive? Would table-top exhibits or exhibit booths be more appropriate? Would tabletop exhibits or exhibit booths be better? Try to clarify what kind of exhibits are desired and the purpose of the exhibit area, then list the requirements:

- **Purpose.** Most exhibit areas are for the purpose of providing resources or information for attendees, but it's helpful if you have a written statement for why the conference is having an exhibits area.

The Exhibits Coordinator handles all details related the exhibits, including making arrangements with exhibitors and preparing the exhibits site.

Recommended skills/qualities

- Administrative skills
- Good people and communication skills
- Attention to detail

Job description

Before the conference

- Attend planning meetings
- Establish exhibit requirements and guidelines
- Coordinate exhibits needs with Site Coordinator
- Arrange for registration of exhibitors
- Plan exhibitors' program (if applicable)

Night before conference

- Oversee setup of exhibit areas and check-in of exhibitors

During the conference

- Be the contact person for exhibitors
- Attend to any exhibitor needs

After the conference

- Compile summary report
- Send notes of appreciation to exhibitors
- Evaluate conference and suggest improvements for next time

Time Commitment

This position's time commitment is:

- **Estimated number of exhibitors.** How many exhibitors do you want to have at your conference?
- **Types of exhibits.** Will there be only tabletop exhibits, draped (booth) displays, or a combination of both?
- **Space.** How much space is needed? How large are the booths? Don't forget to include in your calculation space for:
  - Exhibit booths
  - Aisles between booths
  - Food outlet areas
  - Service areas (audio-visual, utilities, decorator company, etc.)
  - Storage

Once these questions have been answered, you'll have a list of what kind of facility is needed for your exhibits.

RESOURCE TOOLS

At some point you may decide to hire out to a professional company to handle all the exhibit arrangements. Or, you might be required to work with a professional company for certain aspects, such as a decorating company. If you'd like to take a look at what a professional exposition company provides, look at 21st Century Expo Group, www.21stceg.com, 310-386-9771.

VISITING THE SITE

Visit the site with the Site Coordinator to familiarize yourself with the place and to see what the exhibits area will look like. Find out what is provided by the facility, what areas will require outside vendors, and how much the services will cost. A church might provide an empty hall and you bring in your own tables, curtains, or electricity. Convention centers require you to purchase or rent everything, including carpet, drapes, tables, and labor for electricity. Charges also vary from site to site. A convention center might charge $400 to $700 for a booth; usually charges are assessed by the square foot. Even though charges are fixed, don't be afraid to negotiate with the decorating companies in a convention center on signage or other items.

Look at the location of the exhibit site. Is it centrally located? If your exhibit site is off in a remote corner of the property, the exhibitors won't see much traffic and will not return the next year.

Where are the loading docks and how far are they from the exhibit hall? Some places allow a ramp to extend from the truck directly to the exhibit floor. Other locations may have long hallways, which mean plans are needed for transporting the equipment and extra time is needed for move-in.

Check the size of the exhibits area. Is it too small or too large? At this point you will not know exactly how many exhibitors you will have, but look at the area with your target number in mind. If your area is too small, the space will be cramped. If it is too big, it will look like there are too few exhibits. Also account for enough room for smooth traffic flow. Obtain a floor plan from the facility and sketch some rough plans of exhibits in different arrangements to see what would work best.

Ask the facility what kind of requirements exist. Some places require the city or convention center to approve any building codes for exhibits. Factors such as fire safety approval must also be considered.

Find out shipping requirements, such as:
- When materials should arrive
- Address for shipping materials (and the location where they will be delivered)
- How materials will be stored and how exhibitor retrieves them
- If you are allowed to move furniture

ARRANGING BOOTHS

Once you have an idea of where the exhibit area will be and how the area will be roughly laid out, it's time to draw up a map of the booths.

Booths are square or rectangular, usually eight feet or ten feet wide or larger. An adequate aisle usually is ten to twelve feet wide. Professional exhibition companies provide eight foot drapes in the back, and three foot draped divider for booths. A facility that doesn't regularly do exhibits might provide you with a table and maybe dividers in the back if they are available.

Booths located in different areas are called different names. If you're working with a church, it probably doesn't matter what it's called—the people you work with will probably just call them "booths (or tables) against the wall" or "booths in the center" (away from the wall). But if you're working with a convention center, it will be helpful to know the terminology for different types of booths:

- **In-line, linear or standard:** a booth with at least one neighbor on either side.
- **Perimeter:** a booth along the outside wall of the exhibit floor.
- **Island:** a booth that has aisles on all four sides. It stands alone.
- **Corner:** a booth that has aisles along two sides. It is in the corner of a block of booths.
- **Peninsula:** a booth that has aisles along three sides. The fourth side is adjacent to one or more neighbors.

EXHIBIT BOOTHS	Diagram

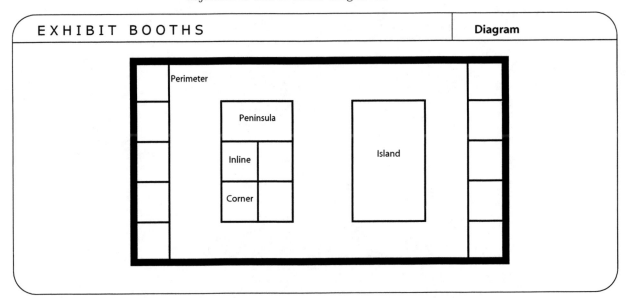

SETTING EXHIBITOR FEES

Discuss the budget amount for each exhibitor with the Finance Coordinator. Setting the fees for exhibitors involves calculating the costs, estimating how many exhibitors will come, and balancing the two so you come out ahead.

Check with the Site Coordinator to determine what the facility can provide and what fees will need to be paid.

- Table top displays cost less than draped (booth) displays. Will you be offering one or the other, or a combination of the two? Find out from the facility if they provide tables or booths.
- Does the facility provide furniture or equipment for the exhibits? What are the fees?

- Does the site set up the exhibits area? What exactly do they set up? Do they charge for setup? Who is in charge of the setup?
- What utilities are available? Electricity, plumbing, satellite hookup, telephones, gas, and drains require setup and extra charges.
- Do they bring in outside vendors such as show decorators that you will have to work with? What are the additional charges?

When you figure out the total for expenses, divide it by the anticipated number of exhibitors to figure out what your break-even cost will be. Then you can determine what you want to charge for fees.

Flat fees are a one-price fee for every exhibitor, regardless of what location they choose. Tiered fees are fees that vary according to location. Prime locations by the entrances or by where food is served may have higher fees since there is higher traffic in those areas. Decide whether you will have tiered fees or one standard fee for everyone.

DRAWING UP THE CONTRACT

Before you contact exhibitors, establish guidelines, policies, and information. This information should be in written form as a letter or contract that the exhibitor can sign and return to you.

- How many booth spaces are available?
- How much is the charge for each booth?
- Are there complimentary booths (for example, for sponsors)?
- How many complimentary registrations are provided for each booth? Can exhibitors participate in the conference? Also, during what parts?
- When do the exhibits open?
- What insurance is required?
- How will the attendees be informed about the exhibits? Will exhibitors be listed in the program? Will there be a separate program for the exhibitors?
- What benefits will exhibitors have for participating? Why should they exhibit with you?
- What kind of screening process is there?
- What is the cancellation policy? Is any insurance required? Clarify any liability issues.

MAKING ARRANGEMENTS

Show decorator

At convention centers, a vendor called a *show decorator* handles many logistics of exhibit halls, such as move-in, move-out, show decorating (drapes, furniture, and equipment), and hiring and supervising the labor installing and dismantling the booths. Contact the show decorator to make the arrangements needed.

Security

The Site Coordinator oversees security on site. Check with the Site Coordinator to see what kind of security is needed in the exhibits area. Include the cost of security in the budget, either under "facilities" or "exhibits."

- What security will be needed at the entrances and exits?
- Does the site provide security or do you need to hire security?
- How much does it cost to hire security?

Food and beverage

Exhibitors at the event the entire time will need to eat. What kind of food and beverage arrangements need to be made. Will food be provided to them? Or are they on their own? Will they join the attendees in the eating area? If food arrangements need to be made, plan them with the Hospitality Coordinator.

Equipment and services

Will booths, tables, curtains, or other equipment be needed? Does the site provide these items? What about support staff, such as electricians to provide for power? Find out if these products or services are provided by the site, and if so, the charge for each. Sometimes you are required to use the site's sources. Whatever vendors you will be using, select and include their information in the letter that you are sending to the exhibitors.

Floor plan

Using the dimensions of the exhibit area, lay out a floor plan for the booths, including spaces for aisles and other areas listed on page 168.

Shipping and storage

Non-local exhibitors will need a shipping and delivery company to handle the transporting of their displays and material to the conference site.

Exhibitor program

Some conferences with many exhibitors plan a program especially for exhibitors so that they have the opportunity to gather together. Determine if this is something you want to provide at the conference.

COMPILING THE EXHIBITOR PROSPECTUS

An exhibitor prospectus is a packet that includes all the information for potential exhibitors.

> We market with an exhibitor prospectus that says what the program will be, what benefits they receive from it, what the cost is, and what the regulations are. In a convention center they will have to call in a decorating company and arrange their own delivery. We try to provide as much information to know the total cost involved; electricity alone is $250 for a single outlet. The exhibitors want the information to make cost analysis.
> ◆ *Andrew Accardy*

An exhibitor prospectus may include:
- Sponsoring organization's information
- Conference purpose, theme (including colors), goals, dates, times and location
- Expected attendance
- Target audience profile
- Schedule of conference, including move-in and move-out dates
- Benefits of exhibiting
- Description of the booth and what is included in the price
- Floor plan of booths
- Limitations on booth height, space
- Show decorator information
- Regulations such as fire, safety, security and insurance
- Forms for utilities and other services
- Listing of labor rates and union regulations
- Registration/housing information
- A contract or letter of agreement

- Cancellation policies
- Ceiling height limitations
- Response date for reply

CONTACTING EXHIBITORS

Once all the arrangements and policies have been made, you can begin contacting exhibitors. Draw up an initial mailing list. List organizations, companies, churches, or other groups that might want to exhibit.

> We begin by creating a "hunt list." We create that list by searching through brochures and their exhibitors. We look at what others are doing, get other conference brochures. We get their addresses and contact them. I don't know any great list out there that you can buy. It's just doing the hard work of finding those people. ◆ *Andrew Accardy*

Call the potential exhibitors to check if the information is updated. Then send them an invitation letter with an exhibitor's prospectus. Don't forget to follow up the information you have sent.

CONFIRMING EXHIBITORS

Exhibitors interested in participating will return the card or contract that you have included in your mailing. You can be proactive in your efforts too: follow up after you send the letter—unfortunately, letters sometimes get lost in the mail. After you have received the registration or contract from the exhibitors, send them a confirmation letter or postcard. Confirm with them once again the dates, the amount that was received, and amount of space that was reserved (booths or tables), and ask them to send you a floor plan of their booth.

The confirmation packet can contain:
- Preliminary conference program information
- Travel arrangements form (airline, ground, and or/hotel reservations forms)
- Shipping information
- Guidelines and requirements. Is food allowed? When is the setup time? When must the booth be cleared? How many people are admitted to the conference free of charge?
- Name badges, if they will not be checking in at the event.
- Let them know that they will be informed of their final space assignments the week before the conference.
- Lay out the expectations so they know what to expect—how much interest they will get from people, what the schedule is, and when they should be at their booths. Be clear up front so that they will not have any unpleasant surprises. Let them know what is allowed and what isn't.

> Judy Byford helped plan a conference where one year an exhibitor brought in an animal as part of his exhibit. The conference planners had to scramble to accommodate this unexpected event. They learned to say no more animals!

> When we send out a confirmation package, we include information such as color of the carpet, drapes, when they need to ship and all the basics they need to know. We give them all the contact information of other vendors they need to contact. ◆ *Andrew Accardy*

Refine the floor plan of the exhibit area. Once you have an accurate count of exhibitors, begin assigning them booth locations. Either assign on a first-come, first served basis, or use a lottery system to do random drawings. Sometimes exhibitors may cancel at the last moment, so be prepared to be flexible.

The Site Coordinator can answer final details about setup and cleanup requirements. As time gets closer, it's a good idea to check in to make sure that everything has been covered. The Site and/or the Hospitality Coordinator should also be asked to help plan for food service during the move-in period. Many exhibitors move in before the actual conference starts and food service often is unavailable. Make plans for how the people moving in will find a place to eat. Even if they are not eating on site, as a courtesy inform them where nearby restaurants are located.

The Registration Coordinator can also help arrange exhibitor badges. Decide whether you want to send the badges in advance or ask them to check in. If they are checking in, prepare a table in the registration area.

When the booth exhibitors and locations are finalized, send the information and map layout to the Program Coordinator to be included in the program. The participants will find the map helpful, especially if they are looking for a particular vendor. A separate list of all the vendors either by type or alphabetically (or both) should also be included.

Your signage arrangements may depend on the facility. Some places, such as convention centers, require you get the signage from the decorating company. If the Site Coordinator is handling signage, work with her to ensure consistency in the signage. Don't forget to make directional signs as well as signage for the different booths.

On-site plans

Make plans for how the move-in will be handled when you arrive at the site.

The show decorator usually handles move-in. He schedules times to move in and out. A general order for move-in is:

1. Tape the floor with the booth dimensions and aisles.
2. Large exhibits, such as islands, move in.
3. Small exhibits move in.

Plan to arrive early to ensure that the exhibits area is ready for setup, supervise the facility staff as they set up the area, and check the electrical and phone hookups to make sure everything is correctly connected.

As soon as the booths are ready, plan to put up the signage so exhibitors can easily find their space.

Make advance preparations for how to return shipping of the exhibit materials after the conference, unless the exhibitors have arranged for it themselves.

Also prepare evaluation forms to give to exhibitors after the event for their feedback on their experience with the event.

C H A P T E R

15 | MARKETING

Your conference is going to be the event of the century—but if no one hears about it, no one will come! Marketing is a crucial area of conference planning because people have to hear about the event in order to attend. The Marketing Coordinator oversees the aspects of the conference that relate to communicating the image and information of the conference to the people.

OVERVIEW

The Marketing Coordinator communicates a positive image to the people attending the conference, helping to motivate them to attend. The more attractive the materials, the more the chance they will be picked up and looked at. Give people enough information so that they can make an informed decision about attending.

Your job is to promote the event positively and establish a consistent image of the conference. Since this covers almost all areas of the conference, you'll be working with almost everybody on the team and getting their information so you can publicize it.

In order to publicize the conference effectively, your job falls into two parts:
1. Setting a strategy
2. Producing marketing materials

STEP-BY-STEP

Because the Marketing Coordinator is involved in so much of the graphic design of the conference, I've also added the task of producing graphics (program handbook, audio-visual design, and signage) to this chapter, although these responsibilities can be assigned to another person. Having these materials fit the "look and feel" of the conference is another way to enhance the image of the conference. At the event, the Marketing Coordinator's main task is to handle signage and banners (*Chapter 18: The Conference*).

After the event, your tasks are summarization of the event, evaluation, and appreciation of those who helped you (*Chapter 19: Wrapping Up*).

PART 1: SETTING A STRATEGY

As you plan, keep foremost the purpose, goals, and theme of the conference. Having a plan allows you to keep to your budget and use your time effectively to get things done on time. An effective plan includes the "W's" of the conference:

The Marketing Coordinator communicates a positive image of the conference to the public by overseeing the establishment of the overall "look and feel" of the conference and producing all marketing- and graphics-related materials.

Recommended skills/qualities

- Marketing or publicity experience
- A good eye for visual design
- Writing ability
- Attention to detail
- Artistic/design ability

Job description

Before the conference

- Attend planning meetings
- Plan and implement marketing strategy
- Oversee production of marketing materials
- Oversee signage and other on-site graphic needs

Night before conference

- Oversee setup of signage and banners

During the conference

- Assist where needed

After the conference

- Compile summary report
- Send notes of appreciation to those who helped in marketing area
- Evaluate conference and suggest improvements for next time

Time Commitment

This position's time commitment is:

1. *Why* market your event?
2. *Who* will you promote to?
3. *What* needs to be publicized?
4. *How* and *where* will you publicize?
5. *When* should everything be accomplished?

1   Why market your event?

Unfortunately, no one has yet found an effective way to get people to come to an event if they don't know about it. You'll need to promote your event in one way or another if you want it to be successful. The more frequently you publicize and the more media you use, the more likely people will hear about the event.

> Businesses use a "Rule of Seven" that says that each person who comes to our event should have heard of it six different times, through a friend, announcement, radio, or a mailing. Few events survive on one mailing. There is too much competition and people are becoming prudent with their time. ◆ *Stephen Macchia*

TIPS FOR SUCCESS

The more people hear about your event, the more likely they will come. It takes time to build awareness and more time for people to decide to attend. That's why it's crucial to market your event!

2   Who will you promote to?

In order to market effectively, you need to know your target market. Who is this conference for? If you were to construct profiles of your potential attendees, what would they look like? What are their demographics, interests, or stage of life? How can you communicate effectively to them and what's the best way to reach them? What's important to them? How can you make it easy for them to respond? What or who influences their decisions?

TIPS FOR SUCCESS

> One of the best ways to publicize a men's event is to talk to women because many of our wives have to give men permission to leave for the weekend. We make sure that the women know about it. Now we have guys come because the wives say, "You should go!" ◆ *Chuck Caswell*

To what groups of people can you target your publicity? The most obvious one is members of your organization. The organization's mailing list is an important tool. To target this group, use a more personal approach such an announcement in your organization's newsletter or a letter sent to them. If your event has been held before, past attendees are another prime group to contact. They came before; they will most likely be interested in coming again. Put this group high on your priority list of potential attendees and frequently remind them about the event.

Ask around for referrals of other people to whom you can send a brochure or contact personally. Your team members or friends will know people. Even the conference speakers may have referrals of people who might be interested in the conference. Ask for contact information of church leaders, media, or people in the field related to your conference.

3   What needs to be publicized?

Obviously, most people won't be interested in details such as how many chairs fit into each meeting room or how many registration packets are needed, so part of your job is to sift through the available information to figure out what people will want to know about the event.

EXAMPLES

List key dates, programs, and benefits of attending. What will help people decide whether they should come or not? Use the *Marketing Information* worksheet on page 176 to track information that needs to be publicized. As you fill out the sheet, ask team members for their input.

MARKETING INFORMATION	Form

Name of event

Date(s)

Location: Facility   City   State

Theme

Organization name

Audience (who should attend)

Program and schedule

Arrival time and location (airport, train station, etc.)

Location: map, directions, details, travel arrangements

Speakers

Workshops/sessions

Benefits of attending

Testimonials

Housing and what's provided

Exhibits

Sponsors

Fee and what it covers

Cancellation/refund policy

Registration form information

Special diet, special needs arrangements

Emergency contact information for attendees to give families

Contact information of Registration Coordinator

What to bring

Artwork needed

Some people prefer general information, but for those who like to know the details before committing, provide more information. If there is no room in the brochure, put it on your Web site.

4 How and where will you publicize?

How you publicize your event will in a large part be determined by how much you can afford. Marketing costs vary greatly, from no-cost to significant financial investment. Those who are in the advertising field will be familiar with the going rates, but if you are not an advertising director, or do not know anyone who handles advertising, you'll have to do some legwork first to find out what you can afford. Call a couple of different competitors (for example, a few local newspapers) to see what their advertising rates are. When you have collected the information, rank your options by value—how effective the method is and how much it will cost.

MONEY SAVERS

Take advantage of all the free methods. Ask for that free listing or exchange a listing in return for a credit byline. These methods are most money-saving—they're free!

Having a creative mind is a great asset to planning publicity for your event. Try to think outside the box for different ways of promoting and drawing attention to your event.

> You have to surprise people. Anything familiar is easily forgotten. It's like television advertising—if my advertising looks like everyone else's, why would you watch it? We always try to come up with something fresh, interesting, new, and interruptive. Publicity starts with something unexpected. I might put a bulletin announcement that says something about how we're going to put an addition to your home. The addition is a husband whose life is changed by the event. ✦ *Chuck Caswell*

WAYS TO PROMOTE CONFERENCE

Word of mouth

Cost: free
Pros: most effective way of promotion
Cons: hit and miss, hard to know who is talking about the event

TIPS FOR SUCCESS

The best and most effective way to promote a conference is by word of mouth. Friends bring friends (since few people enjoy attending a conference by themselves). People trust the opinions of their friends and will be more likely to attend if they hear about the conference in a positive manner.

Have everyone on your team always carry brochures or registration forms with them and tell them always to be ready to talk about the event and to talk about it enthusiastically. Enthusiasm is contagious!

Think of ways that you can leverage the effectiveness of word of mouth. Maybe you can offer a free registration after a certain number of people register—buy ten, get one free. Or offer a prize for the group that registers the most people. Ask people you know to tell other people about the conference. Be creative in taking advantage of this effective means of promotion.

Printed materials

Cost: depends on amount printed. Costs may include fees for design, production (preparing materials for printing), printing and any finishing (stapling, folding, perforating, etc.).
Pros: everything is written in one place and can be referred to easily
Cons: can be expensive to print

Printed materials are a must for every event. The conference brochure is the main tool used for registration (although Web site registrations are gaining in popularity). People will refer to the brochure repeatedly as they consider whether they want to attend. After they register, they will check the brochure again for location and schedule information. Make sure you invest care in the design and planning of the brochure as it will be people's first visual impression of what the conference is about.

Other printed materials add to building awareness about the event. If the details of your event have not yet been finalized, send out an advance postcard to tell people about the upcoming event and ask them to save the date. A postcard is a cost-effective means since it costs less to print and also less to mail. When the brochure is available, do a follow-up mailing.

Printed materials include:

- Brochure
- Flyers
- Letters
- Newsletters
- Postcards
- Posters

Press kit/news release

Cost: printing, assembly
Pros: gets the news out
Cons: you're at the mercy of the media outlet whether they choose to use your news or not

Magazines and news media receive information for news through news releases (also called press releases). A news release for a conference is a short article about the upcoming event. News releases start with an interesting headline, include the five Ws, and end with information on how people can register for the event. Press kits include a news release and other promotional literature such as brochures, flyers, or testimonials from past attendees. For easy handling, stuff them in an attractive folder before mailing. See page 187 for more information on producing press kits.

Mailings

Cost: printing and postage costs; varies depending on complexity of mailing piece and size of mailing list.
Pros: can contact a wide audience
Cons: can be expensive and a low return for money spent

Direct mailings are one way you can inform people about the conference. In the business world, the typical direct mail response is only two to three percent. That means if you mail 100 mailers, expect at the most two or three people to attend your conference as a result of the mailing. However, these statistics are for unsolicited mailings, so if you mail to the people within your organization or people who have attended in the past, then your rate of effectiveness will be much greater.

Brochures (or other mailers, such as postcards) can be mailed to a number of groups:

- The members of your organization
- Past participants
- Referrals
- A mailing list from another organization (either rented or bought). Some organizations provide mailing lists free of charge.

Mailings are most effective when combined with other means of marketing.

> Local pastors help us promote the event. They are the key to making the mailing work. We mail to 2,000 churches. If we get fifty churches that participate, we are fortunate. If you have a connection with the pastor at a church, your event will be perceived as having value. ✦ *Rick Leary*

To maximize your effort, combine mailings with other promotional methods. Remember the Rule of Seven—try to reach your people at least seven different times!

Advertising

Cost: advertising rates vary, from free radio announcements to multi-color advertisements that cost thousands of dollars.
Pros: increases awareness about your event, can reach a bigger market
Cons: can be expensive, may not reach the right audience

Three of the most common media for advertising are:
- Newspapers
- Magazines
- Radio

Advertising in the local paper is usually not effective for Christian conferences. However, if your community has Christian newsletters or radio stations, these may be another way to get the word out about your event. Christian magazines aimed towards your target audience are another good method for advertising your event if it is on a national scale.

Local paper listings

Cost: listings may be free if you put a line in the community calendar
Pros: free
Cons: usually not very effective for Christian conferences.

Though free, don't expect a great response from this method if your newspaper is a local community paper. Your event will be competing with other events and a large part of your audience may never see the small listing.
- Editorials
- Listing on community calendar
- Listing in religious section

Publicity in organization

Cost: free, except for cost of putting together materials for displays
Pros: people are more likely to attend
Cons: may get lost among publicity for other events

Find out about publicity policies your organization might have. Some churches have requirements and deadlines for what can be included in the church bulletin or announced verbally. Plan ahead and ask for the guidelines so you aren't scrambling at the last moment! Here are some forms of publicity within the organization:
- Verbal announcement
- Bulletin announcement
- PowerPoint slide announcement
- Promotional video
- Dramatic sketch

- Display table with brochures or other printed material
- Bulletin board
- Poster
- Personal testimonies

Relationships with other churches

Cost: free; possible cost for giveaways or sending promotional material
Pros: good way for churches to work together
Cons: difficult to cultivate unless you have a key person in the church

- Church liaison
- Pastoral network

Since word of the mouth is the most effective means of publicity, cultivate the relationships that are already developed in other churches if your conference is a community-wide one. If you are able to find one person in each church who would be willing to recruit people to attend the conference, the conference publicity will be so much more effective. The church liaison may either be a volunteer or church staff person. If you can develop a network of pastors, they can help promote the event.

Technology

Cost: Web site registration and development, unless you can piggyback onto your organization's existing Web site
Pros: convenient and accessible
Cons: those who aren't computer savvy are at a disadvantage

- Web site (see page 187 for producing Web sites)
- E-mail lists

With the explosion of Web sites and computers, using technology is another way to communicate to people. An information Web site is a helpful tool to people considering attending your conference. Those who are interested can ask to join an e-mail list where they can receive updates or prayer requests about the conference.

The other part of determining how you will publicize the conference is figuring out who is taking care of what:

RESOURCE TOOLS

- **Do it yourself.** The way of handling marketing preferred by many financially-conscious non-profit organizations is to do the marketing yourself. If someone in your organization has marketing, public relations, or graphic design experience, ask them to volunteer some time in helping. Sometimes there are people with these abilities hidden in your organization and it is just a matter of finding them. Another alternative is using the products of marketing companies that have designed templates that you can customize. For an example, see Outreach Marketing's Web site: www.outreachmarketing.com, 800-911-6011.
- **Use outside sources.** If you have the budget, going to outside sources allows you to work with someone who has experience and industry knowledge of how to market your event effectively.
  - **Graphic designer:** Graphic designers develop a professional image for your publication materials and Web site. They develop a logo that can be used in all applications, building recognizability and uniformity to your event. To find a designer, ask for referrals or check the phone book. Interview them and review their portfolios to find a style that fits what you're looking for.

- **Advertising/marketing agency:** Advertising/marketing agencies help develop an advertising plan that will effectively reach your target market. They handle all aspects of marketing, from concept and design to production and ad placement services. An example of an agency for the Christian market is Manlove Marketing: www.church-marketing.com, 800-825-0845.
- **Mailing houses:** Mailing houses oversee a part of the mailing process or handle the entire job from start to finish. They provide customized mailing lists or only handle the mailing of your brochures using the mailing list that you provide for them. If you are using a mailing house, check their mailing guidelines—some require you to "code" your mailer (put a number on your mailer for identification).

5 When should everything be accomplished?

The key to publicity is to publicize as far in advance as possible, and to promote as often as possible. Set up a timetable of key tasks and when they need to be completed. Since the postal mailing time can be slow and people's schedules tend to book up in advance, don't send the brochure less than two months before the event. Remember to account for bulk mailing schedules—if you want people to receive the brochure two months before the event, allow an additional two or three weeks.

> We try to get our publicity at least a year in advance so that people are scheduling the event ahead of time. People are busy and if you come in with something three months ahead of time, they are already booked. We put out a calendar to let them know about the event. ◆ *Ron Demolar*

PART 2: PRODUCING MARKETING MATERIALS

Once the strategy has been set, begin implementing the plans to carry out the strategy. A major part of this plan is producing the marketing materials to be distributed.

Content

As much as it's important to publicize the information, just presenting facts won't get people to attend. The content of your promotion should be directed and planned. Draw people in and list a course of action for people to follow. Whether you are producing an advertisement, brochure, or promotional video, make sure it does the following:

1 Get their attention. By using an eye-catching visual or an unusual approach, design your materials to stand out among the flood of information that people face every day.

2 Pique their interest. Address needs they have. Why should they attend? How will their problems be addressed?

3 Convince them to come. Don't just list the features ("Ninety-nine workshops available"); instead highlight the benefits ("You'll learn how to be more effective in your ministry!"). Ask the question that your potential audience will have: "What will I get out of this?"

4 Give them an action to take. Tell people to register, call for more information, or save the date.

Keep your audience in mind as you assemble the content. Use words that they can relate to and pictures that interest them. For the workshops descriptions, note the level of experience the workshop is targeted to—those getting started, those who are very seasoned, or something in between.

Logo

Every event should have a designed "logo" or graphic that is a graphic representation of the conference. The logo does not have to be a picture, but can just be type that is set in a visually pleasing format. Plaster the logo everywhere! Put it on the brochure, the letterhead, the postcard, banners, and signage when people first enter. Remind people of the event they are attending. You can never use the logo too often!

MONEY SAVERS

Hire a graphic designer to create the logo since they have training in what is most effective. Or use a design student who can create a logo at a reduced (or even free!) cost. Many students are eager to see their work in print so try to find one who does quality work and who has experience working with printers.

Graphic designers have different styles and you can see examples of their work in their portfolios. As you work with them, develop a logo that fits the theme and mood of the conference. See the following page for examples of conference logos.

CONFERENCE THEME LOGOS	Examples

BUILDING UP THE HOUSE OF GOD

Keys to VICTORIOUS *Living*

EXPERIENCING **H**I**S** PRESENCE WEEKEND RETREAT

Freedom with a Purpose

Brochure

Usually, the brochure is the first impression that people will have of the conference. A visually-pleasing, well-designed, and well-printed brochure goes a long way towards promoting a positive image of the conference. But be aware that a brochure that is too slick might work against you—if you have a small retreat, putting together a full-color, glossy brochure is overkill and inappropriate for the type of event you are having. Make sure the appearance matches the event and audience.

Pictures are an effective tool for promotion. Target your audience by using photos that will attract them. If you are doing a high school retreat, use pictures with action because kids want to be active. Use more relational pictures for senior citizens, such as pictures of seniors around a table or interacting or playing table games. The audience will see it and decide that is what they want to do on a weekend. Be sure to use quality photos, though. It's better to use no photo at all, than to use one that is blurry, over- or underexposed, or that shows people in an unflattering manner!

Content

The registration brochure is both an information-dispensing and information-gathering tool, the brochure informs readers of conference facts as well as collects information on the registration form. A brochure that includes details of the conference helps people make an intelligent decision about whether to attend or not. You can use the information on your *Marketing Information* form (page 176) to make sure that it has all the information.

The amount of information you include depends on the purpose of the marketing piece. Since a poster's purpose is to attract attention and build curiosity about the event, a poster has minimal information—such as the date, theme, location, and speakers. A brochure includes more details.

Spend some time developing the text, too. Some guidelines for effective writing include:
- Use "you" instead of "we" to make it more personal to the reader.
- Use an active rather than a passive voice. Active voices use verbs that show action, instead of passive verbs like "to be." For example, use: "You'll learn practical truths from the Bible," instead of: "Practical truths from the Bible will be learned."
- Be enthusiastic! Write with energy and from a positive point of view.
- Emphasize benefits rather than features.
- Use bullet points for easier reading.
- Use testimonials.

The Registration Coordinator should give you the information needed for the registration form. Assemble the information into a logical, easy-to-fill out design:
- Only collect information needed for the conference. This is not a survey!
- If the form will be faxed or copied, avoid screens (grey areas), very small print, and leave adequate margins so the edges don't get cut off on the fax or copier.
- Don't use a font that is too small and hard to read, especially if your audience is older.
- Try to use checkboxes or circling to avoid illegible handwriting.
- Don't put important information on the other side of the form since the form may be mailed in.
- Test your form when it's done. Fill out the form yourself and then ask your friends to fill it out. Then fax one to yourself. Show it to as many people as possible and ask them to fill one out.

Design

An effective design draws the reader's attention so that the information can be communicated. Whether you are creating the brochure yourself or recruiting a designer to take care of it, it's helpful to know design basics so you know how to put together an effective design. A brochure full of tiny type crammed into a small space is not a good way to get people to read and find out more about your conference! Likewise, the design of the brochure should fit the style and message of the conference. If you're having an event that is lighthearted and fun, a design that looks serious and heavy would do your conference injustice and mislead people about the program. Put together a brochure that is eye-catching and helps give the information needed for the reader to decide. An effective design uses these elements:

- **Format.** Find out from the post office first if there are certain regulations you should follow. If you're mailing a piece, a brochure that is square will cost more than a rectangular piece that fits the proportions set by the postal service. Consider the pros and cons of the different formats. A self-mailer brochure (one that has a panel where you can put an address and postage) may also help you save on cost because you do not need to buy additional envelopes. However, you have one less panel to use, and the brochure may more easily be damaged since it is not protected by the envelope. Discuss with your designer what format is most effective for your event.

  Types of brochure formats using standard paper sizes include:
  - 8.5x11 booklet (11x17 folded in half)
  - 8.5x11 folded twice (a sheet of paper folded into three panels)
  - 11x4.25 booklet (an 8.5x11 sheet folded lengthwise)
  - 8.5x11 size folded twice (producing three panels)
  - gatefold (a sheet of paper folded twice so that the edges meet in the middle)

CONFERENCE BROCHURE FORMATS	Examples

Conference programs using standard paper sizes (left to right): 8.5x14 (legal size) folded twice, 22x17 poster with brochure information on back folded into six panels, 11x17 (tabloid size) folded into four panels.

If your budget allows it, you can experiment with different formats and sizes. Brochures can be made into booklets or posters, and come in every shape and size.

Stay with standard paper sizes to save costs. Using odd shapes or nonstandard sizes may bring up prices or waste paper. Consult your printer to see what they recommend.

MONEY SAVERS

- **Color.** Colors send different messages. Yellow is a bright cheery color, whereas grey may be subdued, peaceful, or even depressing. Think about the message that your color is sending so that it fits the purpose of the conference. Don't use a color just because it's your favorite color; if you like pink, it won't be very appropriate for a men's retreat brochure!

Color is memorable and is an effective tool for building recognition. Think of corporations who have used color for instant recognition: IBM blue, McDonald's red and yellow, Unocal orange, and so on. Using a consistent color in your materials will help people remember your event. Messages that color send:

- Red: exciting, outgoing, passionate
- Yellow: energetic, warm, fun
- Green: natural, fertile
- Blue: peaceful, tranquil
- Purple: royal
- White: pure
- Black: elegant, mysterious
- Grey: stable, conservative

MONEY SAVERS

The more ink colors your brochure uses, the more expensive it will be. Sometimes designs created in one or two colors can be just as effective as full-color designs. You can use colored paper as ink color, too, or even mix two ink colors to create a third. If you are short on finances, spend less money on color and use color on your Web site.

- **Typography.** Even typefaces send messages. Letters that are big and bold convey strength; thin, curvy letters show elegance or artistry. Use a minimum of typefaces in the design because many typefaces confuse the eye and appear too busy. Use simple fonts. Consider your audience too. The older your audience, the larger the type should be. Only use blue or black type since it is most legible.
- **Photographs/illustrations.** Use high-quality artwork. The quality of your artwork adds significantly to how professional your brochure looks. Stock photographs may be obtained from agencies or royalty-free CDs.
- **Paper.** Paper comes in coated (glossy) or uncoated (dull) finishes. If you are using full color photographs, coated paper makes your pictures sharp and bright. Papers are available in all sorts of colors and textures and differing quality. Using colored paper makes your brochure look like it is printed in more than one color.
- **Printing effects.** A reverse is created when the background is the darker color of the ink and the text is the color of the paper. Blue ink printed on white paper shows as white type and the blue ink is the background. Avoid using reverses for large blocks of text because it is difficult to read. Screening is another type of printing effect that uses blocks of color that are greyed behind the text. If you want to color the background, use screening instead of reverses—screens print more clearly and consistently than solids.

Printing

As technology becomes more affordable, a printer that used to cost tens of thousands of dollars can be put on your desk for a couple of hundred dollars or less, expanding your options. The type of printing you use depends on the size of your event and how much you want to spend. If you have a small retreat of only fifty people, it's not cost-effective to print a full-color brochure at a commercial printer's. Here are options for printing marketing materials:

- **Inkjet printers.** Prices have come down significantly on inkjet printers. However, the consumables, such as ink, are still quite expensive. For this reason, using an inkjet printer is a great way to produce a small quantity of brochures and you'll get a brochure that is in full color, too. For best results, use paper specifically for inkjet printers—regular paper tends to soak up the ink and make the color dull. Inkjet printing is best used for small quantities, such as less than fifty brochures.

- **Laser printers.** For larger quantities of brochures, laser printers are more cost-effective than inkjet printing. Laser printing provides crisp text and images. They are great for printing originals and then making duplicates on the copier, which tend to have lower prices per copy. Laser printers are best used for small quantities such as less than fifty brochures.

- **Black and white copiers.** Probably the most commonly used form of printing for most churches, copies are quite reasonable in price when printed in large quantities, sometimes only pennies per page. They make clean copies with fine resolution. However, copiers have certain limitations: the printed image may shift from page to page, the toner may lift if left touching plastic, and you must leave a margin around all the edges of the page.

- **RISOgraph or mimeographed printing.** Risograph printers are similar to mimeograph printers—they make a master template which is used to print the copies. The master may cost thirty cents or so but then after that each copy only costs a penny. The result looks like a printed piece. However, the resolution is limited so you can't get as fine an image as you can on a laserprinter, and the image can also shift from page to page. The advantage is the piece looks like it is offset printed and there is no toner that can stick to other copies or to plastic.

- **Color laser printers.** Color laser printers can be a less-expensive option than offset full-color printing if you are fortunate enough to have one at your organization. The cost of a color print's consumables is about ten cents per copy, but if you go to a copy shop you are charged about a dollar per page.

- **Offset printing.** Commercial printers can take your original and create offset printing. Offset printing is the type of printing that is typically used for business letterhead and business cards. Offset printing gives a high-quality result. However, it's not a good choice for small jobs since most of the cost goes into labor and setting up the press.

- **Process color printing.** Full-color printing is called process color printing. It uses the four process colors (cyan, magenta, yellow, and black) to produce all the colors of the rainbow. Process color printing is expensive since a plate is made for each color, there is a lot of setup time, and the equipment is very expensive and run by trained operators. However, if you are printing tens of thousands of copies, process color is the way to go since it churns out incredible amounts of printing in a very short time.

If you choose to go to a commercial printer, call printers for estimates first. Since prices can vary considerably, call several printers to see what the range is. Don't just decide by cost alone—try to find a printer that specializes in printing jobs similar to yours. Some printers specialize in small runs and orders; others may print hundreds of thousands of brochures at a time. Some charge extra for colors and others include it as standard in the pricing. If you are doing a full color brochure, going to a printer that specializes in one- or two-color printing will be expensive and the quality may be questionable. Call around and find out what is available.

MONEY SAVERS

Printers may print five percent over or under the amount you request (called an "overrun" and "underrun"); this is an industry standard. Allow for this amount in your calculations.

Printers charge for materials as well as labor. That's why it is more cost-effective to print all your pieces at once, since it saves on the time required to set up the press and mix the colors. If you can print the brochure, postcards, letterhead, and other materials at the same time, you will save significantly more over printing each item at a different time.

Cost is determined by size, quantity, paper quality, number of ink colors, whether the design bleeds (goes off the edges), how large the solid areas are, how you provide the artwork to them (whether it is ready for printing or needs extra work). Other ways you can save on cost with printers include:

- Check if they have price breaks at certain quantities. Printing 1000 pieces may be the same price as printing 750.
- Combine two colors to make a third.
- Use colored paper as an additional color.
- Ask what other jobs are being printed and use the same color as the other job.
- Ask for "house" paper—paper that the printer has in stock, so they don't have to order more costly paper.

Before you send your artwork to the printer, be sure to carefully proofread your work! Have someone else proof it—the more people, the better (but not too many so that your schedule slips!). Catch all the errors before going to print, because changing anything after going to print is much more expensive.

Once you submit your final artwork to the printer, the printer will put together a sample of what will be printed, called a proof. They will ask you to review the proof and approve it. Once you sign off on the proof, all additional changes are your responsibility financially. If you make corrections, ask for a second proof to make sure that the changes have been made correctly.

The standard turnaround for printing is two to three weeks; jobs that are more complex may take longer. If you need the piece earlier, you may have to pay rush charges. Getting started early and planning ahead helps avoid any additional charges.

News release/press kit

A news release may be as simple as a typed sheet of paper which is faxed to the local paper, or an entire folder or kit that has multiple pages and examples of brochures and other material. If you have a big event, send the kit out a month before the end of registration. Provide all the pertinent information: the who, what, when, where, how, and why of the conference. After you send the information, follow up—sometimes multiple times!

Web site

Web sites are becoming more effective at promoting conference events. They are a great way of informing people of the latest information; often people will hear of an event and then check the Web site for more information. Another advantage is that people who otherwise might not hear about your event may find your site by looking on search engines.

The opening page of your Web site should be attractive and attention-getting. Present the information clearly, with the purpose, dates, who the event is for, and the benefits of attending. The purpose of the first page is to pique interest so that people will click for further information.

A Web site is a great location to post detailed brochure and registration information. If you can, set up online registration so that people can register directly—this saves you time and paperwork. If your Web site is not set up to take online registrations, there are online registration services available that will process your registrations for a fee.

Here are some ways to make your Web site more effective:

- Avoid graphic-intensive pages which take a long time to load for people who use a modem.

- Make your Web site secure and print your privacy policy so people can register with confidence.
- Give people choices; let them decide whether they want to receive a newsletter or only information related to the conference. People will be assured that they won't get blasted by millions of e-mail messages.
- Make your Web site comprehensive: put schedules, directions, benefits of attending, and anything else that would inform and encourage people to come.
- Set up an automatic e-mail response for online registrations.
- Take advantages of links. Provide convenient links to housing, transportation/travel agent, and city sites.

Set up an e-mail account for the conference so that all questions will be directed to one place. Be sure to check the e-mail regularly!

ON-SITE GRAPHICS

Up until now we have dealt with promotional materials that are distributed before the conference. However, once people arrive at the conference, the graphics at the event should maintain a visual consistency. Whether printed materials, on-site banners and signage, be sure that everything is consistent in style and tone. Here are different areas of on-site graphics to check:
- Conference program
- Audiovisual design
- Signage (Banner, welcome sign, registration materials)
- Stage sets

Conference program

The conference program can vary from a single sheet of paper with the schedule and information, or a multi-page, bound book that has evaluation forms, space for taking notes, and advertisements. Some conferences bind all the sheets needed (speaker biographies, evaluations, schedules) in one book for convenience. Conference handbooks contain the following information:
- Schedule
- Map

PROGRAM MATERIALS	Examples

Programs come in an infinite variety of formats (clockwise from left): 8.5x5.5 booklet (Fremont Evangelical Free Church), 9x12 binder with plastic insert to hold audio cassette tapes (North Coast Church), 9x12 envelope that functions like a folder (Willowcreek Association), spiral-bound 8.5x11 notebook with tabbed dividers (Hawaiian Island Ministries).

Programs used with permission.

- Welcome note from director
- Speaker bios
- Speaker notes
- Recreational activity information
- Sponsor information
- Local information

Work with the speaker coordinator to solicit the speakers early for their outlines and biographical information to include in the program. Set a deadline and follow up often if they do not respond.

> People tell us that the notebook is one of the most valuable things they get at the conference, because it has everything. It has the nuts and bolts of where to go, speaker profiles, and profiles of exhibitors. We put our evaluations in and people just tear one out. It's a tool that evolved over the years so that we use what works best. ◆ *Pam Chun*

Audiovisual design

Audiovisual design includes projection slides, videos made for the event, overheads, or other graphics that are projected. Some simple design rules should be kept in mind when creating visuals.

- **Typography:** A common mistake made with slides is using too much text on one slide. Approach slide design from the perspective of the person sitting in the back row. Will they be able to see the letters clearly? Don't use more than six words per lines or six lines per slide. If you are making an overhead, put it on the floor and stand over it. If you can't see what the type is saying, then it's too small and should be made larger. Be sure your type contrasts with the background so people can read it clearly.
- **Colors:** Use a few, simple colors. Colors convey emotions and moods, too. If you are having an upbeat, encouraging event, don't use only dark grey and maroon on all your visuals—it will have a depressing effect. Also, don't overdo using colors; the human eye can only process only so much information at once. Using lime green, orange, yellow, brown, blue, and fuschia as text colors in one slide will cause confusion and possible motion sickness. Using two or three colors is usually more effective than going through the colors of the rainbow.
- **Artwork:** Keep the artwork or photographs simple. Watch that the background doesn't clash with the artwork. Photographs with neutral or simple backgrounds are most effective. Avoid mixing drawings and photographs on the same slide. Limiting art or photographic elements to one or two on a slide is usually more than enough.
- **Transitions:** Some slide or video editing programs have a lot of neat effects and you may be tempted to try a different transition for each slide. Don't! If you watch the transitions they make on TV or in movies, you'll see that they are usually just simple cuts used at strategic times. Don't let the graphics or transitions be distracting—you want your audience to concentrate on what the speaker is saying, not think, "Wow, what a cool transition!"

Signage/banners

Signage is another area that is often missed. Posting clear signs at every hallway intersection or stairway helps attendees find their way with minimal confusion. Use the same lettering on all signs and the same background color. This makes the signage instantly recognizable. Most facilities will already have signage in place, but it's helpful to walk through and supplement the signs with additional ones if necessary.

Work with the Site Coordinator to determine what signage is needed. Some teams may prefer to have the Site Coordinator handle the signage requirements.

Consider making a generic sign that can be used over for workshops or sessions. Add a name plate on the bottom to customize it for the different speakers. Then it is simple to update the signage since it only takes a few seconds to change the plate.

Types of signage include:
- A large banner to welcome attendees
- Parking
- Registration area
- Sessions/workshops
- Directional
- Exposition
- Restrooms

Some tips for effective signage:
- **Keep it simple.** Eliminate *the, a, please, thank you.* Avoid punctuation. Make it short. Include only necessary information. There's no need to say "Wednesday January 10" if your conference is only being held one Wednesday. Shorten times; use "10 am" instead of "10:00 am."
- **Don't use all caps.** Lower case letters are easier to recognize and read, and using all uppercase letters is an indication of shouting to e-mail savvy readers.
- **Make all signs consistent.** Keep the same order for all signs. If you decide to list the topic first, the time next, and the location last, do so for all the signs.

EXAMPLES

Drawing a map of where the signage can be posted will simplify the process when you arrive on site and begin posting. See pages 191-192 for a sample *Signage Map* and *Signage List* of where signage was placed at one of our conferences.

Signage can be simple sheets printed off your computer printer, or big banners that are made at a signage company. Check the yellow pages for such companies in your area. If you are using a company, ask for bids from different ones so you can compare prices.

FINALIZING ARRANGEMENTS

The month before the conference, double-check any preparations that need to be made. Ask the Volunteer Coordinator to arrange for volunteers to help post signage. Schedule the delivery of the conference programs to the Registration Coordinator to put in the welcome packets. If there are any other arrangements that need to be made, take care of them as soon as possible.

SIGNAGE MAP

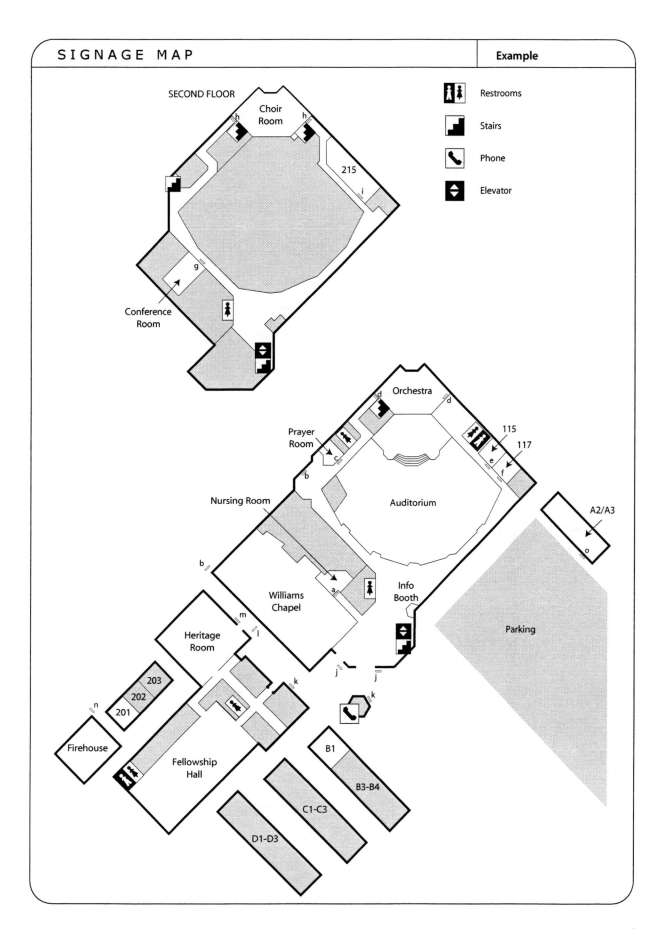

SECOND FLOOR

Choir Room

215

Conference Room

Restrooms

Stairs

Phone

Elevator

Orchestra

Prayer Room

115

117

Nursing Room

Auditorium

A2/A3

Williams Chapel

Info Booth

Parking

Heritage Room

203
202
201

Firehouse

Fellowship Hall

B1

B3-B4

C1-C3

D1-D3

SIGNAGE LIST					Example

Area	Qty	Map	Arrow pointing to	Description	Notes
Nursing room	1	a	door	Nursing Room	
Down window	1	b	right (in window)	Registration	
				Please Use Courtyard Entrance	
Prayer room	1	c	door	Prayer Room	
Orchestra	1	d	door	Workshop: Special Needs/Conflict	
Rm 115	1	e	right up	Rm 115	
Rm 117	1	f	door	Rm 117	
Conference room	1	g	door	Workshop: Teens/Prayer	
Choir room	1	h	door	Workshop: Aging Parents/Workplace/Parenting	
Rm 215	1	i	door	Workshop: Women's Ministry	
Outside	1	j	left	Registration	
Outside	2	k	right	Registration	
Outside	2	l	up (Hanging 2-sided)	Registration	
Heritage room	1	m	door	Workshop: Mentoring Women	
Firehouse	1	n	door	Workshop: Brokenness	
A2/A3	1	o	door	Workshop: Got Christ?/Worship	
Inside	9			Women's restrooms	Various locations
Inside	2			Men's restrooms	One downstairs
					One in fellowship hall
Outside	5			No Food Allowed In Sanctuary	On sanctuary doors
Outside	2			Fellowship Hall →	In patio, sanctuary
	3			Fellowship Hall ←	
Sanctuary	1			Workshop: Christian Courtship	
	1			Workshop: Education Choices	
	1			Workshop: Grief/Loss	
Information	2			Information	Hang from ceiling
Registration	2			TABLE #1 Walk-In	
	4			TABLE #2 NameTags	
	1			TABLE #3 Conference Staff & Volunteers	
	1			TABLE #4 Handbooks /Packets	
	1			TABLE #5 Questions	
Food	4			Water	
	8			Coffee	
	4			Tea	
	8			Juice	
	2			Vegetarian	
	4			Trash	
	3			Lunch →	
Lobby	1			Tape Orders	
	1			Guest musician CDs	
	1			Information	
Workshops	30			5 minutes	One per workshop, 1 emcee
	30			1 minute	One per workshop, 1 emcee
Pews	1			Reserved For Speakers/Worship Team	

C H A P T E R

17 | **VOLUNTEERS**

Every Christian conference uses a good number of volunteers, and some events are entirely volunteer-run. Therefore a key to a successful event is managing volunteers for maximum productivity and efficiency. God made people with different gifts and abilities and it's an awesome thing to see everyone working together in areas that they enjoy and being more effective together than when they are alone.

> The difference between a good event and a great event is the volunteers you get.
> ✦ *Doug Yonamine*

OVERVIEW

STEP-BY-STEP

The Volunteer Coordinator oversees the volunteers who serve in every area of the conference. Initially, you get an idea of what will be happening in the conference as the planning team coordinates the plans. Since you will be helping to provide and coordinate volunteers for all areas, it's important for you to be knowledgeable about what will be happening and where volunteers will be needed.

Your responsibilities include:
1. Determining volunteer needs
2. Recruiting volunteers
3. Assigning volunteers
4. Making arrangements
5. Preparing training
6. Interacting with volunteers

At the conference, you'll check in the volunteers and direct them throughout the day (see *Chapter 18: The Conference*).

After the conference, your tasks are summarizing, evaluating, and expressing appreciation to the volunteers (see *Chapter 19: Wrapping Up*).

DETERMINING VOLUNTEER NEEDS

EXAMPLES

About halfway through the conference planning process, the other coordinators will have a better idea of what volunteers are needed. Get an initial list from them of what positions are needed and how many are needed for each position.

Use the *Volunteers Needed* worksheet on the page 195 to list the volunteers needed for your conference. The total at the bottom is the number of volunteers that will need to be recruited for the job.

The Volunteer Coordinator recruits volunteers and organizes them into carrying out tasks.

Recommended Skills/Qualities

- Administrative skills
- Able to function under pressure and make decisions
- Team builder and good people skills
- Attention to detail
- Able to delegate responsibilities and follow-up on task delegation

Job Description

Before the conference

- Attend planning meetings
- Work with conference staff to determine volunteer needs
- Recruit volunteers and keep records
- Assign volunteers to positions
- Make arrangements for volunteers
- Prepare volunteer training

Night before conference

- Coordinate volunteers to set up signage, tables, and chairs

During the conference

- Check-in, orient and train volunteers
- Direct and assist volunteers
- Redistribute or reassign volunteers as needed

After the conference

- Update volunteer job descriptions for next year
- Compile summary report
- Send notes of appreciation to technical operators and helpers
- Evaluate conference and suggest improvements for next time

Time Commitment

This position's time commitment is:

VOLUNTEERS NEEDED | Worksheet

Number needed

Setup

Before conference set up signage, decorations, tables, chairs, and stage.

Greeters

(Outside building) Greet people as they arrive. Help direct people to registration area. Provide assistance.

Ushers

(Inside building) Greet people and pass out programs. Be sure attendees have name badges. Provide assistance to people with directions and questions about the facility. Help seat latecomers, and collect offering and evaluation forms.

Information

Assist people who need directions, information or any assistance. Take messages and post them on the bulletin board.

Sales crew

Assist in selling merchandise items.

Registration

Register people as they arrive. Check in people who have already registered and direct them to the correct location. Help check in speakers, volunteers and conference staff.

Speaker Hosts

Help speakers feel welcome and assist them with any needs.

Workshop Hosts

Assist workshop speakers with any needs. Adjust environmental controls if room is too hot or too cold. Help seat latecomers. Record workshop on tape. Keep time for workshop speaker. Return supplies to Information Booth.

Prayer Intercessors

Pray for the conference while it is in sessions, provide prayer ministry time for conference participants.

Technical team

Assist Equipment Coordinator in setting up and operating sound, lighting and video equipment. May need to attend rehearsal the night before the conference. Take down and return equipment after the conference.

Transportation

Direct attendees towards transportation, help drive buses, assist attendees with ground and air transportation.

Photographer/videographer

Help take photographs or videos during the conference.

Food crew

Assist caterer and Hospitality Coordinator in preparing and serving food.

TOTAL VOLUNTEERS NEEDED

After the volunteers have been listed, write a job description for each position with the following information:
- Person to whom they report
- Schedule for when volunteers are needed at the event
- Amount of time expected for the position
- Responsibilities. Be specific about what they will need to do so they know what they are getting into. List responsibilities before, during, and after the conference.
- Volunteer Coordinator's contact information

You may also need to recruit volunteers for any tasks that must be done before or after the conference. Pre-conference tasks might include database entry or stuffing welcome packets. Post-conference jobs are returning rental equipment or entering evaluation information.

EXAMPLES

Beginning on the page 197 are some sample *Volunteer Job Descriptions* that are given to potential volunteers considering the positions.

RECRUITING VOLUNTEERS

After you have compiled the list, it's time to start recruiting! Having a system in place will streamline the process.

Qualifications

What kind of people should you look for? The ideal volunteer has a good mix of gifts, personality, and passion that fits the job. As you recruit volunteers, look at what their working styles are. What kind of job would be a good fit for how they work? Look for people who are willing and capable and who have been proven in their abilities, especially for the leadership positions.

> Don't look for new folks; look for people who are already invested in their ministries. Empower and develop the people that you have and they get excited and bring people that they serve with or are good friends with because they want the right people under them. Empower and develop existing volunteers. It's about challenging them, sometimes developing them, and giving them the authority to make decisions to walk alongside you. ✦ *Terry Toro*

Sources

Volunteers can come from many sources:
- Ask the planning team to recommend people they might know.
- Ask people at your church.
- Ask friends.
- Put an announcement in the bulletin.
- If the event involves more than one church, check other church contacts for recommendations or ask them to get the word out that volunteers are needed. Give them guidelines of what you are looking for.

Recruiting

Begin by recruiting leaders and then have the leaders recruit their own volunteers. This allows the leaders to work with people they know and are comfortable with.

> The key to approaching volunteers is saying, "The reason I thought of you for this role is because you have these gifts and these experiences." Not, "Twenty-eight people have turned me down and you are the twenty-ninth." Help them feel that this has been intentional and prayerful. Say, "This is the unique thing about you, that I feel you would be great on the team. Here's the value you are to our organization." It's win-win. You sell them on what that life experience is going to mean to them and the people they will meet. ✦ *John Pearson*

House Manager

Reports to at conference: Volunteer Coordinator

Times needed: Saturday, March 1 • 8 am-5pm

Responsibilities:
- Oversees volunteers in greeting, ushering, and information table areas.
- Assists greeters and ushers in their tasks.
- Reassigns volunteers to another area if an area is short of volunteers.
- During the day, help people needing assistance.

Contact: John Jones, Volunteer Coordinator, 111-2222.

Greeter

Reports to at conference: House Manager

Times needed: Saturday, March 1
Morning registration: 8 am - 9:15
Morning break time: 10:15 - 10:45
Lunch time: 12:00-1:00
Afternoon break time: 3:00-3:30
May sign up for one or multiple shifts.

Responsibilities:
- Greets and directs arrivals to registration area.
- During day, help people needing assistance.
- Be ready a few minutes before the end of the sessions to help people needing directions to other parts of the facility.

Contact: John Jones, Volunteer Coordinator, 111-2222.

Usher

Reports to at conference: House Manager

Times needed: Saturday, March 1
Morning registration: 8 am - 9:15
Morning break time: 10:15 - 10:45
Lunch time: 12:00-1:00
Afternoon break time: 3:00-3:30
May sign up for one or multiple shifts.

Responsibilities:
- Greets people as they enter main meeting room.
- Assist with late seating and those needing assistance.
- Help collect offering.
- During day, help people needing assistance.
- Be ready a few minutes before the end of the sessions to help people needing directions to other parts of the facility.

Contact: John Jones, Volunteer Coordinator, 111-2222.

Setup Manager

Reports to at conference: Volunteer Coordinator

Times needed:

Friday, April 30, 6pm - 9pm.	General facility setup
Saturday, March 1	Registration area: 7:30 am - 8 am
	Morning break: 9:45 - 10:15 am
	Lunch: 10:45 - 11:45
	Afternoon break time: 1:00 - 2:45
	Break down eating area: 3:30-4:30
	Break down stage: 5:00-6:00

May sign up for one or multiple shifts.

Responsibilities:

- Assists Volunteer Coordinator in overseeing setup of different areas the night before the conference.
- During the conference, oversees setup and breakdown of eating areas.
- Help break down stage area after conference is over.

Contact: John Jones, Volunteer Coordinator, 111-2222.

Setup Crew

Reports to at conference: Setup Manager

Times needed:

Friday, April 30, 6pm - 9pm.	General facility setup
Saturday, March 1	Registration area: 7:30 am - 8 am
	Morning break: 9:45 - 10:15 am
	Lunch: 10:45 - 11:45
	Afternoon break time: 1:00 - 2:45
	Breakdown eating area: 3:30-4:30
	Breakdown stage: 5:00-6:00

May sign up for one or multiple shifts.

Responsibilities:

- The night before conference help put up signage, set up stage, workshops, exhibit hall, eating areas, and registration area.
- Assist Volunteer Coordinator in overseeing setup of different areas the night before the conference.
- During the conference, oversees setup and breakdown of eating areas.
- Help break down stage area after conference is over.

Contact: John Jones, Volunteer Coordinator, 111-2222.

Sales Table

Reports to at conference: Volunteer Coordinator

Times needed:

Saturday, March 1	Before conference: 8:30 am - 9am
	Morning break: 10:15-10:45 am
	Lunch: 12:00-1:00
	Afternoon break time: 3:00-3:30
	After conference: 5:00-6:00

May sign up for one or multiple shifts.

Responsibilities:

- Help sell merchandise.

Contact: John Jones, Volunteer Coordinator, 111-2222.

If you make the initial request through a phone call, follow up the request in writing. Send a letter with details, job description sheet, application form, and a commitment form. Spell out as many details as possible. Let them know what expenses are covered and what they will have to pay or provide, such as if the conference fees or their travel costs are covered.

EXAMPLES

For larger events where you may be working with unknown people, a screening process may be necessary. Give each volunteer a *Volunteer Application* form to fill out (page 200).

As the applications are processed, inform people of their final status. Try to select a wide range of volunteers, varying in age, ethnicity, and geographical location. For those who are accepted, confirm that they are still interested.

ASSIGNING VOLUNTEERS

Tell the planning team members not to try to do everything themselves at the conference! Remember to delegate, delegate, delegate. Focus on tasks only you can do. Volunteers are stepping forward because they want to help, so take advantage of it!

EXAMPLES

As volunteers sign up, keep their information in a spreadsheet. Use the *Volunteer Information* form on page 201 or create your own spreadsheet.

Break down the volunteers into manageable units. If you have 100 volunteers, don't have them report to you for everything. Assign leaders to oversee groups and concentrate your time on working with the leaders. Have a House Manager oversee ushers, greeters, and information booth; or a Workshop Manager to oversee the different workshop hosts. It's helpful to create a chart of how many volunteers are needed in each area and what time slots are available so you can get a big picture of where volunteers should be. See the sample *Volunteer Needs Schedule* on page 204.

EXAMPLES

Begin assigning people to different areas according to their abilities and interests. As you make assignments, assign them by blocks of time rather than for the whole day and include breaks and rest time. Make sure the work is varied so they don't get bored. Try to balance your volunteers' desires to have a good time and to feel productive, but not get burned out or overwhelmed by too much work.

If you have the opportunity, a great way to assign volunteers is to set them all on doing a group task. See who seems to be the natural leaders and delegate larger responsibilities to them. Observe what strengths people have and make assignments afterwards.

Match responsible people with key areas. For example, you need a responsible volunteer to oversee the registration area since it is one of the first impressions delegates will have at the conference. You need to know that your volunteer will show up on time and be there! If you are able, assign leadership positions to volunteers who have worked at the event two or three years. Because of their experience, they are better able to direct other volunteers who may be new to the event.

Don't insult a volunteer by giving them something too easy. Stretch them in an area that they want to be stretched. Some volunteers are looking for significant responsibility and opportunity.

When Doug Yonamine coordinated the logistics for Willowcreek Management Association conferences, he learned how to give volunteers significant responsibility. Jim and Bob first started volunteering and Doug assigned them simple tasks such as posting signage, counting attendance, and moving boxes. Later it became clear that they had many more gifts and wanted to do more. In the end, Doug assigned Jim one half of the

VOLUNTEER APPLICATION	Form

Name ☐ Male ☐ Female

Address

City   State   Zip code

Phone (W)   (H)

Best time to call   E-mail

Church

City where church is located

Emergency contact name   Phone

Dates and times available

Gifts/abilities, any special positions desired

Do you have a personal relationship with Jesus Christ? (Please explain)

Have you attended this conference before?   ☐ Yes   ☐ No   If yes, when?

In what capacity?   ☐ Attendee   ☐ Volunteer   ☐ Other:

References (18 years or older, no relatives, please)

Name   Phone

Name   Phone

Name   Phone

Office Use Only

Date received application

Date interviewed

Reference check dates: 1.   2.   3.

☐ Accepted   ☐ Denied (explain):

Date contacted with results

Volunteer position placed

Times

Comments

Sent: ☐ Confirmation letter   ☐ Evaluation form

VOLUNTEER INFORMATION Form

Status		Last Name	First Name / City, Zip	Address / E-mail	Phone / City	Church	Comments	Time Available	Assignment
App. Rcvd	Ref. Chkd	Approved	Assigned							

App. Rcvd	Ref. Chkd	Approved	Assigned	Last Name	First Name / City, Zip	Address / E-mail	Phone / City	Church	Comments	Time Available	Assignment
x	x	x	x	Johnson	Dave	123 Main Street / Main City, CA 94555	(510) 111-2233 / davej@example.com	Community Church / Main City	High recommended by references	All day	House Manager

©2003 *The Christian Conference Planner*, by Angela Yee.

building and Bob the other half and they made sure everything ran smoothly. Often they didn't even call Doug and directly called the person who could fix the problem, saving Doug a lot of work!

MAKING ARRANGEMENTS

The month before the conference, work with the the other team members to oversee the preparations for your volunteers.

- Work with the Hospitality Coordinator to provide drinks, snacks, and meals for the volunteers. If volunteers are coming the night before the conference to help setup, provide a dinner for them, especially if they are coming directly after work.
- Develop any special name badges for the volunteers with the Registration Coordinator or make your own nametags.
- Work with the Site Coordinator to assign a lounge where volunteers can go for their breaks.
- Ask the Program Manager for any final details that the volunteers should be aware of.

Prepare other items that volunteers will need. If they will wear the same clothing, order the shirts or uniforms needed. Decide how you will orient and train the volunteers and put together any training materials needed.

Information packet

Assemble a packet of information to be given to the volunteers when they arrive at the event:

EXAMPLES

- Program and schedules
- Map of facility
- Times, locations of sessions
- Instruction sheets of their responsibilities (see sample *Volunteer Instructions* on page 203)
- Timetable of who will be doing what
- Name badges

PREPARING TRAINING

Training can be held on-site when volunteers arrive. Or, if tasks are more complex, you may hold training ahead of time.

Put together a training plan for your volunteers. Ask volunteers to arrive early to meet you for orientation, training, and prayer. If possible, do the training the day before. Gather the volunteers and give them an overview and orientation for the day. Give clear guidelines and make the briefing fun.

Familiarize them with the facility as well as the program. Show them where they will be going.

Clearly give instructions on what needs to be done. Inform them who is responsible for what and who they report to. If volunteers will need to make decisions, make sure that they have what they need to make an informed decision and that they are given the authority to make decisions.

Give safety guidelines and go over contingency plans in case something goes wrong.

Pass out their name badges.

Be ready for no-show volunteers! Whether due to transportation issues, illness, or just sheer forgetfulness, sometimes volunteers will not arrive. Have a back-up plan in case all the volunteers do not show up. If short of people, you

GREETER

Instructions

Look over the facility map carefully to be familiar with the locations of key areas such as meeting rooms, workshop rooms, information booth, restrooms, and the eating area. Carry the map with you throughout the day.

In the morning, greet all arrivals with a smile. Direct them to the registration area. Breakfast is available in the fellowship hall.

As people are leaving the registration area and entering the main meeting room, make sure they have a name badge. If they do not, send them to the registration area to register. If they have already registered, remind them politely to put on their name badges.

During the day, assist anyone who has questions, needs directions, or information. If you are unsure of the answer, direct the person to the information booth.

Be ready a few minutes before the program is over to help people with directions or questions.

Lunch/Breaks

A volunteer break room is available in Room 100. Between periods that you are needed, please feel free to use this room. Lunch will be served at 1:00 in the dining area.

Dress Code

Business casual.

Report to

Dave Johnson, House Manager. If you need to reach him, go to the Information booth and ask them to contact him via walkie-talkie.

Contact Information

Medical emergencies: Call the information booth immediately. Medical personnel is on call.

Facility address and phone number:

This conference would not be possible without your service. Thank you for helping to make this conference a success. In appreciation, we ask you to pick up your thank you gift afterwards at the information booth.

Attachments

- Travel directions
- Map of facility
- Program schedule
- Volunteer assignment timetable

VOLUNTEER NEEDS SCHEDULE | Example

Location   **Time/# of volunteers**

Location	7:00	8:00	9:00	11:00	12:00	1:00	2:00	3:00	4:00	5:00
Lobby										
Registration		10								
General Session			5	5		5	5	5	5	
Technical		3	3	3		3	3	3	3	
Workshops				30		30		30		
Food	25	25	25		40	40		25		40
Sales	5		5		5		5		5	
Transportation	10				5					10

VOLUNTEER EVALUATION | Form

Name

Address

Phone   E-mail

Volunteer position

Changes to make to job description:

I would rate my experience at this conference as:

What I most enjoyed about this conference:

Suggestions for improving the conference:

may need to recruit willing helpers on the spot. Or if too many volunteers show up, you may need to reshuffle them to areas of need. One conference coordinator has found an average of five to six percent no-show volunteers per event.

Evaluation forms

EXAMPLES

Prepare evaluation forms to give to volunteers after their conference is over. The evaluations will help you to know how the conference experience was for them and how it can be improved for future volunteers. See page 204 for a sample *Volunteer Evaluation* form.

INTERACTING WITH VOLUNTEERS

Throughout the event, you will be directing and helping volunteers in their jobs. Observe them to see if they have particular strengths that might be better utilized in another area. Get to know your volunteers. What do they enjoy doing? Volunteers who are put in a position that fits their interests and personalities are set up to be successful!

Motivating volunteers

Volunteers are not being paid to do their job, so you must rely on other methods of motivation to keep them going. Everyone is motivated in different ways and an effective Volunteer Coordinator tries to discover what motivates the volunteers. Motivating volunteers will help in the long term. A volunteer with a negative experience is not likely to return.

Give them a sense of purpose and accomplishment in what they are doing. Sometimes it's easy to get caught up in the little responsibilities without understanding how it all fits into the big picture. You can help them find purpose and fulfillment in what they are doing by:

- explaining how their service fits into the big picture and helps meets the goals of the conference.
- showing them their unique contribution to the team and why they make a difference.
- welcoming them as a team member and helping them fit in.
- giving them t-shirts or use other ways to identify them as part of the team. Another advantage of using t-shirts is that it helps people know who is officially volunteering.
- giving them clear instructions for what they are to do. Challenge them to do their best, yet appreciate their efforts and acknowledge them.

Utilize their abilities and give them opportunity to grow and be challenged. Know your volunteers and encourage them by recognizing their contributions. Make your rounds in the different areas throughout the day and encourage and appreciate people. Thank them publicly for what they've done.

> One of the most important things is for each volunteer to feel special, like they were significant contributors to the success of event. We made sure that Volunteer Central, where they showed up, was decorated significantly. It looked like a mountain lodge. We had trees, waterfalls, and it looked really special. Volunteers said, "Wow, is this for us?" We had a TV in there so they could watch the event and put their feet up. During lunch time the associate pastor prayed for them and said thank you. At the end of the event, each of them also got a thank you letter from their leader and from me. Nurturing starts in the beginning with recruiting but you continue it and they return cheerfully. ✦ *Peggy Brems*

Put those who have returned from previous conferences in areas of greater responsibility, such as leadership roles. Tell volunteers not to quit without having trained their replacements and challenge them to consider a volunteer role for more than one year.

Also, keep in mind that no matter how much you motivate or encourage them, not all volunteers will stay on forever. Most volunteers will help out for two or three times before feeling the need to do something different. Don't look at it as a failure on your part, but as a normal part of managing volunteers. In fact, if people are looking for something new to do, encourage them to try out a different area in volunteering.

FINALIZING ARRANGEMENTS

One or two weeks before the conference, send a confirmation letter with the following information:
- Date and time of conference
- Location of facility and driving directions
- Times they will be working
- What to wear
- Where to park
- Where to go
- Who they report to
- Your contact information

For smaller events, it might be easier to make personal phone calls to go over details (although it is also helpful to have written materials so people can refer to them easily).

Collect the items that you need before you head to the site:
- Volunteer packets
- Name badges
- Evaluation forms

17 | ADMINISTRATION

Sometime during the planning process, the Conference Director should make arrangements for the following administrative areas (or assign them to a team member):

- Crisis Management
- Schedules
- On-site communications
- Evaluation

CRISIS MANAGEMENT

Although we hope that our conferences have no incidents, it's still best to be prepared, given the uncertainty of our world.

Be prepared

No matter how well an event is planned, something unexpected will happen! Throughout the whole planning process, plan as if you won't be there the next day. If you happen to break a leg and end up in the hospital in surgery, what will happen to the conference? How will it go on and who will carry it through?

> The one rule of thumb that I always teach my staff is to work with the Mack truck rule— even if you are hit by a Mack truck, someone should be able to pick up your work the next day. We use an archives binder. In the binder, they are twenty-five different tabs. They are all the same so that next year the person who picks up he event can see the footprint of what was done to arrive at the final event. Event managers keep the binder clean and updated every day. If they can't come in, someone else can pick up the event where they left off. ◆ *Terry Toro*

TIPS FOR SUCCESS

Being prepared for a crisis is the best situation when an emergency arises. Expect a disaster and be pleasantly surprised when everything goes smoothly! Ways you can plan ahead are:

- **Make plans ahead of time.** Think through the event beforehand and list contingency plans for when things go wrong. What if there is a medical emergency? Where are the phones in case you need to call 911? Is there a doctor you can have on call? Be prepared for crises such as inclement weather, medical emergencies and transportation issues.
- **Know the site's emergency procedures.** Present different scenarios to the staff and ask them what the procedures are. At the initial meeting on-site meeting with site staff, clarify that there is adequate space for all attendees (if you are working with a facility that overbooks), and ask what will happen if there is not enough space.

- **Establish a clear responsibility structure.** Review as a team who is responsible for what when a crisis happens. Divide the responsibilities and clarify the decision process. For example, if the rooms are over-booked, who is the one who ultimately makes the decision on what to do? Is it the Site Coordinator? Or is it the Conference Director?
- **Have medical staff on site.** Some facilities (such as convention centers), require medical staff to be there. Some conferences ask for volunteer doctor, nurse, or paramedic to attend, pay their registration fee, and give them a pager throughout the conference. At the very least, find have a person who is CPR-certified. It's even better to have a CPR-certified person on your conference staff!
- **Invest in a portable radio.**

> You can buy a national weather service emergency radio for $49 at Radioshack. We have one that we take with us to major events. It's a phenomenal tool to have. It comes on immediately and you know what is going on. ◆ *Brad Weaber*

If you're a resident of California (like I am), buy a radio for your home earthquake kit and then bring it to the conference!

When a crisis happens

Sometimes an emergency arises and there is no plan as to what to do. That's when you use these guidelines:

- **Be calm.** When emergencies arise at the conference, it's a great advantage to have a clear head during moments of crisis.
- **Work with your vendors.** Ask them what to do and if they have any suggestions. They may have plans in place or they will work with you to resolve the problem.

> On the day of arrival, which is the most critical in terms of logistics, we ended up having to deal with a gas line issue in two separate instances. One was along the train line that we were using. There were significant delays because people had to get off the train, get bused around the track, and hop on another train. Then one of the hotels had a gas line problem and ended up shutting down; fifty people ended up without a hotel. The hotel helped us secure another area where they found rooms. ◆ *Keith Hirata*

> [If you are in a new or unfamiliar site] and you need to call 911, don't call 911 yourself. If I don't know the building, I have no idea how to tell them how to get there. Call the site's operator and let them call 911. ◆ *Brad Weaber*

- **Be honest.** Don't try to hide the problem; communicate it in a timely fashion. Sometimes it's wise to wait a little to resolve some problems. Other times, communicating what's happening immediately will put people's minds at rest.
- **Keep emergency contact information on hand.** Your registration form should have a space for emergency contact information in case something happens. Have the person's phone number and room number, and even their flight information so you know who to contact. A number of conferences now have attendees write their emergency information on the back of their badges, and some print the phone number of the local police or fire department.

> In San Francisco, during the 1989 quake, the general session had just started and there were about 3000 people in room. The earthquake hit but fortunately the area of Moscone Center was not directly hit. There were no phone lines [at first], but we were able to secure one phone line. Instead of having a mad rush of 3000 people getting to the phone, we already had registration lists in place with contact information, and we made the calls and made an announcement we were going to contact everyone. It

would take hours, but it kept the panic down. Then people made their own calls as more lines became available. ◆ *Brad Weaber*

- **Make a person with a medical crisis comfortable and respect their privacy.** People will want to help or watch, but limit the person's exposure to others.

We had someone have a heart attack in the ballroom during a general session. We pulled some high tables around him. The ballroom had a separate entrance and we redirected everyone to go around to the other entrance. Be respectful of that person. ◆ *Brad Weaber*

Having insurance is also another way to prepare for unexpected events.
- **Liability insurance.** Some facilities (such as churches) require the sponsoring organization to have liability insurance for the attendees. Usually, providing proof of insurance from your organization's insurance company is sufficient.
- **Conference insurance.** Insurance companies offer a form of insurance called *conference insurance* or *event insurance.* Although it may be too costly for smaller conferences, conference insurance provides peace of mind in case a conference is cancelled. Conference insurance covers natural catastrophes, or even problems like the facility going bankrupt and being unavailable because it was not built in time.

SCHEDULES

SCHEDULING

As each staff member puts together a schedule for their particular area, their schedules can be combined into a master schedule so the Director knows what is happening in each area. All the schedules can be maintained in a binder that can be carried around on the day of the conference. The Director should hand out a copy of the schedule to all the staff, as well as a list where each coordinator will be during the conference.

If the Director needs to assign responsibilities, keep in mind when people function best. Give morning people the early duties and night people the late jobs. Then everyone will not only be efficient, but awake too!

At one of our retreats, someone had to go around and wake up everyone. We assigned the Fellowship Coordinator the job because he liked to get up early. Waking people up had nothing at all to do with his duties overseeing fellowship, but he was the best one to do it because the rest of us would have slept through breakfast and the whole morning program!

ON-SITE COMMUNICATIONS

Begin planning for how the team will communicate with one another when you are all at the site.

The easiest way is for everyone to have wireless radios (walkie-talkies) or headsets. Having a headset reduces the noise and makes communication easier. If the site does not provide radios, you'll need to rent or buy your own. If you have a limited number of radios, the most important people to have a radio are:
- the Director
- the Program Coordinator
- the Logistics Coordinator. If you don't have a Logistics Coordinator, then provide headsets to:
  - the Registration Coordinator
  - the Hospitality Coordinator

- the Transportation Coordinator
- the Volunteer Coordinator
- the Site Coordinator.

A list with each person's cell phone number and contact information is also extremely helpful, so give one to everybody on staff.

Make plans to check the communications system once you are on site. Test out the radios and check cell phone reception in different parts of the facility. Make contingency plans for alternate forms of communication in case the radios or cell phones don't work.

Plan to give the contact person on site a radio with the frequency you'll be using. This keeps them updated with what is happening and will enable them to give you prompt service.

On-site office

Before heading to the conference, designate a location to be the on-site office, "command center," or "headquarters" during the event. This is where a temporary office space will be set up, holding all the materials needed for the conference. Store your supplies here, and put a copier, telephone, printer, walkie talkies or other equipment that the team will use. Here everyone can check in and pick up their headsets and information needed during the conference.

The Site Coordinator can find a space for the office—perhaps a suite or a complimentary room. Some facilities can provide a space where you can have a desk to handle paperwork and where the team can meet. If you have a conference with over 100 people, you'll find it helpful to have a central location for the office space. If you are using multiple hotels, one hotel is designated as the headquarters in which the office area is located.

EVALUATION

TIPS FOR SUCCESS

An important part of the program is to build in evaluation opportunities to get feedback for improvement. Evaluations are crucial if you want to improve your event next time. They allow people to give feedback about what they experienced and express any ideas they may have.

Make sure evaluations are easy to fill out and that they have both quantitative (numerical) and qualitative (subjective, usually in the form of written comments) ratings.

Develop a system for data entry and find volunteers to help (ask the Volunteer Coordinator for assistance). Have a plan for analyzing the data and communicating it to the people involved. Do you want to send out a brief letter, a report, a spreadsheet? Send out the information in whatever format people will find easiest to read. Pie charts and other visuals are great if you have the time and the means to put them together. Keep the results simple.

While you're at it, develop a follow-up plan for those who accept Christ or who want more information about becoming a believer and finding a local church.

Attendee evaluations

Include an evaluation form in each person's packet. The evaluation form should cover major areas of the event but not be so detailed that it is unwieldy to fill out. Don't try to cover everything! Only cover what is most important and helpful for future conferences. Evaluate in relation to your goals. Were they met?

Make the evaluation easy to fill out by including responses that can be circled or or checked. The shorter the form, the more likely people will fill it out. If you find that there are too many things you want to evaluate, you can also break them up by giving an evaluation at the end of certain time periods (such as at the end of every workshop).

To encourage a response, give people a time to fill out the forms and pass them in or have someone at the door to collect them as they leave; be aware that sometimes the end of a long day is not the best time for filling out evaluations, as people are tired and will give lower marks. Or if your program cannot allow for such a time, then remind people of the evaluation throughout the conference and have them turn it in when they return their key. Offer a drawing for the prize from the evaluations submitted. The key is to have people fill out the evaluation when they are still at the event, because most people won't take the trouble to mail in an evaluation.

See pages 212-213 for a sample *Evaluation Forms*.

EXAMPLES

Speaker evaluations

Give each speaker an evaluation form, too. How was the conference experience for them? What did they find positive or helpful? How could the experience be improved for them?

Exhibitor evaluations

Don't forget to ask the exhibitors how the experience was for them. How was the registration process? What kind of attendance did they get? What are suggestions for improvement?

EXAMPLES

Volunteer evaluations

Ask volunteers about their experiences, too. Give the Volunteer Coordinator a form to give to the volunteers (see page 204).

Team evaluations

You'll want to hear from your team members about how the conference planning experience and event was for them (see page 231).

Drop this form in the baskets in the foyer. Thank you! Your comments are greatly appreciated.

How did you hear about this conference? Check all that apply. For answers with blanks, please specify name:
- ❑ Friend
- ❑ Previous conference
- ❑ Internet site
- ❑ Newspaper
- ❑ Church: _____
- ❑ Other: _____

How did this conference most help you?

_____

_____

_____

_____

What are suggestions for improvement?

_____

_____

_____

_____

_____

Pleases evaluate the speakers as well as any comments: (rating of 1-5; 1=poor, 5=excellent)

#1 _____

_____

#2 _____

_____

#3 _____

_____

Evaluate the following, as well as any comments (rating of 1-5; 1=poor, 5=excellent)

Registration procedure _____

_____

Worship time _____

_____

Food quality _____

_____

Food service _____

_____

Tell us about yourself:

Age ❑ <18 ❑ 18-22 ❑ 23-34 ❑ 35-49 ❑ 50+

Marital status ❑ Single ❑ Married
How many children under the age of 18 are in your family? _____

What are their age ranges? (check all that apply)
❑ 1-3 years ❑ 4-10 years ❑ 11-14 ❑ 15-18 years

What are topics, speakers, or locations would you like to see utilized in future conferences?

_____

_____

_____

_____

_____

Would you come to this conference again? ❑ Y ❑ N

Have you visited our website? ❑ Y ❑ N

Please use back for additional comments. Thank you!

WORKSHOPS

Name of workshop _____

Rating and comments _____

_____

_____

Pleases evaluate the workshop teachers, as well as any comments (rating of 1-5; 1=poor, 5=excellent):

Name of workshop _____

Rating and comments _____

_____

_____

EVALUATION FORM (RETREAT)

Example

Rank the following aspects of the retreat. Feel free to add comments about the speaker, food, activities or other.

	Poor				Excellent
Welcome package	1	2	3	4	5
Written programs (organization, appearance, space for notes)	1	2	3	4	5
Main sessions	1	2	3	4	5
Worship	1	2	3	4	5
Childcare/children's program	1	2	3	4	5
Free time activities	1	2	3	4	5
Quiet time	1	2	3	4	5
Evening activities	1	2	3	4	5
Talent show	1	2	3	4	5
Housing	1	2	3	4	5
Meals	1	2	3	4	5

What was especially good about the retreat?

_____
_____
_____
_____

What would have been better if it were different?

_____
_____
_____
_____

What steps do you plan to take as a result of attending this retreat?

_____
_____
_____
_____

Are there topics, sessions, or workshops you'd like implemented?

_____
_____
_____
_____

Any suggestions for next year's retreat (site, speaker, theme, etc.)?

_____
_____
_____
_____
_____
_____
_____

PART 3 | CONFERENCE

THIRD STAGE

18 | THE CONFERENCE

The big event is here! All your many months of preparation have been preparing for this moment. This chapter will go over the on-site coordination and conducting of the conference. Please note that I've called out specific responsibilities for each member of the team, but everyone should read over the entire chapter so that the responsibilities can be coordinated.

At the last staff meeting before leaving for the site, cover the details covered in this chapter to make sure that all the details are assigned to at least one person.

BEFORE YOU LEAVE

Director

Before leaving, make up an information sheet to be distributed to every person on staff. Include the following information:
- Name and title
- Address
- Phone number, including cell phone
- Arrival time
- Where person will be staying (such as the room of the hotel)
- Facility address and phone number
- Where to go upon arrival and check-in instructions

Every staffperson should receive a copy of the sheet and carry it around at all times so that people can easily reach each other. Encourage everyone who has a cell phone to bring it so that they can be easily contacted at the facility.

What to bring

Divvy up the following responsibilities among the staff:
- Conference schedule (programs/events), as well as a dress code list
- Cue sheets
- Rehearsal schedule
- Emergency kit
- Registration materials/welcome packets
- Decorations
- Signage
- Any equipment needed
- Tape
- Staplers

Finances: Honorarium checks, payments to vendors and site
Prayer: See list on page 66.

Site: Your notes and information.
Program: Anything additional items needed during the program.
Speakers: Speaker packets, speaker information.
Technical: Technical equipment, cables, power strips.
Hospitality: See information on page 147.
Transportation: See information on page 153.
Registration: See list on page 164.
Exhibits: Exhibitor information, evaluation forms.
Marketing: Signage, banners, marketing materials.
Volunteers: See list on page 206.

MOVE-IN

The planning team arrives at the location before the event actually begins. How early you arrive depends on the nature of your conference. For a retreat, you may actually arrive early the first day in order to set up for the event the same night. From a multi-day, extensive conference, sometimes more than one day is booked for setup.

Remind everyone to check in at the command center where they will be given their headsets for communicating with one another.

Some conference planners like to drop off advance thank you gifts to site staff to develop a positive relationship from the beginning. Small gifts like chocolates or promotional items work well.

SETUP

The major task upon arrival is setting up the site. The staff members set up their particular areas.

Conference Director and Logistics
- Greet staff and volunteers as they arrive
- Oversee and help the staff in their areas.
- Set up office/administrative area or command center.
- Check radios and cell phones to make sure they function (or have whoever is in charge of that area take care of it).
- Be sure information center is stocked with brochures and supplies.
- Attend staff meeting.

Finances
- Be on hand to pay any outstanding bills.
- Attend staff meeting.

Site
Although the staff will oversee setup of their particular areas, you can help them check their areas to make sure that they have everything they need and that everything is in place.
- Check a sampling of the housing accommodations. Are they clean and ready? Do all the lights work?
- Direct volunteers as needed.
- Attend staff meeting.

Check in with the following people:
- Program Coordinator: How is setup of the meeting rooms going? Have all the chairs and tables been set up correctly? Are stage sets in place?
- Technical Coordinator: Has all the equipment been set up in all the rooms?
- Registration Coordinator: Has the registration area been set up? Are directions or signage to the registration area clearly marked so people can get there quickly.

- Hospitality Coordinator: Is everything in place and working correctly? Are tables set correctly and is the right cutlery available?
- Marketing Coordinator: Check signage to make sure it is posted correctly. Are there signs outside every room and major use areas? Is directional signage in place?
- Exhibits: Make sure the exhibit hall is set up and ready for the exhibitors.

Hospitality/Food
- Set up eating areas: serving areas, dining areas, and any décor needed.
- Meet with the caterer to check food arrangements.
- Prepare any food or beverages to be ready before people arrive.
- Direct volunteers as needed.
- Attend staff meeting.

Technical
- Oversee the equipment setup and operation.
- Review the equipment bill to make sure it is accurate.
- Direct volunteers as needed.
- Attend staff meeting.

Registration
Set up the registration area the night before, if possible. The registration area can be added to the setup list so check with the Logistics Coordinator beforehand to make sure it is on schedule.
- Direct volunteers to help set up the registration area.
- You may also want to enlist volunteers in helping you deliver the registration packets if there are too many for you to bring yourself.
- Store any valuable equipment or money in a secure area, especially if you are setting up the night before.
- Direct volunteers as needed.
- Attend staff meeting.

Exhibits
- Set up the exhibits area.
- Supervise the facility staff as they set up the area.
- Direct volunteers as needed.
- Check electrical and phone hookups.
- Put up booth signage.
- Attend staff meeting.

Volunteer
- Coordinate volunteers to handle any setup of tables, chairs, or signage.
- As a courtesy, provide dinner for the volunteers if they are rushing over after work.
- Attend staff meeting.

Program
- Check the meeting rooms to make sure that everything is in place.
- Furniture setup: chairs, tables correctly positioned
- Stage setup: location, equipment in place, screens, lighting
- Speakers: all speaker requirements are set
- Other people involved in the program: check with worship team, entertainment, creative arts and make sure their needs are met
- Run through the rehearsal schedule.
- Test headsets for operation the next day.

Speaker

As speakers arrive, help make them successful. Make sure the host is prompt in greeting the speaker.

- Check speakers' rooms to make sure everything is prepared, in working order, and that the location is a quiet one.
- Orient any hosts.
- Greet speakers (or have the hosts do it) as they arrive and help them get checked in.
- Introduce speakers to their hosts.
- Give speakers their packets and show them to their rooms.
- Take them to dinner.
- Bring them back to the facility to pray with the planning team. (Or pray with them before you go to dinner.)

Marketing

- Post signage and banners around facility.
- Direct volunteers as needed.
- Attend staff meeting.

Prayer

- Lead the prayer time during the staff meeting.

STAFF MEETING

At some point during the day (or night), the staff should gather for a staff meeting. The purpose of the meeting is to cover last minute details and pray together. If you are at a hotel, gather the heads of the different departments as well as your staff to review details; you may choose to pray with your staff after this meeting.

Prayer

TIPS FOR SUCCESS

Sometime during the setup, gather together as a team to pray for each other and for the event! There's nothing that brings peace more than putting everything in God's hands! Even if things are crazy and everything is going wrong, it's good to stop and pray to get a good focus on what is going on. It's ideal to have the speakers and worship join the team during this time so that they can receive prayer. If the group is too big, break down into smaller groups to pray.

Conference Director

TIPS FOR SUCCESS

This is also a good time for the Director to give last minute details, an encouraging talk, and a reminder of what to expect. Inspire the group and get everyone excited that all the months of work is going to be paid off soon! Pass out any schedules and changes that might have been made.

Make sure that there is a clear understanding of what the lines of responsibility are at the event. For example, the staff should know who is calling the program and who makes the decision on what to change if the program is running late. Don't have everyone respond to you for everything—divide the responsibilities but don't have overlapping decision makers on the same area. The Site Coordinator should be the contact with the site instead of having different team members going to the site and requesting different things. This will help everyone and cause less confusion! Make sure people know who the emergency contact person is!

You may also choose to give thank you gifts to the staff now.

Then everyone should go home and try to get a good night's sleep—usually a difficult task! Don't be surprised if you or your team have conference dreams all night!

THE CONFERENCE

Setup

The staff should arrive early to make sure that everything is set up correctly. Some special notes:

Facilities: Make your rounds thirty minutes before the program begins to make sure that items have not been moved and everything is in place.

Equipment: Pass out headsets to all team members involved in the program or logistics during the event: Director, Logistics, Site, Hospitality, Volunteer, Registration, and Exhibits. Double check all equipment and settings to ensure that they are correct.

Hospitality: Be on hand to meet the caterer and help with any food preparation.

- Arrive early to meet the caterer and check the setup of food, break, and décor areas.
- Prepare any food or beverages to be ready before people arrive.
- Double check serving areas occasionally to make sure they are well stocked and clean.

Don't check a room for a major dinner or reception too early. There is nothing worse than [checking a room early, seeing some activity, then] leaving—and when you return to the event, what you saw three hours earlier hasn't changed. There could be a shift change in the middle of the setup of your meeting, and then the next group doesn't have paperwork [on how to set up the room]. Ask the banquet person, "Will there be a shift change during my event?" ◆ *Brad Weaber*

Registration: The day of the conference, arrive early and make final arrangements to set up the area. Hopefully there will not be much to do but if you arrive early, you'll have plenty of time to deal with any last-minute problems that come up.

As volunteers arrive, greet them and then train them on the registration procedure and process. Be available to direct and encourage the volunteers as well. The attendees may have questions so be sure you have a good grasp on the layout of the facility as well as program details.

Volunteer: Arrive early to set up the volunteer check-in table before the first volunteer arrives. Check in, orient, and train volunteers and then send them off to their areas. Be available to direct and encourage the volunteers as well. Sometimes volunteers will not show, in which case you should be prepared to re-distribute people.

Exhibits: Be available to greet exhibitors and answer any questions.

Arrival

Now people begin arriving! As people enter the facility, they register and then go to where they are directed: breakfast, dinner, or the program.

Registration

Process registrations as people arrive. Make sure the line is going smoothly—if there are any backups, shift volunteers to that area.

Have plans for late arrivals; some people always arrive late no matter what you do. Since they will need to be registered, the registration coordinator can move all the registration materials to the central information booth and check people in there. This allows volunteers to begin taking down the registration area. Make sure there is signage for people so they know that they can go to the information booth.

For late people who arrive in the dark and have to walk to their cabins, try to find a holding place for their luggage so they can join the program immediately. Then after the program is over, they can pick up their luggage and head to their cabins.

When registration is over, close and break down the area. Bring any additional registration materials left to the information booth in case people arrive very late.

Program

As much as possible, set a good precedent for your conference by starting the first session on time. Sometimes you may have to delay the starting time, such as if traffic is particularly bad, or weather has delayed many peoples' flights. But in general, try to stay with the schedule out of respect for peoples' time.

Conference Director

The Conference Director is the schedule keeper during the event. He oversees the conducting of the conference. It's crucial to have either a wireless radio or headset to use to communicate to the rest of the team.

EXAMPLES

Program

The Program Coordinator calls the cues for the program by following the cue sheet (page 107). Usually seated in the technical booth, she calls out any cues needed, such as who goes next, any lighting or sound cues, and makes on-the-fly adjustments to the program schedule. If the emcee is seated near the front of the audience, it's a good idea to give the emcee a headset too, in case certain program elements must be dropped or the order changed.

- Keep the programming on schedule in order to give the speaker enough time without feeling time pressure.
- Keep an open eye for background things that need to be attended to within the meeting room: changing the temperature of the room, closing doors to reduce distractions, and making sure there is enough light for people to take notes during the message.

Emcee

The emcee keeps the program flowing smoothly and serves as a timekeeper for the speaker.

- If your schedule is tight, prepare time notification signs ("Five minutes," "One minute,") to warn the speakers. As a courtesy, ask the speakers ahead of time if it is okay to use the signs.

Speaker

The Speaker Coordinator attends to the needs of the speakers. The day they are to speak, stay on top of the background details to make sure that your speaker has a positive conference experience:

- Check the lectern to make sure it is the right height. If the lectern is too high, provide a step for the speaker to stand on.
- Prepare a glass of water.
- Check their equipment to ensure it is functioning properly. Have emergency supplies on hand (extra bulbs, power cords, and other supplies).
- Plan the intro for the speaker to make sure the information is accurate. If the speaker gives you an intro to read, don't ad lib. If the intro is to be made by another person, introduce the speaker beforehand. Let the speaker know what the previous speakers have said.
- Keep the program on schedule so that the speaker has adequate time.
- Make sure the room environment is at comfortable settings.

- If your speaker is presenting during a meal, make sure the tables are cleared before they begin so that there is minimal distraction.
- Don't spring surprises on your speaker. If you want them to say a closing prayer, then communicate that beforehand. Prepare them by reminding them of the theme and audience. Help them understand the different personalities and the importance of communicating creatively to the audience with different learning styles.

Communication is key to a well-functioning conference. Staff and attendees all should be updated on the schedule. Communicate things clearly to the staff, especially changes made on-the-fly as the conference is being conducted. Communicate with the people involved in the program, too. Let speakers know what's working great and what might need to be changed.

Throughout the event, communicate your program to attendees in advance so they know what to expect. Give them a program agenda so they know what is coming next; people don't want to be trapped. During sessions, before the break time, remind people what is ahead the next hour. People are forgetful and need to be constantly reminded. Also be sure people understand what the purpose of the conference is.

> When you're on the operational side, you can sometimes lose what is actually happening; a lot of work being done is behind the scenes. That's sometimes hard because when you're an event manager, if you do your job well, people don't see you. You miss a moment and the reward. One of the things I always like to do is take my staff through the backstage … so they can see the faces of the people that they are affecting. Otherwise they don't get to experience that special moment. Especially during worship, I have them see their part. ✦ *Terry Toro*

Bringing the team to watch the program gives them a chance to experience the results of their labor and see how God is using it to bless others.

Operations and Logistics

Conference Director
During a multi-day event, have a daily communication time for the team to gather together and update one another. Go over anything not working effectively and ask what changes need to be made.

Site
As the conference nears the end, help attendees with their checkout. Arrange storage for luggage, putting it in one area. If you have many pieces of luggage to take care of, assign a volunteer to stand by the door with tickets. She tapes one ticket to the bag, and gives one to the attendee. When the attendee returns for the luggage, she compares the tickets. If the room is a small one, try using tables to stack the bags higher.

Hospitality
The Hospitality Coordinator oversees the break times and the meal times:
- Double-check serving areas occasionally to make sure they are well stocked and clean.
- If there are any complaints or issues, talk to the caterer immediately so that they can be resolved.
- If your event is a multi-day event, meet at the end of the day with the caterer and site manager to be clear on any adjustments that need to be made. Pay the invoices while everything is still fresh in your mind.
- After the meal, have a plan for leftover food. Additional food from meals may be donated to shelters or distributed to staff and volunteers.

- Find out where the trash disposal is. Does the venue provide trash disposal services?
- Clean up the preparation, serving, and eating areas. Don't forget the volunteer area or staff break room if food was served there.
- Be flexible with schedule changes. If something doesn't run on schedule, think of ways to make things go more smoothly for the attendees.

Brad Weaber gives the example of what to do if the dinner preparation is running late and people are arriving. If the reception is part of the dinner, ask the hotel to roll it into the foyer so people feel that something is going on and their basic needs for food and drink are being met. Or, ask the hotel to provide something simple, like coffee, which they may pay for if they are not ready in time for the dinner.

Exhibits
- Be available all day to assist exhibitors.
- Attend to any last-minute requests.

Transportation
- Communicate with the transportation vendors any changes in schedule or plan.
- Help attendees with transportation issues.

Volunteer
- Direct volunteers during the day. Reshuffle people to different areas as needed.
- Encourage and motivate volunteers in their work.

Technical
- Oversee equipment operations.
- Oversee audio/video recording.

Move-out
When the conference ends, it's time to begin moving out of the site.

Director/Site Coordinator
At the end of the event, meet with the site staff to review the bill.

At every event, require the hotel to bring you the check at the end so there aren't ; you're able to change it right then. At every event, we tell the hotel, "If you don't have the signature on it by end of the day, then we are not responsible." They will find you. Resolve all your disputes prior to leaving the facility. ◆ Brad Weaber

Volunteers
At the end of the event, help the volunteers clean up their respective areas and inventory any supplies or equipment that need to be returned. Give them a feedback form to fill out. Give one to all your volunteers, or if you have a large number, select a few. You can give the forms to them personally or mail them afterwards. Another way of soliciting feedback is to ask the staff or volunteer leaders to speak to each volunteer to hear how the experience was for them.

Give them expense forms to fill out and have them return the forms with receipts so they can be reimbursed.

If there are thank you gifts at the conference (such as centerpieces used in the dining area), give them to the volunteers. Be sure to let them know ahead of time to pick up the gifts so they don't leave before you have a chance to tell them! A good idea is to include a note about the thank you gift in their instructions.

Exhibits

At the end of the day, give the exhibitors evaluation forms to fill out and return. Or you may choose to mail them afterwards when you send them a thank you letter.

All staff

At the end of the day, help clean up the different areas and take down equipment and signage.

Celebrate with each other comments that have been heard and positive things that happened.

Then everyone go home and sleep for a week straight!

PART 4 | CLOSURE
FOURTH STAGE

19 | WRAPPING UP

TIPS FOR SUCCESS

The event is over, but the work isn't! You may wish it was done, but the follow-up of an event is important if you're planning another event next year. The extra work you put in afterwards will pay off the next time planning begins because it will serve as the foundation for the next event.

The three main tasks after the event are:

- Returning items
- Summarization
- Appreciation/celebration
- Evaluation

RETURNING ITEMS

Some tasks need to wait until after the conference is over. If the conference is held during the weekend, returning rented equipment or other items can't be done until the business week starts.

Some areas that might need to return borrowed or rented items include:

- **Hospitality:** linens, rented kitchen or serving equipment
- **Technical:** equipment, cables
- **Exhibits:** ship back materials, equipment, or other items from the exhibit area, unless the exhibitors have arranged for the shipping themselves

SUMMARIZATION

Another job for the staff is to collect all the information from the conference and to summarize it in such a way that it will be helpful for next year's team.

- **Registration:** Compile registration records and information for next year's mailing list. Find out why people did not attend. If people registered and then cancelled, contact them to find out why; the information they provide will be helpful for the future.
- **Exhibits:** At the end of the conference, give the exhibitors evaluation forms to fill out and return. Or you may choose to mail them afterwards when you send them a thank you letter.
- **Director:** Putting together a summary report of the event will be a tremendous asset for next year's Director. Even if you are coordinating the event next year, the report will be a helpful reminder of facts and a record of what worked and what didn't. Include in the report copies of:
  - The budget and actual costs
  - Planning meeting agendas and minutes

- Schedules and lists (cue sheet, rehearsal schedule, contact information)
- The conference brochure as well as any mailings or publicity materials
- The contents of the registration packet
- Notes of what to do differently next time in order to improve the planning process or to improve the event itself
- Evaluation results summaries
- Statistics: how many people registered and attended (overall and broken down by event), number of meals served (and minimum guarantee numbers that were submitted to the site), vendors who participated, sponsors
- Answers to prayer

APPRECIATION/CELEBRATION

After the conference, send thank you notes to all the people you worked with. Let them know how much they were appreciated! Each person on the team should take the time to write thank you notes to the people they were involved with. You may want to include any reports or interesting quotes. If the Director wants to, she can sign the notes, too. The more the merrier!

> After the conference, we send out a volunteer newsletter giving them final statistics and fun quotes from guests, and a listing of every volunteer's name. It goes to them with a thank you and this year we gave them a special offer to a Christian magazine. The volunteer tells ten people, "I just got a nice letter from Christian Managment Association and all I did was volunteer." It helps build attendance for the next event. ✦ *John Pearson*

Have a celebration party or send a gift certificate for coffee or other affordable item. Hold a drawing for the volunteers, give awards, or give them a gift with the conference logo or their name printed on it.

Have them review their job description and update it so that next year's volunteer knows what to expect.

Send notes of appreciation to these groups:
- Speakers: speakers, speaker hosts, workshop facilitators, entertainment
- Program: small group facilitators
- Equipment: equipment operators and setup crew
- Worship: worship leader, worship team members
- Hospitality: facility staff, caterer, and volunteers.
- Site: staff members at the site who made your job easier
- Exhibitors: organizations or companies who held exhibits, any site staff that were especially helpful
- Prayer: prayer partners/intercessors
- Financial: sponsors, donors
- Volunteers: everyone who volunteered time to help before, during, and after the event.
- Director: vendors/suppliers not covered by other staff. Don't forget to write notes to your conference staff, too!

Don't forget to give great thanks to the One who this conference was for. Spend some time together praising God for his goodness and faithfulness through the whole process.

Conference Director
Have a big celebration party or dinner for your team and get them thank you gifts for their numerous hours of labor. Bless them in their ministry and share a prayer of thanksgiving together at the end.

EVALUATION

The Director should get feedback from each staff member. This can be done either individually—by talking to people and seeing what their experience was like—or by meeting as a group. It's helpful to meet as a group so you can discuss what went well and what didn't. A follow-up meeting for the entire staff lets everyone meet together to evaluate the conference. Review the event. How did it go? What went well? What was most challenging and how can you prepare for those challenges next year? What did you learn? What can be improved next time?

One interesting result of discussing these items is that people aren't aware of what happened outside their area so the discussion helps others get a sense of what went on at the conference. You may even combine this meeting with your celebration party. It's an encouraging thing to see the results of God's working at the event!

> Surveys came back saying, "I came here with a little deal with the Lord—this is the last shot. I am so tired. I was ready to quit until this conference." Then we know it was the Holy Spirit. It wasn't us and we know that the goal was met to have these women encouraged and challenged. ◆ *Yvette Maher*

RESOURCE TOOLS

Evaluations may either be collected at the event, or after the event with surveys. You'll get more responses from people at the end of the event, because the event is fresh in their minds and you can remind them to fill out the form. After the conference you can do online surveys that collect the data for you so you don't have to enter in the responses by hand. One Web site which provides a free survey tool is www.zoomerang.com. You can enter in the questions you wish and e-mail the survey to your participants.

Go over the evaluations that were collected from the participants. As you look at them in relation to the goals that were set for the conference, were the goals accomplished?

Sometimes an evaluation or two will be off the deep end; take these evaluations with a grain of salt. One or two comments about something may not be worth worrying about, but if a large number of evaluations bring up an issue, take a careful look!

> Reading the evaluations after the conferences was always a humorous event. Without fail, we would get the comment, "More general session speakers, less workshops," and then another one that said, "More workshops, less general session speakers." "Longer worship," and "Worship too long." "Too much food." "Not enough food." Most of the times the comments cancelled each other out and then we dealt with the others that were repeated by a lot of people. The best comments were the ones where people shared how they had been impacted. Be sure to leave room in your evaluation sheet to hear positive statements, too!

TIPS

TIPS FOR SUCCESS

When you're planning your schedule, it will seem like your calendar is suddenly empty the few days right after the conference. Remember that it's helpful to block out a few days afterwards to recover from the conference. The days or weeks right before the conference can sometimes be intense, so it's nice to have a little buffer to catch up on some sleep, clean up your messy house, or start patching up relationships with ignored friends. It's also useful to have the extra time to collect information for your evaluation or write thank you notes.

There's also a phenomena (documented somewhere, I'm sure) called "post-conference depression." Although it doesn't hit everyone (after my first conference I was on such a high I couldn't sleep for two nights!), people have reported a sudden sense of loss and depression after the conference was over. Since the conference planning has taken such a large part of your life, don't be surprised if you suddenly feel a bit blue that all the excitement, work, and experience has come to an end. It really hasn't. God continues to work in ways we can't see as a result of the conference!

THE END

Congratulations! You are done! You have survived the conference experience! It's been a long process but hopefully you have found it to be rewarding and educational.

As a result of the work that you have done:
- others have been blessed
- new relationships have been formed
- participants have learned more
- people were drawn closer to God
- you and your team have grown in experience and faith
- all of which will work together for life change that will make an impact for all eternity!

I think the work is worth it, don't you?

R E S O U R C E S

The following is a short list of professional organizations that provide resources for conference and meeting planning.

The International Association of Professional Congress Organisers (IAPCO)
42 Canham Road
London W3 7SR
United Kingdom
44-20-8749-6171
www.iapco.org
IAPCO is a non-profit organization that represents professional organizers and managers of international and national congresses, conventions and special events.

International Congress & Convention Association (ICCA)
Entrada 121
Amsterdam   NL-1096 EB
Netherlands
31-20-398-1919
www.icca.nl
ICCA is an organization in the world of international meetings, with members from more than seventy-six countries around the world. Its membership represents the main specialists in handling, transporting and accommodating international events.

Meeting Professionals International (MPI)
International Headquarters
4455 LBJ Freeway, Suite 1200
Dallas, TX 75244-5903
972-702-3000
www.mpiweb.org
MPI is a global community committed to shaping and defining the future of the meeting and event industry. MPI helps its members enhance their professional value by providing them with practices, education, research and trends, professional development and networking opportunities.

Professional Convention Management Association (PCMA)
2301 South Lake Shore Drive
Suite 1001
Chicago, IL 60616-1419
312-423-7262
www.pcma.org
PCMA is a nonprofit international association of professionals in the meetings industry whose mission is to deliver breakthrough education and promote the value of professional convention management.

Religious Conference Management Association (RCMA)
One RCA Dome, Ste. 120
Indianapolis, IN 46225
317-632-1888
www.rcmaweb.org
RCMA provides resources designed to enhance the professionalism of its members and to improve the experience of religious meeting attendees worldwide.

BIBLIOGRAPHY

"Administrative Information, Forms and Procedures." *Texas Library Association.* < http://www.txla.org/groups/officers/toc.html >.

"A Little Change of Space." *Religious Conference Manager.* August 2002.

Allen, Judy. *Event Planning.* New York: John Wiley & Sons Canada, Ltd. 2000.

"Annual Conference Planning Guidelines." *Canadian Association of Colleges and University Student Services (CACUSS).* 1999. < http://www.cacuss.ca/en/reports/html/conference manual.html >.

"Appendix II: Sample of VLDB Conference Plan and Checkpoints." *VLDB.* 1999. Very Large Database Endowment, Inc. < http://www.vldb.org/sample.html >.

Avery, Christopher M., Ph.D. "Anatomy of a Small Meeting." *Religious Conference Manager.* August 2002.

"Avoiding 'Death by PowerPoint.'" Corbin Ball Associates. 2000. < www.corbinball.com/articles/art-powerpoint.htm >.

Ball, Corbin. "High-Tech Site Inspection Checklist." *Religious Conference Manager.* 2000. MeetingsNet. < http://www.meetings net.com/rcm/0200/0200siht.asp >.

Barish, Rachael. "ACM SIG Conference Manual." ACM. 1993. *Association for Computing Machinery.* < http://www.acm.org/ sig_volunteer_info/conference_manual/ >.

Barmore, M. "Planning A Group Retreat." *University of California, Irvine.* < http://www.dos.uci.edu/publications/guides/b6.html >.

Bastian, Lisa. "Planning Mega Events." *The Meeting Professional Digital Edition* 19:5 (1999). < http://www.mpiweb.org/news/tmp/1999/05.htm#1 >.

Boehme, Ann J. *Planning Successful Meetings and Events.* Amacom.1999.

Brian, Marshall. "How House Construction Works." *How Stuff Works.* < http://www.houwstuffworks.com/house.htm >.

Brunet, Pere and Ivan Herman (ed). "Eurographics Association Conference Planning Guide." European Association for Computer Graphics. < http://www.eg.org/EG/DocArchive/exb_006/NewGuide >.

Carrier, Thomas J. "How to Get More for Less." *Religious Conference Manager.* Feb 2001.

Chinappi, Anna. "First Aid for Meetings," *Religious Conference Manager.* Feb 2001.

"Client Information." *Conference Services.* 2002. University of Virginia. < http://www.virginia.edu/housing/conferences/SummerConf/clientinfo_coord.htm >.

Collins, Martha. "Conference Centers: Meetings By Design." *The Meeting Professional Digital Edition* 21:6 (Jun 2001). < http://www.mpiweb.org/news/tmp/2001/06/conf.htm >.

"The Compleat Planner." *Meetingsnet.com.* < http://www.meetingsnet.com/rcm/0896/compleat.html >.

"Conference Cost-Cutting Concepts—222 Budget Cutting Ideas." *Corbin Ball Associates.* 2000. www.corbinball.cm/articles/art-costcuts.html.

"Conference Planner." *AMC Corporate Communications.* < http://www.amc.net.uk/html/choosing_a_venue.html >.

"Conference Planning." 2002. Association of Faculty Clubs International. < http://www.facultyclubs.org/host.html#mat >.

"Conference Planning!" 2002. National Council of Teachers of English. < http://www.ncte.org/tyca/conference/index.shtml >.

"Conference Planning Manual." Art Libraries Society of North America. < http://www.arlisna.org/planningmanual.htm >.

"Conference Planning Manual." Montana Library Association. < http://www.mtlib.org/manual/confmanual.html >.

"Conference Planning Manual." International Association of School Librarianship. < http://www.iasl-slo.org/confmanintro.html >.

"Conference Planning Manual." 2002. Wisconsin Association of Academic Librarians. < http://www.wla.lib.wi.us/waal/conferences/confmanual.html >.

Creative Programs for Life-Changing Camps and Retreats. Grand Rapids: Zondervan Publishing House.

"Crisis Strategy Checklist," *Religious Conference Manager.* Jun 2002.

Dana, Margie Gello. "Save a Bundle on Printing." *Religious Conference Manager.* Feb 2001.

Davidson, Harvey Paul. "Small-Meeting Timeline." *Religious Conference Manager.* 2000. MeetingsNet.

Davis, Louisa. "Audiovisual/Technology." *Religious Conference Manager.* 2000. MeetingsNet.

—. "Budgeting." *Religious Conference Manager.* 2000. MeetingsNet.

—. "Personnel." *Religious Conference Manager.* 2000. MeetingsNet.

—. "Food and Beverage." *Religious Conference Manager.* 2000. MeetingsNet.

—, "More Than 300 Ways to Improve Your Meeting's Bottom Line." *Corbin Ball Associates.* 2000. < www.corbinball.com/articles/art-300costsavers.htm >.

—. "Negotiating & Contracts." *Religious Conference Manager.* 2000. MeetingsNet.

—. "Registration, Setup & Decor." *Religious Conference Manager.* 2000. MeetingsNet.

—. "Site Selection." *Religious Conference Manager.* 2000. MeetingsNet.

—. "Transportation." *Religious Conference Manager.* MeetingsNet.

Davis, Louisa and Sandy Biback. "87 Cost Saving Tips." *Religious Conference Manager.* Feb 2001.

Dobrian, Joseph. "All-Inclusive Resorts Gain as Meeting Destinations." *Meeting Professional Digital Edition* 21:8 (Aug 2001). < http://www.mpi.web.org/news/tmp/2001/08/resort.htm >.

Dodson, Dorian. *How to Put on a Great Conference: A Straightforward, Friendly and Practical Guide.* Santa Fe: Adolofo Street Publications. 1992.

Elliott, Ralph. "Marketing Your Meeting. *Religious Conference Manager.* Feb 2001.

Edmondson-Yurkanan, Chris. "ACM SIGCOMM Conference Planning Assistance." University of Texas at Austin. < http://www.cs.utexas.edu/users/chris/sigcomm/conf/index.html >.

Ensman, Richard. "From A to T: Building Committee Participation." Corporate Meetings & Incentives, 1 April 2001.

"Exhibit Specifications." International Autobody Conference and Exposition. NACE. < www.naceexpo.com/content/NACEpdf/exhspecs.pdf >

Finkel, Coleman Lee. *New Conference Models for the Information Age.* Washington, DC: American Society of Association Executives. 1998.

Fripp, Patricia. "How to Get the Most Out of Your Speaker Investment." *Speakers Platform.* 2002. Prometheon. < http://www.speaking.com/articles_html/PatriciaFripp,CSP,CPAE_552.html >.

Garsee, Berniece. *Program Handbook for Women's Ministries.* Kansas City: Beacon Hill Press. 1984.

"Getting Started." *The Complete Event and Meeting Planner.* < http://www.where-events.com/gettingstarted.html >.

Gilgen, Read. "Conference Planning Guidelines." International Association for Language Learning Technology. < http://iallt.org/confplan.html >.

Harrington, Wesley, and Hugh K. Lee. "Aiming for a Great Meeting." *Religious Conference Manager.* Feb 2001.

Hemming, Janet K. "Think Small: Budgets and Lead Times." *Meeting*

Professional Digital Edition 19:9 (Sep 2000).
<http://www.mpi.web.org/news/tmp/1999/09.htm#3>.

"How Do You Get Volunteers to Work At Meetings, and How are They Rewarded?" Religious Conference Mananger, August 2002.

"How to Plan A Retreat." The Mountain Retreat and Learning Centers.
<http://www.mountaincenters.org/planaretreat.html>.

Kasabian, Judy, Ph.D. and Jacqueline M. Dewar, Ph.D. *Future Teacher's Conference Planning Handbook.* 2002.Los Angeles Collaborative For Teacher Excellence.
<http://www.lacteonline.org/Teacher/FTC/ftc.PDF>.

Kaufman, Ron. "10 Tips to Make Your Corporate Conference More Successful." *Speakers Platform.*1999. Prometheon. <http://www. speaking.com/articles_html/RonKaufman_311.html>.

Keltto, Larry. "When Youth is Served." *Religious Conference Mananger.* October 2002.

Knox, Alan B. *Planning and Marketing Conferences and Workshops.* San Francisco: Jossey-Bass Publishers, 1990.

"Large Meeting Timeline." *Religious Conference Manager.* 2000. MeetingsNet.
<http://www.meetingsnet.com/rcm/0200/0200lmtl.asp>.

"Liability and Meeting Planning." *Corbin Ball Associates.* 2000. www.corbinball.com/articles/art-liability.com

Mandel, Jed. "Sponsorship: The New Rules." *Religious Conference Manager.* Feb 2001. Primedia Business Magazines & Media Inc.

"Meeting Makers Checklist." *Meeting Planner Survival Guide.*
<http://www.meetingsnet.com/mpsg/speakers.asp>.

"Meeting Planner Guide." Marconi Conference Center.
<http://www.marconiconference.org/planner.htm>.

Meeting Planner's Handbook 1998. 1998. Meeting News.
<http://www.meetingnews.com/meetingnews/images/pdf/Handbook1998.pdf>

Meeting Planner's Handbook 1999. MeetingNews.com. 1998. Meeting News. <http://www.meetingnews.com/ meetingnews/images/pdf/Handbook1998.pdf>

Meeting Planner's Handbook 2000. MeetingNews.com. 1999. Meeting News. <http://www.meetingnews.com/ meetingnews/images/pdf/Handbook1999.pdf>

Meeting Planner's Handbook 2001. MeetingNews.com. 2001. Meeting News. <http://www.meetingnews.com/ meetingnews/images/pdf/Handbook2001.pdf>

Migliore, David. "Conference Planning Guide." *Office of Justice Programs.* U.S. Department of Justice. 2001 <http://www.ojp. usdoj.gov/ovc/publications/infores/res/confguid/>.

Nadler, Leonard and Zeace Nadler. *The Comprehensive Guide to Successful Conferences and Meetings: Detailed Instructions and Step-by-Step Checklists.* San Francisco: Jossey-Bass. 1987

Nixon, Stephanie. "Retreat Planning Manual." 1997. University of Missouri.
<http://www1.umn.edu/cic/resources/retreatmanual.htm>.

Norris, Joye A. "Five Keys to Facilitating Learning." *Corporate Meetings & Incentives,* 1 April 2001.

Ovenell-Carter, Julie. "Beating the Perfect Retreat." *Globe and Mail.* Apr 1999.

"Planner's Instruction Guide." Special Libraries Association.
<http://www.sla.org/documents/conf/2003planners instructionalguide.doc>.

"Planning A Conference." *Amsterdam 2000.* 2000. Billy Graham Evangelistic Association.
<http://www.amsterdam2000.org/pg_planning.asp>.

"Planning A Retreat." Cal State San Marcos.
<http://www.csusm.edu/srl/fast_tips/planning_retreat.htm>.

"Planning A Retreat." National Association of College and University Residence Halls. <http://www.nacurh.com/resources_benefits/ Publications/president/planning_a_retreat.htm>.

"Planning A Retreat." Orthodox Church in America. <http://www. oca.org/pages/youth/youthpage/Planning/Retreats.html>.

Rawland Gabriel, Anne. "Official Airlines: First-Class Strategies." *Meeting Professional Digital Edition* 20:10 (Oct 2000).
<http://www.mpi.web.org/news/tmp/2000/10/airlines.htm>.

"Retreat and Conference Planning Packet." *Women's Ministry Support Department.* Worldwide Church of God.
<http://www.wcg.org/womensministry/Brainstorm.htm>.

"Retreat Planning Guide." Timber-lee Christian Center.
<http://www.timber-lee.com/html/retrserv.htm>.

"Retreat Planning, Resources and Ideas." VaLLLey Camp.
<http://vallleycamp.lutherans.net/rplanning.htm>

"Retreat Planning Worksheet." Cannon Beach Christian Conference Center.
<http://www.cbcc.net/retreatplannningworksheet.htm>.

Rowe, Megan. "Adventures in Downtown." *Religious Conference Manager.* June 2002

—. "Meetings Take Center Stage." *Religious Conference Manager.* June 2002.

"Scheduling Interpreters for Conferences: Guidelines for Conference Planners." *Sign On.*
<http://www.signonasl.com/conferenceplanning.htm>.

Sherman, Patricia D. "Catering Managers Blow Off Steam." *Meeting Professional Digital Edition* 20:16 (Oct 2000).
<http://www.mpi.web.org/news/tmp/2000/10/catering.htm>.

"Site Inspection Checklist." *Religious Conference Manager.* 2000. MeetingsNet.

Sprague, Sally Knox and Jayne M. Becker. *Planning Effective Programs.* Oakland, CA: New Ventures. 1979.

Stiteler, Rowland. "Smooth Sailing: Cruises Offer Surprising Bargains." *Meeting Professional Digital Edition* 21:8 (Aug 2001).
<http://www.mpi.web.org/news/tmp/2000/08/sailing.htm>.

"Student Organization Retreat Planning." Marshall University.
<http://www.marshall.edu/student-activities/retreat planning.htm>.

"Ten Dos and Don's of Conference Planning." *Business Traveller Express.* 2002. Indian Express Group (Mumbai, India).
<http://www.businesstravellerindia.com/200202/mice.shtml>.

"38 Ways to Use Internet to Promote Meetings." *Corbin Ball Associates.* 2000. www.corbinball.com/articles/art-promote.html.

2001 IAESTE Regional LC Conference Planning Guide." International Association for the Exchange of Students for Technical Experience (IAESTE). 2001.
<http://www.aipt.org/subpages/iaeste_lc/presentations/ Outbound/IAESTE%20Regional%20LC%20Conference%20 Planning%20Guide2001.doc>.

Voso, Michele. *The Convention and Meeting Planner's Handbook: A Step-by-Step Guide to Making Your Event a Success.* Lexington, Massachusetts: Lexington Books. 1990.

"What Marketing Techniques Work For Your Meetings?" *Religious Conference Manager.* June 2002.

Wierzgac, Michele. "Marvelous Marketing." *Religious Conference Manager.* August 2002.

INDEX

ORDER FORM

Order copies to give as gifts for your team members and friends!

Buy five or more books and get a 10% discount! *

(That means if you buy ten, you get one free!)

❑ Yes, I want to order The Christian Conference Planner.

❑ Yes, I want to be informed when The Christian Conference Workbook is available.

❑ Yes, please put me on your e-mail mailing list. (We promise we will not inundate you with e-mail or give your

e-mail address to other companies!)

Name		
Address		
City	State	Zip
Phone (H)	(W)	
E-mail address		

The Christian Conference Planner Order Form

A	Quantity ordered	$
B	x $19.99 per copy (1-4 copies) x $17.99 per copy (5+ copies)	$
C	Subtotal (A x B)	$
D	Taxes California residents 7.25% (C x .0725)	$
E	Shipping $3.50 first book, $1.50 each additional copy	$
F	Total (C + D + E) Make check payable to SummitStar Press	$

For credit card payments, please use our Web site at www.summitstarpress.com.
Payment must accompany orders. Allow three weeks for shipping.
• In order to qualify for discount, five copies of the same book must be ordered at the same time.

Please send form to SummitStar Press, 2140 Sunsprite Drive, Union City, CA 94587